NORMAL
1 2 BRIGHT

VOLUME TREBLE MIDDLE BASS

VIBRATO
1 2 BRIGHT

VOLUME TREBLE MIDDLE BASS REVERB SPEED INTENSITY

Twin Reverb-Amp

FENDER MUSICAL INSTRUMENTS

DESIGN & CIRCUITS
PATENTED 63-5

AMPED

The Illustrated History of the World's Greatest Amplifiers

DAVE HUNTER

Voyageur
Press

Contents

INTRODUCTION

A 1964 Rickenbacker 360 rests atop a 1964 Vox AC30 six-input copper-panel model.

In a world where technological progress for the sake of "the product" seems to outstrip genuine cultural and social advancement, it's refreshing to still be able to fire up a chunk of archaic technology and make some rock 'n' roll.

Seemingly daily, our lives are depleted of depth and dimension as new developments in the name of convenience and speed disguise a steady decline in pure quality—camera phones over cameras, ear buds over speakers, MP3s over CDs—even CDs over vinyl. And it is all heartily accepted, so long as it's faster, sleeker, *newer*.

But however much digital technology has made inroads into guitar amplification, offering thirty-two amp emulations, sixteen effects, and twelve cab sims at the twist of a menu dial, this apparent new world order will never really make a dent in a technology that is rooted in the early part of the last century and that still delivers up the goods simply and virtually by its very nature.

In addition to their pure sonic beauty, vintage tube amps hook many of us for the window they provide onto an era when rock 'n' roll was young, when life was simple, and when the world as we know it today was really just forming.

An "Accordion" input on an old Ampeg or Sonola combo? You betcha. Independent channels for "Instrument" and "Mic" on your 1950s tweed Fender? So much the better to cover that sock hop gig in style.

Of course, these amps also had a major hand in shaping popular music, in addition to having been shaped by it—even as the guitar gets louder, the band gets smaller, the sound gets rattier and more aggressive, and the saxophone fades from center stage. These amps forged the sound of an era of popular music that, despite the Black Eyed Peas, Lady Gaga, and Justin Bieber, has remained consistent in its core sound and instrumentation longer than any era of popular music before it. And it's all thanks to that beat-up little electronic suitcase over there in the corner—*that's* where the tone came from, and that's why we still love it.

There are many, many great modern amps, and we honor several of them here, too. The early successes of what has become known as the "boutique amp movement" were produced by makers who were among the first to perceive and accept the glory of vintage amplification and to seek to recapture that in reliable, contemporary formats suited to the modern guitarist. The tube amp is, thankfully, not a dead art, and great designers are introducing better and better examples all the time.

Alongside these, this book also celebrates a handful of vintage solid-state guitar amps that have attained at least a modicum of "classic" status.

Still, few things can or ever will surpass the sheer sonic beauty of a great vintage tube amp in good condition. Fire up an exemplary 1959 Fender Bassman, 1965 Vox AC30, or 1968 Marshall JMP50, plug in, and attack it with some attitude, and you'll still discover worlds of tone that can't really be bettered, only altered.

Now, if they could just bottle that vintage tube amp smell, we would really be getting somewhere. ●

The amps make the band. The Beatles onstage in Germany in 1960 with a varied back line of great amps. Paul McCartney's Selmer Truvoice Stadium amp is on the far left. (This amp originally belonged to George Harrison, who sold it to McCartney.) Harrison's Gibson GA-40 Les Paul is in the middle, with John Lennon's Fender 5E3 Deluxe on the right. The band mates include, from left, McCartney, drummer Pete Best, bassist Stuart Sutcliffe, Harrison, and Lennon. *Astrid Kirchherr/ K & K/Redferns/Getty Images*

The greatest Masterpieces
the complete new line of
MAGNATONE
Golden Voice AMPLIFIERS

FEATURING A MONUMENTAL ACHIEVEMENT IN
DISTORTION-FREE HI-FI DIMENSIONAL SOUND

MAGNATONE
the world's finest amplifiers & guitars

Musical Merchandise Corporation
WHOLESALE DISTRIBUTORS
POST OFFICE BOX 4135   Greensboro, N. C.

Vox:
it's
what's
happening

Go over big with
MARSHALL

GRETSCH Guitars

Gibson

guitars

amplifiers

GIBSON, IN

AMPLIFIERS | THE VERY BEST IN | SOUND

PARIS
Corporation, Inc.

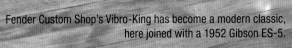

Fender Custom Shop's Vibro-King has become a modern classic,
here joined with a 1952 Gibson ES-5.

ELECTRONIC SUITCASE

Mention the name Rickenbacker and most guitarists conjure up images of John Lennon's 325, George Harrison's 360/12, or Pete Townshend's smashed export models—in short, some form of thrang and jangle from the British Invasion or from artists who sought to emulate those tones in the years that followed. Probe Rick's earlier history, though, to way back before its efforts in the 1960s to hold onto third- or fourth-tier status behind Fender, Gibson, and arguably Gretsch, and you find a company at the forefront of electrification and amplification, bold voyagers in tumultuous and uncharted waters.

The name as we know it today didn't land on the headstocks of guitars until around 1949, but Adolph Rickenbacker's associations with inventors George Beauchamp and Paul Barth began in the late 1920s (as a natural course of the trio's work with National resonator guitars). By 1931, Beauchamp and Barth had put their "horseshoe pickup" on Rickenbacker's cast-aluminum Electro-String-branded "frying pan" guitar, and this early electric guitar naturally needed an amplifier to go with it. By 1934 these guitars and amps carried the Rickenbacher name, the Germanic *h* adopted to milk the popularity of Adolph's war-hero cousin, Eddie, the ace fighter pilot. And toward the late 1930s, all of this had evolved toward the amp we have before us: the Rickenbacher M11.

While this 1930s Rick has the "electronic suitcase" appearance of its day—an image that brings to mind archaic circuitry and brown, warm, tubby tones—the M11 packs some surprises in both departments. Certainly its cab is made of thinner panels than most contemporary amps, being constructed of 3/8-inch pine. Its crude top-mounted, folded-steel chassis is bolted right to

1937 RICKENBACHER M11

- Preamp tubes: One 6SJ7 and one SN7
- Output tubes: Two 6V6GTs
- Rectifier: 5Y3
- Controls: Volume, Tone
- Speaker: Rola alnico
- Output: Likely 12 to 15 watts RMS

The soothing sound of the Hawaiian Isles was music to woo by. This band was outfitted with a full range of rare Rickenbacker electrics, from "frying pan" lap steels to horseshoe-pickup four- and six-string Spanish electrics.

the back panel, and its preamp tubes are the Old World pairing of 6SJ7 and SN7 octal-based types, but other elements are surprisingly forward looking.

The amp here has received the bits of maintenance necessary to keep it operational (the replacement of filter caps and a few drifting resistors, new handle, new speaker), but it is otherwise original. A look underneath the hood reveals a surprisingly tidy point-to-point circuit, with less of the rat's nest look of some other amps of the era. Its dual 6V6 output stage looks very much like that of Fender's Deluxe of a full decade later (the oft-bandied opinion being that Leo took a little inspiration from the several Rickenbacher amps that came through his radio repair shop), and where we'd expect to find the field coil speaker that so many other amps of the 1930s and 1940s carried, the M11 held forth with an alnico, permanent magnet, 12-inch Rola with a *chassis*-mounted output transformer no less. Controls are limited to Volume and Tone, but again, that's more than plenty of amps offered back in the day.

In the looks department, the M11 is simple yet elegant. The sultry white art deco knobs are worthy of any vintage-o-phile's lust, and take a closer gander at the grille slats in the front of the cab and you'll see that the cutouts subtly spell out "RICK" in tall, narrow letters. As for tone, the M11 offers some surprises. Where we were expecting the woolly, dark sound of so many early jazz recordings (a sound we can partly attribute to the guitars of the day, our course), Steve Olson reports that his Rick is "pretty punchy, crisp, and clear sounding, and kind of bright too, with the tone rolled all the way up. And because the cabinet is so lightweight, it really resonates."

Hal Lindes, the former Dire Straits guitarist (1980–1985) and film soundtrack composer, also owns a 1937 M11 and declares it "a killer amp, one of my main recording amps, and the one that we refer to as my secret weapon." Lindes' amp was likewise brought back up to spec with just a few cap and resistor replacements (by Fred Taccone of Divided by 13). Its fragile woven orange grille cloth was replaced, but it is otherwise as it was made more than seventy years ago, and it still earns its keep as a working tool for this busy composer and studio guitarist. "It's got its own unique

thing going on," Lindes adds. "At low volumes it's fat, compressed, clean, sweet, and punchy. At full volume it just sings. It's an especially great companion to the Fender Stratocaster, producing simple yet highly complex tones." *Now* you want one, right?

Naturally, given the early circuit topology and transformers, the 6V6s and 5Y3 rectifier, and the great-sounding but inefficient Rola speaker, the M11 isn't going to put out much in the volume department, although Olson reports that he has gigged regularly with his in small clubs, and you could pump it up on any larger stage by miking it through the PA, of course. For recording in particular, though, amps like this one frequently do offer the "secret weapon" that Lindes raves about, and maybe that's just what you need to make a little musical history of your own circa 2011 with a piece of guitar history circa 1937.

Could Adolph, George, and John have foreseen that? Probably not, but you can bet they'd be proud. 🎱

EARLY EXPERIMENTER

Before Leo Fender's rise to prominence, which is to say before anyone knew what the platonic form of the electric guitar amplifier would ultimately be, a broad free-fire zone existed between general purpose amplification, PA amps, and guitar amps.

Many companies covered all bases, as did Masco, a name that has come to prominence again largely in blues harp circles, where vintage-minded blowers are fond of converting Masco PA heads into amps of the style Little Walter purportedly wailed through in the early days. Old Masco PAs can make great guitar amps too, but the company did manufacture dedicated guitar combos right alongside its PA production in the 1940s and 1950s.

Our MAP-15 combo isn't a rare bird as such but is a lesser-seen example of the species. This one comes to us courtesy of pickup-maker Jason Lollar, who says it was his first real gigging amp. "I played a lot of gigs with it when I was seventeen to twenty years old," Lollar relates. "No mic, just straight amp with a boost pedal when I needed a little more volume and treble."

With that vented speaker grille, buffalo covering, and one of the most wistful control panels in guitar-amp history, it's a groovy contraption to have cut your teeth on, and it was a gutsy move for any kid to plonk it down on stage alongside the Peaveys, Fenders, and Ampegs.

A Sams Photofact Folder from 1947 tells us that Masco amps were manufactured in Long Island City, New York, by the Mark Alan Simpson Company (M-A-S-Co). Akin to the department-store brands that proliferated in the day, they were sold through electronics catalog retailers such

1946 MASCO MAP-15

- Preamp tubes: Two 7F7s
- Output tubes: Two 6L6GAs, cathode-bias, no negative feedback
- Rectifier: 5Y3
- Controls: Volume, Tone
- Speaker: Jensen PM P12T
- Output: Approximately 15 watts RMS

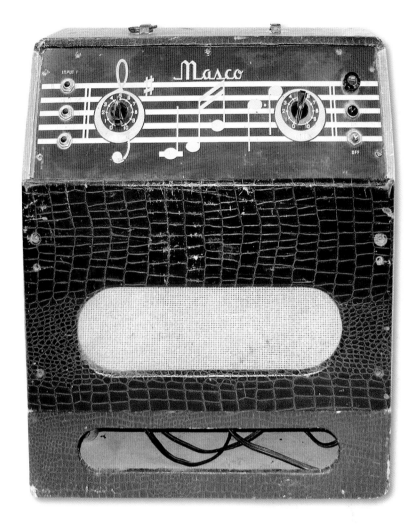

as Archer and Lafayette and were a semigeneric amp option at brick-and-mortar retail outlets as well.

For all its prehistoric looks, this MAP-15 is a pretty well-constructed beast—as are all Mascos—and not entirely as archaic as its aesthetics might imply. Where you'd expect a fiddly field coil speaker, the MAP-15 carries a permanent magnet Jensen P12T alnico speaker (although the Sams sheet indicates that a previous field coil version might have existed), and the transformers, including choke, are of a decent quality. These are true point-to-point amps, however, and WE don't mean the good kind (as in the Matchless format) but the kind that is a real rat's nest of connections, with caps and resistors linking components directly and no circuit board or terminal strip to impose order on the clutter.

A pair of 6L6GAs occupies the output stage, but with only 320 DC volts on the plates and grids, these big bottles wouldn't have put out more than around 15 to 18 watts (and early 6L6s weren't capable of the output levels their descendents would muster anyway). Thus their cathode bias is set with a relatively low-value 200-ohm resistor, and they're fed by a humble 5Y3GT rectifier tube and a soft-filtering network consisting of a 16uF electrolytic cap either side of the choke—standard stuff for their day.

More unusual tube choices arise in the 7F7 dual triodes that take preamp and phase inverter (PI) duties. These old octal tubes aren't too dissimilar to the 6SL7s that would replace them in the MAP-15 in later years and are fairly high-gain and chunky-sounding tubes. Good NOS examples are still readily available at just a few bucks each. Inputs 1 and 2 go to one half of the 7F7, and input 3 goes to the other half, with a hotter signal seen in the latter thanks to different biasing configurations for each of the two triodes. Despite the independent input circuits for inputs 1–2 and 3, they share a single Volume control, as well as the simple treble-bleed Tone control. From here it's straight on to the soft and squishy (but rather fat-sounding) paraphase inverter, then onward to the 6L6s.

The OT in the MAP-15 is specced for 4 ohms, a fact that has probably escaped plenty of players who have replaced their flimsy Jensen P12Ts with sturdier speakers,

but a lot of this old iron can be fairly tolerant of an impedance mismatch that isn't too far out of the ballpark. In any case, a thoughtfully restored Masco with a good contemporary speaker is likely to sound better than the same amp with its original speaker, which is barely up to the task of reproducing the full 15-watt output anyway. All this comes in a fairly flimsy cab, and the chassis doesn't appear to have been built to last twenty years, much less sixty. But, hey, it's a light lift, and if you avoid knocking it around, this Masco combo can make a surprisingly good-sounding club rig.

"The amp works best with brighter single-coil pickups," Lollar says of his MAP-15. "It never gets plinky at lower volumes with cleaner tone settings. It always has a smooth, softish attack with lots of sustain. When you turn it up halfway, it starts to get creamy and dirty, and the tone turns from one with full-range clarity to one with a prominent, tubey mid-range." He adds, "For two 6L6s, it's not very loud—somewhat like a Princeton Reverb volume-wise."

But who needs volume anyway? Some, perhaps, but probably not as much—or as often—as we think. No matter how you slice it, it makes for a tempting chunk of smoky sixty-five-year-old tone. ◉

Amp and photos courtesy Jason Lollar

THE WORLD'S FIRST "TWIN"

What's in a name? Regarding early Fender amps, the Dual Professional says it all. After the early "woody" amps, this was the fledgling company's first jump up into the truly professional amp league. It was also the world's first production amplifier with two speakers. It's Dual, it's Professional—and back in early 1947, your aspiring steel or electric-Spanish guitarist couldn't ask for much more.

For that matter, Leo Fender's Dual Professional was also arguably the first venture by the guitar amp world into professional products that would pave the way for the industry's direction through the second half of the century.

In addition to these major firsts, it was also among the earliest amps to feature a top-mounted control panel. It was the first Fender to offer easy access

to the inside of the chassis through a removable back panel, to be covered in the enduring and popular tweed (though a whiter, more linen-like variety), and to carry a tube chart. And, as John Teagle and John Sprung point out in their excellent book *Fender Amps: The First Fifty Years*, it was the first Fender amp to be built in a finger-jointed cabinet.

With all these innovations in its corner, the Dual Professional is usually most notable today for its wedge-fronted cabinet design with central metal support bracket, a feature necessitated by the split-V baffle arrangement. Fender clearly determined that if you were going to go so far as to put two speakers in one amp, you might as well go whole hog and maximize their sonic dispersal by angling them slightly away from each other. This arrangement, along with the otherwise traditional open-backed cab, gives this amp a very

1946–1947 FENDER DUAL PROFESSIONAL

- Preamp tubes: Two 6SJ7 preamp tubes, 6N7 phase inverter tube
- Output tubes: Two 6L6s
- Rectifier: 5U4
- Controls: Mic Volume, Inst Volume, Tone
- Speakers: Two 10-inch Jensen PM10C alnico
- Output: Approximately 18 watts RMS

"surround sound" feel and is part of what makes a Dual Professional sound bigger than its meager wattage rating.

Most documentation indicates that Fender introduced the Dual Professional in 1947 and produced the model only until the fall of that year, when it became the Super, which remained a 2x10 combo for sixteen years. The owner of serial number 43 here, however—Mark Watson of Amwatts Amps in Australia—reports that it was made with Stackpole potentiometers that all date to the thirty-ninth week of 1946. Certainly, the amp could have been assembled in 1947 from pots made the year before, although Fender was also unlikely to keep large stocks of parts on hand in the early days the way it did in later years. Either way, it's an early one—and an excellent example too.

Watson also tells us that the circuit used in this amp—which he obtained unmodified—is different than the period schematic available for the model, although Fender's amp designs were constantly evolving in the late 1940s, 1950s, and even well beyond, so perhaps that's no great surprise. Whether a standard Dual Professional or an early transitional example, these are quirky beasts when compared to later tweed amps, but they already display plenty of Fender traits for solid design and stellar tone.

The lone Mic input goes straight to the grid (input) of one 6SJ7 octal pentode preamp tube, and the two Instrument inputs are joined following a 40k "grid stopper" resistor each to hit the grid of a second 6SJ7. These channels share a simple passive treble-bleed Tone control, but there's also an odd Lo Gain input, presumably designed to receive a line-level signal, that routes through the signal post-preamp tubes and straight into the Volume pot of the Instrument channel and from there into the phase inverter, a 6N7 octal twin triode. All this fed a pair of metal envelope 6L6 output tubes, but wattage levels were likely to be only in the upper range of later 6V6-based amps. After this, the signal hit a pair of output transformers, one attached to the frame of each 10-inch alnico Jensen PM10C speaker. An unnecessary extravagance,

it might seem, but you have to give young Leo Fender a break: this was perhaps the world's first two-speaker amp, so the minor details were still up in the air.

We think of early guitar amplifiers as sounding fairly woofy and flubby, but the word is that this Dual Professional's performance is quite to the contrary. "The amp has amazing tone," raves Watson. "It has relatively clean headroom up until twelve o'clock, then starts to break into a creamy, woody overdrive. It compresses into a nice distortion, and with a combination of the two [10-inch speakers], it doesn't flub out as much as the later narrow-panel tweeds. I only use Strats, Teles, and P-90 guitars, and it has the most organic tone of all my vintage amps. The angled, split-front baffles create a spacious room-filling sound—the player can stand and move around in front of the amp and not lose any tone or volume."

And he's not the only enthusiastic supporter of the breed. One Billy F Gibbons has long been a fan of the Dual Professional and similarly enthuses over the tone of these early amps, perhaps another reason they are so hard to come by these days.

Early in the Super's reign, the preamp tubes were changed to 6SC7 octal dual triodes, dropping the creamy, thick tone of those 6SJ7 pentodes, and several other distinctive features of the Dual Professional were also dropped. So while V-front and wide-panel tweed Super amps can also sound fantastic (again, surprisingly buoyant and playable), these alterations meant that the *first* V-fronted Fender model's rare and unusual tone was lost for good.

Of course, the Dual Professional wasn't even designed for the solid body and semiacoustic electric guitars that can sound so good through them. It would have accompanied a Fender Dual Professional steel guitar, a twin-neck model that survived well beyond the amp that briefly shared its name. Alternatively, it might have been pirated to amplify a big-bodied Gibson, Epiphone, or other arch-top electric (known as a Spanish electric back in the day). But, as with so many things Fender, a fortuitous virtue of design cast these archaic V-fronted beauties as surprisingly enduring tone machines, a fact that makes their rarity all the more bittersweet.

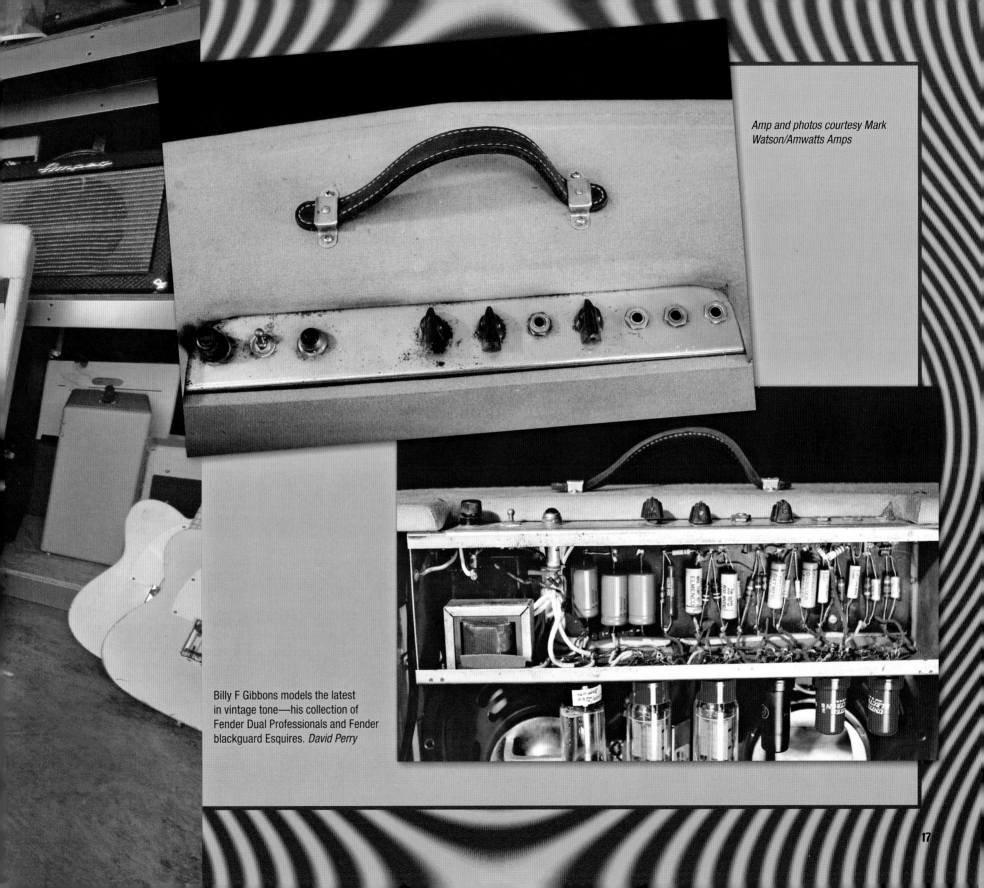

Billy F Gibbons models the latest in vintage tone—his collection of Fender Dual Professionals and Fender blackguard Esquires. *David Perry*

A TRIP BACK IN TIME

Before founding Danelectro in Red Bank, New Jersey, in the late 1940s, Nathan I. "Nat" Daniel was making amps for a number of large department stores and catalog outlets, most notably supplying Silvertone-branded amplifiers to Sears, Roebuck and Company. This amp is a rare beauty from this formative period in the maker's history. Something like it is seen more often— though not very often—as the Model 1344, which ran from 1950 to 1954.

Our featured piece here is a model 1304, most likely from 1949, and although the two have a lot in common, and the 1304 is often considered the short-lived predecessor to the 1344, there are a few interesting differences between them.

On the outside, the two models look much the same, although a metal trim ring seems to have been added around the speaker cutout and grille cloth on the 1344. Both have that "antique radio" look that seems to promise (and in this case delivers) fat, primitive, electric blues tones, with a subtly stylish two-tone covering of oxblood with silver stripe. While the 1304's groovy speaker cloth looks somewhat like spun silk, the 1344 had a more proper "grille." Other details changed surprisingly rapidly, even during the ultrashort life span of the 1304, and you can find examples with green pilot lamp jewels rather than the red here and with more art deco–looking knobs with a stylized *S* in their centers. By the time of the 1344, the Silvertone logo had also been added to the front, in a narrow parallelogram stenciled in the right side of the broad silver stripe.

CIRCA 1949 SILVERTONE 1304

- Preamp tubes: One 12SJ7 for gain, one 12SN7GT phase inverter
- Output tubes: Two 6L6Gs
- Rectifier: 5U4G
- Controls: Volume, Treble, Bass, Tremolo on/off
- Speaker: Jensen PM P12T
- Output: Rated at an optimistic 18 watts RMS

There are a few more differences under the hood, though both models certainly take us back into the realms of archaic amplification technology, with several obscure tube types onboard, separate top- and bottom-mounted control and chassis sections, and the soon-to-be-extinct field coil speaker topology. But check it out: tremolo and separate Treble and Bass controls! Pretty advanced stuff for 1949, even if the tremolo is only a basic early configuration with just an on/off switch and no depth or speed control. Fender wouldn't bring either of these features to the table until 1955, so hat's off to Nat Daniel. The simple tremolo circuit is powered by a hard-to-find 7C7 tube, which is a sharp-cutoff pentode with a nine-pin loctal base (a mounting that looks something like the more common eight-pin, or octal, base but with an extra pin where the octal's guide channel is located). Another but quite different sharp-cutoff pentode in the form of a 12SJ7 takes preamp duties. This metal tube is a cousin of the more familiar 6SJ7 pentode that appeared in some early Fenders, but it uses a 12-volt heater rather than the more familiar 6.3 volts required by most tubes used in guitar amps. Other than that, it yields the fat, rich sound that many pentode preamp tubes are known for, octal types especially, and is a big part of this old combo's magic. Also like more familiar nine-pin pentode preamp tubes, such as the EF86 and the 5879, the 12SJ7 can be rather microphonic, a tendency that Daniel sought to combat with the use of rubber grommets around the mountings of this tube's socket on the 1304, a trick that several makers use to this day.

The split-load phase inverter carries another 12-volt tube, this one a 12SN7GT, a dual triode that provides a driver from one side and a phase inverter from the other. Beyond the PI, we find another surprise that the 1304 has to offer when compared to the 1344. Instead of the 6V6GTs you'd expect to see, this early rendition carries a pair of big Coke bottle–shaped 6L6Gs, with a beefier 5U4G rectifier tube to ramp up the voltages a little higher than a 1344's 5Y3 would manage. That said, the whole shebang doesn't provide the output tubes a whole lot of steam to

run on, and with just a little over 300 volts in the system, a pair of these old-style 6L6s aren't going to put out much more than 15 to 20 watts or so, at very best.

The 1304 has a beefy, thick tone that is extremely mid-range rich, and it excels at vintage jazz tones when kept in the clean zones, or at greasy blues and early rock 'n' roll when wound up a little higher. This combo, and those of its ilk, can be a lot of fun and will often be found selling for fairly modest prices, partly because many players don't want to mess with field coil speakers.

For that reason, if a field coil–loaded combo isn't working well, you really might just want to walk away, unless it's wearing a dirt-cheap sticker price or you relish a project. Field coil speakers can be replaced by standard permanent magnet speakers, but since their circuits usually include the presence of a couple hundred volts or so at the field coil itself, they can be dangerous to work on if you don't know what you're doing, and making such a swap isn't a matter of simply putting the new speaker in for the old. If you feel like getting behind such a conversion, it's best to take it to a tech who has experience with field coil speakers. He will usually need to place a large resistor in series with the wires that had previously supplied voltage to the speaker's second coil, the field coil, in addition to connecting the signal feed to the new permanent magnet speaker's connection terminals in the traditional way. This is one way of breathing new life into an archaic old combo like this one, but trying to do it yourself—and doing it wrong—can result in zapping both your new speaker and yourself.

Fortunately, our sweet 1304 on display is working just great as is, and if you ever encounter one in similarly clean condition, it behooves you to plug in and give it a taste. This is a combo from the tail end of the first real era of electric guitar amplification, and its tone offers a quick trip back in time. ◉

Amp and photo courtesy Terry Scarberry

RIDING A SWEET HAWAIIAN SONIC SWELL

Back in the day when the Hawaiian steel guitar ruled the amplified roost and Spanish electric guitar was still a dirty word (or moderately soiled, at least), any company that wanted in on the game—and there were plenty—couldn't just offer "a guitar" or "an amplifier." No, no—you had to offer a set. And if you weren't in a position to manufacture your own amplifier, chances are good you bought it from the Valco company.

Such was the case with a Cleveland-based music publisher named Oahu, which specialized in Hawaiian guitar method books, sheet music, and steel guitar lessons taught at any of the more than the twelve hundred schools this franchise operated at its peak. Along with all the schoolin' and the steel guitars themselves, for a time in the middle of the last century, this Valco-made

Tone Master 230K amplifier was also a major item in Oahu's lineup, as partner to the Tone Master guitar. This one carries two Instrument inputs (each with its own Volume control), one for Micro (microphone) with its own Volume and a shared Tone control with integral power switch. Two 6V6GTs, a 6SN7GT and 6SL7GT, and a 5Y3 rectifier do the good stuff inside and pump it through an 8-inch Rola field coil speaker.

Oahu had a number of amps called Tone Master, and circuits of even similar-looking examples varied somewhat, but this one from around 1950 is one of the more common designs (the same chassis layout appeared in many Harmony H200 combos). Most that you stumble across are in the two-tone brown-and-fawn covering rather than this relatively rare black-and-white with blue grille design. In either dress it's an extremely cool and sporty looking little fella that's instantly evocative of a bygone age. Most of the original sets—from Oahu and others of the era—have been broken up by now, with the steel guitars often falling out of use, while the amps have frequently migrated to duties belting out Spanish electric guitar at the hands of players who have discovered what fierce

- Preamp tubes: 6SN7GT and 6SL7GT
- Output tubes: Two 6V6GTs, cathode-bias
- Rectifier: 5Y3
- Controls: Volume for two Instrument inputs and one Mic input; shared Tone (with built-in on/off switch)
- Speaker: Single 8-inch Rola field coil
- Output: 10 watts RMS +/-

An Oahu-equipped orchestra poses circa 1950 with guitars and accordions, all run through three Oahu combo amps.

little recording tools they can be. Very often, they have been conscripted into service amplifying blues harp, a task they perform with grace and gusto.

Although many Valco-made amps of a few years later were migrating toward more modern (or early modern) designs, this 230K really is a throwback to a previous era of tube electronics. There's no circuit board here at all, just a somewhat chaotically cobbled rat's nest of point-to-point connections, with the relatively few resistors, coupling, and filter caps soldered directly between other components, such as input jacks, potentiometers, and tube sockets. Of course, early Fender amps were wired in a similar manner, and Gibson continued to build many of its small and medium-size combos in this point-to-point fashion right into the early 1960s. But these groovy little Oahus still manage to have a more archaic look and feel, and a sound that's all their own.

One more big part of that "archaic look and feel" is the field coil speaker these models still used. Rather than carrying a permanent magnet like the speakers we're all familiar with in the vast majority of amps post-1950 or so, field coil speakers use electromagnetic coils that require a voltage from the power transformer (PT) to operate. Many vintage amp buffs avoid models with field coil speakers because they can be a bit of a hassle to deal with; the original speakers often don't do justice to the potential of the amps themselves, and you need to find an experienced repairman to rebuild the coil if that is required. Swapping them for a more efficient or more tuneful replacement isn't as straightforward as with a modern amp either, but it can be done. Mainly, you have to deal with the PT, which is expecting to handle the resistance from this field coil, so you'll need to have a qualified tech (who also understands what you're trying to achieve) add a resistor of the correct value to the DC supply chain to fool the PT into thinking it's

still seeing that resistance from the missing field coil. Not a job to take on yourself if you don't know exactly what you're doing.

Another thing that marks this as an amp from days gone by is its use of octal (eight-pin) preamp tubes. The 6SN7GT that provides the first gain stage for the Instrument and Mic inputs and the 6SL7GT that performs phase inverter duties are both dual-triode types that would be replaced by miniature nine-pin preamp tubes like the 12AX7 in most amp designs by the mid or late 1950s. They can be a bit more prone to microphony than the miniature tube types (although less so than the metal 6SN7 and 6SL7 that preceded them), but they also have a flavor all their own—one that some players describe as a bit fatter, warmer, and juicier than a 12AX7.

The plate voltages on this Tone Master's 6V6GT output tubes are a low 260 volts DC, give or take a few volts (the typical 5E3 Deluxe runs around 350 volts; a Deluxe Reverb around 415 volts—way beyond the spec for this tube!), so this amp probably puts out only about 10 watts at most. It also used a cathode-bias resistor of a mere 200 ohms, a much lower value than you'd find on better-known two-6V6 amps such as the tweed Fender Deluxe, to turn again to that familiar example, which used a 250-ohm bias resistor. Low voltages predominate throughout the circuit, in fact, and this is definitely a brown-sounding little beastie, with chewy, chocolaty tones at the fore. It's also a very tactile, touchy-feely amp, with plenty of squash but also decent body when you rein it in a little. Crank it and it rewards you with a smooth, sweet, soothing breed of vintage tube overdrive. In all, a fun little number—and one that is lately showing some escalation in value, from around the $150 mark just three or four years ago to double that or a little more in recent sales. Snap one up while you can. 🌀

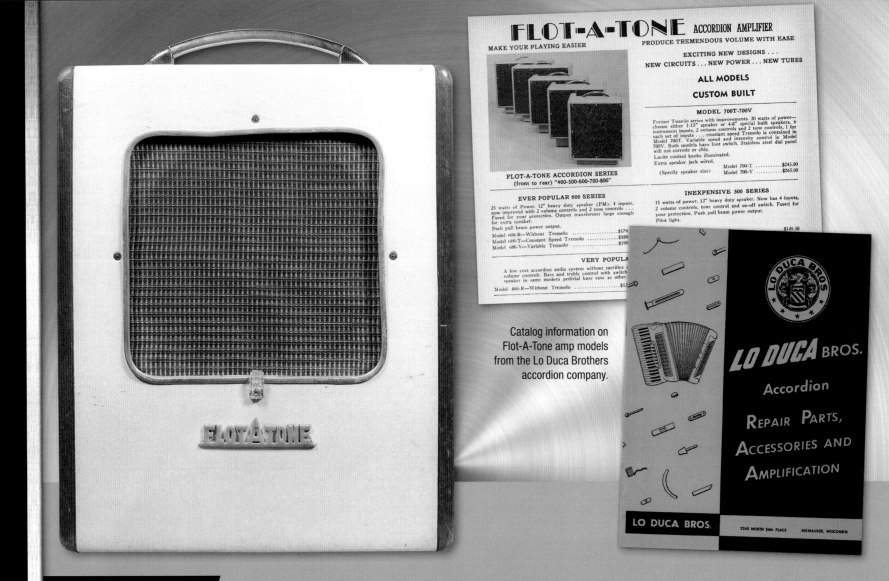

Catalog information on
Flot-A-Tone amp models
from the Lo Duca Brothers
accordion company.

LET'S POLKA!

Flot-A-What? That's Flot-A-Tone, baby. It just trips off the tongue, doesn't it? Okay, the truth is we're not sure what the filament a "flot" is anyway, and in the mind's ear, the word certainly doesn't inspire sonic simulacrums of unearthly tone. But when an amp looks this groovy, one is willing to forgive a slight schism in the marketing department. The nifty red-and-white two-tone covering, slanted rear control panel, upright cabinet structure, and refrigerator handle all reek of a Chicago-made Valco amp. But, in fact, this is not a product of that esteemed jobber.

Flot-A-Tone amps were manufactured in Milwaukee beginning in the late 1940s and lasting into the late 1950s or early 1960s, sold by accordion importers

Lo Duca Brothers. Thomas and Guy Lo Duca retailed accordions and related equipment via local stores and nationally through their catalogs, founded accordion schools in Milwaukee that boasted of teaching thousands to play the instrument (they held recitals in Milwaukee Auditorium with up to twenty-five hundred accordionists performing at a time), and later imported Eko guitars from Italy. Were it not for their use for guitar by a handful of esteemed tonesmiths, however—Ry Cooder and G. E. Smith in particular—these funky combos might have left nary a footnote in the annals of guitardom. That's because the Flot-A-Tone, good readers, as you have likely guessed by now, was made to amplify the accordion.

Fret ye not. Just as Fender, Gibson, Valco, and others applied generic amplification circuits from many tube manufacturers' application notes to their early guitar amps, so did the rest of the tube audio world. Particular

1950s FLOT-A-TONE

- Preamp tubes: One 6SC7GT in preamp, one 6SN7 in PI
- Output tubes: Two 6L6GCs, cathode-biased
- Rectifier: 5U3
- Controls: Two Volume, one Tone (disabled tremolo control)
- Speaker: Single "heavy duty" 12-inch
- Output: Approximately 25 watts RMS

Flot-A-Tone fan and guitarist extraordinaire Ry Cooder. *Mick Hutson/Redferns/Getty Images*

stages might have been adapted to suit the frequency range of the intended instrument, but these circuits were all so simple back in the day that nothing strayed too far from its roots, and you can stick an electric guitar into just about anything with two knobs and a handful of tubes with a reasonable expectation of decent—or at least interesting—tone. Heck, get lucky and you might even achieve Flot-A-Tone (it's hard to stop saying that).

Our amp in question looks for all the world like an example of the 600 series, but there's no model name or number anywhere to be found here. As it happens, the model designation is likely to be moot anyway, because just about every Flot-A-Tone you will encounter appears to be a bit different inside. Word is that the manufacturer built them on sort of an on-the-fly basis, using whatever suitable components were handy at the time an order came in.

The design uses an upper-rear-mounted control panel, with an umbilical cord descending to a main chassis mounted in the bottom of the cab, which reveals a semi–rat's nest, point-to-point circuit job. This one carries 6SN7GT and 6SC7GT octal preamp tubes, two 6L6 output tubes, and a 5U4 rectifier, and it puts out something in the region of 25 watts through a single 12-inch speaker. The 6SC7GT in the first gain stage is a medium-gain dual triode that appeared in many early tweed Fenders, and others, and is known for its thick, rich tone. The 6SN7GT in the phase inverter was an extremely popular low-mu dual-triode tube of the 1940s and 1950s, with a low gain similar to that of a later 12AU7.

Other Flot-A-Tone models used other tube types, and they are more commonly seen with a pair of 6V6s in the output stage and a 5Y3 rectifier, for about 15 watts. The speaker in our featured Flot is a replacement, but original drivers would most likely have come from Jensen, perhaps Rola, or a similar maker.

Dig, if you will, the comely control panel—something right out of radio days. And check out the knobs—they go all the way to . . . nine. Each of the two channels has a volume control and two inputs (one via a 1/4-inch jack and one via a screw-on terminal). There's a shared passive Bass–Treble control (really just a standard treble bleed tone pot). A fourth knob is either a control for a dead tremolo circuit or is just there for show. Oh, and there's also our candidate for "coolest superfluous feature" in the form of the knob-embedded pilot light. Rotate it and your lamp goes from dim to bright. Super!

Ah, but how does it sound? Well, despite the semirandom construction and no-fixed-address circuit topologies, most Flot-A-Tones sound surprisingly good when in decent condition and carrying living tubes. This one is no exception. It has that meaty, smoky tone that so many early 1950s octal-preamp-based amps are known for, but with a little more bite and definition than you might expect and plenty of compression when you dig in. Cooder and Smith are clearly on to something.

Crank it up and it's easy to induce a throaty wail out of that tubey breakup, and while it's not especially loud, even for a supposed 25-watter, it's enough for smaller clubs with a diplomatic drummer, and it would be a boon in the studio for sure (where a smaller 15-watt Flot is likely to really shine). All of which is pretty impressive for a girlie-colored amp that was original marketed to the accordion crowd. That said, we would expect nothing less from an amplifier that boasts the catalog-copy platitude "A modern electronic miracle." (We jest not.) What else can we say other than, "Let's polka!" 🎱

Amp and photos courtesy Tommy's Guitar Shop

23

PRICE LIST

Gibson FAVORITE of the STARS

PIONEERING SOPHISTICATION

Get your classic 1950s electric jazz guitar tone right here, folks—warm, smooth, woody, and round . . . and positively dripping with "the juice." For all that it looks like a cheap suitcase, this 1952 Gibson GA-50T was a surprisingly sophisticated amp for its day—right up at the top of its class—and its features hold up to scrutiny sixty years later.

Jim Hall used a GA-50 (we don't know whether he used the tremolo-version GA-50T) for many years and declared it responsible for the best tone he ever achieved. This is an amp from the heart of Gibson, looking to be Gibson, with little regard for what California upstart Fender was up to and stuffing a design full of the quirks and upgrades that at the time represented a genuine effort to move the art forward. An amp conceived before the birth of rock 'n' roll, and

with a fully fleshed bias against the existence of any such music, the GA-50T was for purring and singing, not roaring and wailing. Let's poke around inside to see what makes it stand apart from the madding crowd.

The cab design and mismatched speaker configuration catch one's attention first, so let's start there.

Amp makers were still getting a handle on what they were dealing with regarding the frequency range of the electric guitar, and to many, a multi-speaker setup, something that might seem more at home in a hi-fi system, still seemed like a good idea. In the case of the GA-50T, which was introduced in 1948, we've got one 12-inch and one 8-inch. Although the little 8-inch in this mismatched set wouldn't be entirely happy with cranked-up rock 'n' roll, it could actually add some fidelity and sharpness to the overall tone when playing the music of its day, and the odd pairing worked together to add extra dimension and shimmer. Gibson used the mismatched formula on a number of

- Preamp tubes: Three 6SJ7s; 6SL7 tremolo; 6SN7
- Output tubes: Two 6L6GAs, cathode-biased
- Rectifier: 5V4
- Controls: Gain on each channel; shared Bass and Treble, tremolo Frequency, and Intensity
- Speakers: One Jensen P8P 8-inch and one P12P 12-inch
- Output: Approximately 20 watts RMS

The paraphase inverter, employing a 6SN7 dual triode, is pretty standard for its day, but the GA-50T's power stage incorporates two chokes. The first, mounted right after the initial filtering stage, is rated at 10 henrys and 175mA (and, very unusually, it has a 10uF filter cap bypassing it). Following it is a second of 30 henrys and 30mA. We've never seen that before, but it no doubt helps keep this old Gibson impressively quiet, and smooth and firm along with it—or relatively so for an amp that employs so many ingredients that normally contribute to serious squash and mid-range dirt.

In all, this is one upmarket amp for 1952. The cabinetry might be a little flimsy, with thinner side panels than you'd see in most quality tweed-era amps of a few years later, but a protective back panel that enclosed the entire rear section of the combo (and made it look even more like a suitcase from the posterior view) offered grab-and-go gigging convenience, and that six-knob control panel—mounted to the floor of the cab, of course—looked pretty impressive up against most of what the competition was putting out. Crank it up and you can certainly get a sweet little bluesy grind out of it, but keep our GA-50T in her comfort zone and there's arguably nothing better out there for sublime lounge jazz tones. ⦿

models throughout the 1950s and has returned to it again for some members of the revamped GA lineup of the modern era, starting with the Trace Elliot–designed Gold-tone series in the late 1990s.

Most people are more familiar with the ratings of the Jensens commonly used by Fender—the R, Q, and N ranges—but here we've got a P8P and a P12P. The P could handle more than the R and about the same as the Q (documentation varies, but it's usually around 20 watts) but was less efficient than the Q or N, decibels-wise. Together, these two speakers wouldn't pump out a lot of oomph, even with the dual 6L6 output stage behind them, but of course this is an old-school 6L6 circuit anyway. It's cathode biased, with a shockingly low bias resistor made possible by the relatively low voltages seen here, and we're guessing you could expect to see only between 18 and 22 watts here—and again, it would sound like even less, given the Jensen P's inefficiency. But it's about tone, not volume, and the GA-50T rolls it out in abundance.

Along with the odd speaker pairings, Gibson displayed an occasional fondness for pentode preamp tubes. This penchant is seen most prominently in the 5879 of the desirable GA-40 Les Paul Amp of a few years later but is represented here in the octal 6SJ7 tubes found behind the Microphone and Instrument inputs of the amp's two channels. It's a rich, full-sounding preamp tube, not dissimilar to the nine-pin EF86 (6267) in some ways. It also has a higher gain than the familiar 12AX7 or the 6SC7, 6SN7, and 6SL7 octal dual triodes that were popular in the late 1940s and early 1950s. But in this GA-50T, it's used more for fidelity and breadth than for pure gain.

Beyond the preamp, there are a few surprises. First—shock, horror—there's a two-knob EQ stage with controls for Bass and Treble, something we didn't see from Fender until the top-of-the-range Twin in 1952, although Gibson had been putting it into the GA-50T for some time. There's also a fairly complex and good-sounding tremolo circuit using both halves of a 6SL7 dual triode with another 6SJ7 as a booster stage. It's pretty deluxe stuff for 1952—and there's more to come.

Photos courtesy Vintage Guitar *magazine*

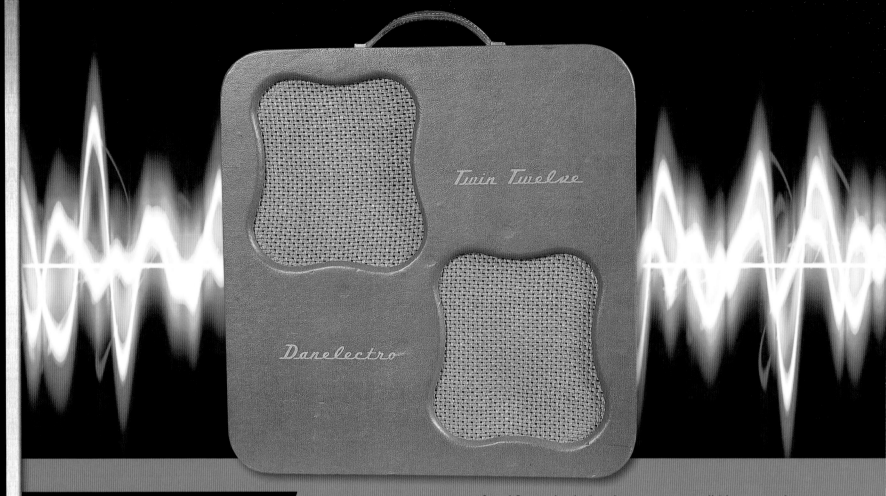

LOW-BUDGET LO-FI COOL

Sometimes an extremely funky old amp that wanders in makes you wish you had paid more attention as a kid to what was lurking in garage sales.

This Danelectro Twin Twelve from the mid 1950s is certainly one of them. It's an extremely unusual design, powerful for its day, and it has the kind of lost-era looks and grimy phat sound that makes it perfect for anything from proto-grunge to garage rock to low-end blues. It's also just so darned funky that it draws a lot of attention.

Danelectro amplifiers are often referred to as a poor man's Fenders, but company founder Nathan I. "Nat" Daniel was making amplifiers for a large New York department store in the 1930s, when Leo Fender was still learning to repair radios. Daniel followed by supplying Epiphone with early Electar amplifiers. He founded the Danelectro brand in Red Bank, New Jersey, in the late 1940s, and until he sold the company to MCA around 1966, he manufactured a range of amplifiers under the Danelectro name—as well Silvertone and a range of other brands.

As storied a career as Daniel had in the business, the history of Danelectro amps is considerably underdocumented. (Even finding schematics for these amps is tough.) And despite predating Fender—the grand establisher of guitar amplification standards—Danelectro and Silvertone products were almost universally second- or third-choice options for musicians who couldn't afford the professional-grade products Fender supplied to western swing and early rock 'n' roll players up and down the West Coast. Players who acquire one of these old fellas (or something similar) today will often declaim, "Wow, a vintage 1950s amp with four 6L6s and two 12-inch alnico speakers for a tenth the price of a tweed Twin!" But as cool as these Danos are, there are plenty of reasons for their affordability, even now that their collectibility is increasing.

Make no mistake, this Twin Twelve sounds extremely groovy—with a soft, smooth low end, throaty and slightly raspy mids, silky highs, and plenty of compression and saturation when cranked. But it's definitely garage-grade fidelity compared to the bandstand-grade performance of a 1950s Fender. For

CIRCA 1955 DANELECTRO TWIN TWELVE

- Preamp tubes: 12AX7, 6AU6, 6FQ7 (the latter as PI)
- Output tubes: Four 6L6GCs in class AB, fixed-bias
- Rectifier: 5U4GB
- Controls: Channel A Volume, Channel B Volume, Amplification, Bass, Treble, Vibrato Speed, Vibrato Strength
- Speakers: Two 12-inch CTS alnico
- Output: Approximately 40 watts RMS

starters, check out what the amp is housed in: no finger-jointed solid-pine cabinet here but a cab and baffle of rather flimsy particleboard covered in faux-bronco sticky paper (or a textureless brown covering) with a—*gasp*—diagonally mounted chassis and control plate. The latter feature seems like a lot of trouble to go to for a visual gimmick, but mounting the chassis across the diagonal provides more room for all those tubes and transformers than traditional horizontal positioning, so maybe there was more to it—or not.

Another notable feature is the use of two output transformers (OTs), one for each speaker, which would seem pretty deluxe except that they're each about the size of, well, a tweed Deluxe's OT, and even melted together they are far less weighty than the OT in an 80-watt Twin. Compared to higher-end amps, this Dano also has rather more gramophone-grade circuitry and components inside the chassis, but it does sport individual Bass and Treble controls rather than just the Tone of most amps of the 1950s, in addition to vibrato (tremolo) with Speed and Strength controls. None of Fender's larger amps carried the effect at the time.

Another drawback of many Danelectro designs—and those of plenty of other manufacturers when you consider them with hindsight in the light of Fender's foresight—is that they tended to use a lot of tubes that were fast on their way to becoming obsolete. Similar models also tended to jump from tube to tube through rather swift evolutions, as if the Dano techies just couldn't decide which types to favor. In addition to the four nifty Sylvania "Coke-bottle" 6L6s in this example, this electrified suitcase carried a 6AU6 for tremolo, a 6FQ7 in the phase inverter, a 5U4GB rectifier, and a 12AX7 in the preamp. The oddball tubes are one of the challenges faced by contemporary players who want to bring such an amp up to gig-worthy status. You've got to either find scarce (and potentially expensive) NOS parts or trust a good amp tech to convert certain portions of the circuit to use more conventional and readily available tubes.

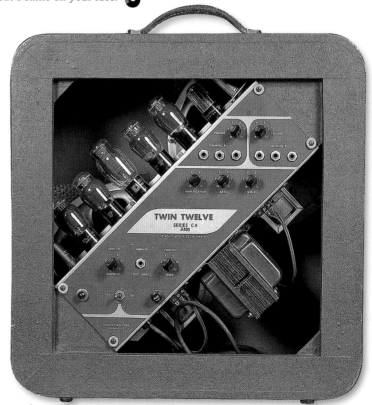

Photos courtesy Vintage Guitar *magazine*

But to hell with it. That exceedingly spiffy diagonally mounted chassis and control panel arrangement makes up for just about all this baby's shortcomings. It's impossible not to keep coming back to this feature because the format makes the amp such a conversation piece. Every guitarist who has encountered one of these amps has experienced at least a temporary bout of raw animal lust.

Don't kid yourself about this putting out anything close to a high-powered tweed Fender Twin's 80 watts, though. Just a glance at those diminutive OTs pegs them as being in the 15- to 25-watt camp, at most, so the Twin Twelve probably puts about that much power into each speaker, providing the Dano a maximum total output somewhere in the 30- to 50-watt range. Through a pair of well-worn CTS alnico speakers, it tends to sound like even less than that, and these were never efficient drivers to begin with. Never mind. Volume isn't king in Toneland, and the juicy, thick, ever-so-slightly raspy and gritty soundstage that the Twin Twelve whips up is as much of an attention getter as the amp's unconventional looks, and it could be just the thing to help plenty of players establish a distinctive voice in a range of genres.

A lot of guys have turned on to the lo-fi beauty of Danelectro and Silvertone amps over the years. While obvious examples of players tapping into this exact model may not spring to mind, Jon Spencer of the Jon Spencer Blues Explosion, Jack White of the White Stripes, and Mark Arm of Mudhoney have all indulged in the garagey growl of the 1960s Model 1484 Silvertone Twin Twelve (which has a head that fits neatly into the speaker cab for ease of cartage). Whichever evolution of the model you encounter, if it's in playable condition when you get there, it's guaranteed to put a smile on your face. ◗

28

1955 DANELECTRO TWIN TWELVE

Jack White of the White Stripes played later evolutions of this Danelectro amp, branded under the Silvertone name and sold by Sears. Here, the White Stripes perform onstage at the Fillmore in San Francisco, California, on June 4, 2002. *Anthony Pidgeon/Redferns/Getty Images*

AMPLIFIERS
by Danelectro

Illustrated above, our newest model:

The
Challenger

Giant 15-inch speaker — 30 watts — Vibravox* — $189.95

Two channels with separate volume controls, four inputs, two tone controls for bass and treble, two vibrato controls and remote control included.

Slip cover $8.25.

The Danelectro Corporation, Red Bank, N. J.

*Patent nos. 2466306, 2534342, 2550336

Twin-Twelve

TREMENDOUS POWER. Fifty (50) watts delivered by two pairs of pushpull 6L6 tubes to two heavy duty 12 inch speakers, makes this model the most powerful portable amplifier for musical instruments ever created. Vibravox*. Two channels with separate volume controls and three input jacks in each channel. Two tone controls, one for bass and one for treble. Vibrato has speed control, strength control and connection for remote control cable. Size 22" x 22" x 9½". Weight 40 lbs.

Slip Cover $8.25   Remote Control $4.25   Amplifier List $219.95

Maestro

THE STANDARD PROFESSIONAL MODEL. Vibravox* Seven tube chassis delivers 25 watts to 12 inch heavy duty speaker. Total of four inputs divided in two channels with separate volume control for each channel. Two tone controls for individual regulation of bass and treble. Vibrato has speed control, strength control and connection for remote control cable. Size 19" x 19" x 8½". Weight 30 lbs.

Slip Cover $8.25   Remote Control $4.25   Amplifier List $164.95

*Patent nos. 2466306, 2534342, 25503

PRO-AMP

This is the amplifier which has become a standard in the musical world. It has been in use for a number of years and has proven itself by its many durable performances throughout the years the Pro Amp has been on the market. It has been constantly changed and brought up to present day standards until today it represents the most modern circuitry possible. It is capable of excellent power and fidelity and has proven itself as a favorite among all classes of players.

The Pro Amp features the solid wood lock jointed cabinet, covered in brown and white striped airplane luggage linen. It features the top mounted chrome plated chassis with the following controls: bass, treble and presence tone controls, two volume controls, four input jacks, ground switch, on-and-off switch, and stand-by switch. It employs a heavy duty 15" Jensen speaker and is capable of producing considerable power without distortion.

It features the extension speaker jack mounted on the chassis providing instant connection for a separate or remote speaker. This is a fine feature which many professional players are using.

Tubes used: two 12AY7, one 12AX7, two 6L6G, one 5U5G. Three of these tubes are dual purpose tubes making it the equivalent of a nine tube amplifier. It produces high quality audio power and is truly an exceptional buy in its price class.

Size: 20" high, 22" wide, 10" deep.

Fender
fine electric instruments

1954 CATALOG

TV-front Fender Pro with a sunburst Gibson Les Paul Standard. *Amp and guitar courtesy Nathaniel Riverhorse Nakadate/photo Kerry Beyer*

DELUXE HEADROOM

We think of Fender amps from the 1950s as generically "tweed"—a word that has become synonymous with chewy, rich, slightly brown tones and superb touch sensitivity. Yet there is no single template to credit with all these characteristics but rather three different incarnations of tweed-covered amps through the course of the decade, with even more circuit variations hiding behind this simple cosmetic description. Our 1955 Pro sits right in the center of this evolution, both chronologically and developmentally, and thus makes a great jumping-off point for studying both its predecessors and its successors, and how its siblings in the lineup advanced through the decade too.

The Pro was one of Fender's first amplifier models, arriving in the form of the "woodie" Professional in 1946. It was the company's top-of-the-line amp at the time, with a big 15-inch speaker and two metal 6L6 output tubes (for around 20 watts of power), compared to the Deluxe's original 10-inch speaker and two 6V6s. It was aimed at the electric guitarist and steel player who really needed the optimum in amplification. The name was shortened to Pro in 1947 with the arrival of the TV-front cab and the loaning of its former moniker to the 2x10-inch V-front Dual Professional. The TV-front styling ushered in the new decade—though it had gained the more familiar diagonal tweed covering by 1949—but the circuit behind it advanced bit by bit throughout the early 1950s.

Notable archaisms of the 5C5 circuit of the late TV-front and early wide-panel models, which arrived in 1953, were its three octal 6SC7 preamp tubes and the grid-leak biasing of the first two of these, which provided the single gain stage for each of four inputs (from the two dual-triode tubes). The 5D5

- Preamp tubes: Two 12AY7s, one 12AX7 phase inverter
- Output tubes: Two 5881s (6L6 equivalents), cathode-biased
- Rectifier: 5U4G tube
- Controls: Volume, Volume, Tone
- Speaker: One 15-inch Jensen P15N
- Output: 30 watts RMS +/-

its own triode). Think about it a moment: How many players have raved about the tweed Deluxe's juicy compression and seductive overdrive yet bemoaned its crippling lack of headroom? Well, here's your big-boy Deluxe.

The 5E5 Pro has the cathode-biased output stage with no negative feedback (a topology often referred to as class A), two interactive volume controls with a single tone control, the cathodyne (aka split-phase) inverter, and several other little elements between them that help make the 5E3 a preeminent tone machine. Yet its two 6L6GBs, firmer 5U4GA rectifier tube, and bigger output transformer give it a stouter voice and significantly more volume. Aficionados of these amps will tell you that the tweed Pro is one of the great sleepers among tweed Fender amps. Perhaps the ultimate Tele amp for twang meets snarl with Volume set just shy of noon, and an unbeatable roadhouse blues shouter cranked to early afternoon or beyond, this amp can still be had for less cash then the smaller Deluxe, and it offers significantly more volume, plenty more headroom, and an overall bigger voice.

In 1956 the 5E5-A Pro gained improvements that its brethren, the Super, low-powered Twin, and Bandmaster, had received as much as a year before. Among these were the cathode-follower tone stack with independent treble and bass controls, a presence control, a fixed-bias output stage, and a negative feedback loop returned to the fold to tighten it all up a little more. This is many players' concept of the archetypal tweed amp—the fully featured narrow-panel model of the late 1950s—though that 12-month period during which Fender seemingly let the Pro lag behind design-wise did provide us a sweet cathode-biased, 6L6-based 30-watter, something that would forever after be missing from the lineup now that so many models were extremely similar, if not identical, other than in speaker complement.

For those who see the virtue of the rare 5E5 circuit but can lay their hands only on a more readily available 5D5, a conversion can be made. It takes a little creative thinking on the part of your amp tech, but twisting the self-balancing paraphase inverter into a cathodyne inverter with preceding gain stage involves only a handful of solder joints and cap and resistor changes, and removing the negative feedback loop, or making it switchable, is easy as pie. We hesitate to recommend modifying any collectible vintage amp, and a good 5D5 should sound outstanding—in its own way—just as it stands, but if you have a beater that needs internal work anyway and have long had your heart set on a 5E5, the mod is there as an option. The alterations give the amp a little more bite, broaden the frequency response slightly, and are easily reversible should you decide they're not for you or you want to sell the amp later in more original condition.

that followed in the wide-panel cab still had a version of the paraphase inverter seen in the 5C5, but this was now "self-balancing," a slight improvement, and the amp also gained a standby switch and a negative feedback loop to help tighten up the cathode-biased output stage. In addition, all preamp tubes were now the new nine-pin miniatures, a pair of 12AY7s for gain and a 12AX7 in the phase inverter, all cathode biased. Although the Pro hadn't yet become what the 6L6-based tweeds would embody by the end of the 1950s, it was a bigger, more powerful amp than it had been on its arrival eight years earlier. It now put out something in the region of 28 to 35 watts and had a broader frequency range and better note definition overall.

The Pro here typifies Fender amp production for its day, with a date stamp of "ED" signifying April 1955—making it an extremely late wide-panel example—an original Jensen P15N from a full year before, and an output tube alteration penned in on its chart (5881 in place of 6L6GC, though the two are interchangeable). It also carries the faded signature of "Lupe" on a piece of masking tape in the bottom of the chassis between the first two pre-amp tubes, a little piece of history that lets us know who wired it all together fifty-five years ago. Very shortly, however, 5D5 would become 5E5 and shed its wide-panel cab for its new narrow-panel shell, adopting a fleeting incarnation that some fans of the breed consider the sweetest of all tweed Pros.

In the short-lived 5E5 Pro of mid 1955 to early 1956, the circuit was identical to the ubiquitous 5E3 Deluxe once you got beyond the 1-meg input grid resistors and the independent 12AY7 for each channel (which still offered each of the four inputs

Bob Wills and His Texas Playboys plugged into at least a trio of Fender tweed amps, including what looks to be a TV-front Pro behind Wills himself. Guitarist Junior Barnard with his big Gibson ES-5 likely used the wide-panel Fender behind the pianist.
Michael Ochs Archives/Getty Images

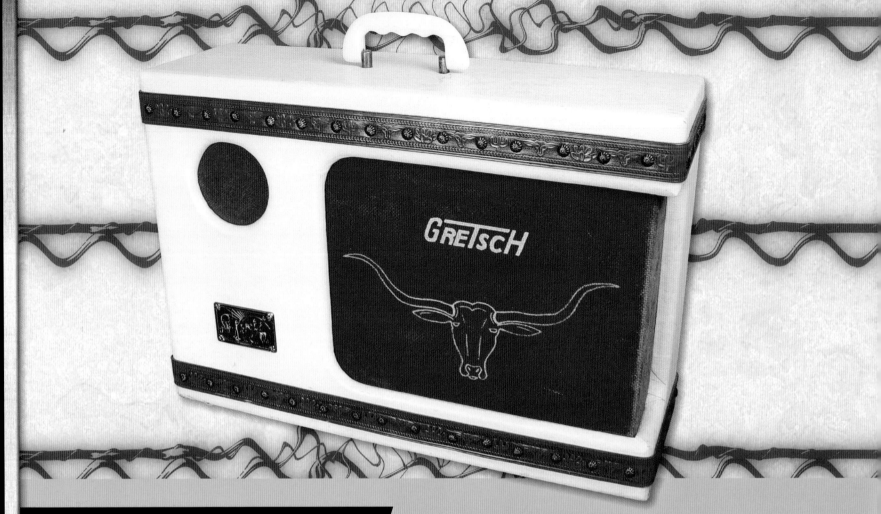

ONCE UPON A TIME IN THE WILD WEST

What good was selling a newfangled electric guitar back at the dawn of the revolution if you didn't have an electric guitar amplifier to go along with it?

Any significant brand that offered a lap steel or electro-Spanish model in the early days of rock 'n' roll also needed to offer an amp to make a "set" or "combo" out of the package—an obvious strategy from the marketing department's point of view—and by the mid 1950s Gretsch was one of the hottest names in electric guitars. Trouble was, the hallowed Brooklyn instrument maker didn't have its own amplifier production facility, so it did what plenty of others before and after it did: it turned to Chicago OEM supplier Valco to provide a range of spiffy-looking amps to partner with its bodacious guitars.

Valco was formed in the early 1940s out of the remnants of the National Dobro company, which had been transplanted from California to Chicago in the mid 1930s by legendary resonator guitar manufacturer Louis Dopyera. Named

for the first initials of its owners at the time (Victor Smith, Al Frost, and Louis Dopyera, plus "co" for "company"), Valco was soon cashing in big time on the Hawaiian music craze's shift from acoustic in the 1930s to electric in the 1940s. It supplied lap-style instruments, amplifiers, and even plenty of standard six strings sold under the Airline, Oahu, Supro, Danelectro, National, and other names. While Gretsch was doing just fine making its own guitars, the Valco products fit the bill very nicely for that critical second half of the combo, and wearing the well-considered Gretsch look and logo, they came out arguably the coolest of all the amps to roll out of the Chicago plant.

Even in the standard dress given the 6160 and 6161 models that accompanied many Gretsch guitars in the mid 1950s, these amps still looked damn spiffy. But swaddled in the ivory mock leather, burgundy wraparound grille cloth, and tooled leather trim of the 6169 Twin Western version, the workaday Valco was transformed into a total knockout. This amp was partner to the original 6120 Chet Atkins Hollow Body and 6121 Chet Atkins Solid Body models introduced in 1954, and the 6130 Roundup Solid Body of the same era, and it shares the western motif regalia that Atkins objected to from the

CIRCA 1955 GRETSCH 6169 ELECTROMATIC TWIN WESTERN

- Preamp tubes: Two 6SC7s
- Output tubes: Two 6V6GTs, cathode-bias
- Rectifier: 5Y3
- Controls: Volume, Tremolo (rate), Tone
- Speakers: Two elliptical 6x11-inch speakers, plus a 4-inch tweeter
- Output: 14 watts RMS

start (and eventually had removed from his signature guitar). You can clearly see the links between the longhorn steer on the grille cloth and the guitars' headstocks, and the "cow and cactus" tooled-leather trim on both the amp and the sides of the two solid-body guitars. And if you've ever seen an original hard shell case from any of the early Chet models, it's like encountering a twin that was separated at birth from the 6169 amp.

Despite the trendsetting looks (or should that be trendstopping?), the 6169 was an extremely basic amp inside, even for its day. This was one of the company's flagship models, intended to accompany what was arguably Gretsch's most important guitar line to date, yet it put out only about 14 watts and carried minimal tone-shaping facilities, all housed in a rather archaic vertically mounted chassis. The amp carried three inputs—two standard and one treble—but all went to the same gain stage formed at one side of a dual-triode 6SC7 octal (eight-pin) preamp tube. A simple treble bleed network formed the amp's lone Tone control, then it was on via the shared Volume control to a 6SC7 phase inverter and through a pair of 6V6GT output tubes to a field coil speaker configuration (these amps—and similar—were later offered with 6L6 and 6973 output tubes). Power conversion came courtesy of a 5Y3 rectifier tube. All in all, the tube complement is not unlike Fender's Model 5C3 Deluxe of the early 1950s, which is also cathode biased like the Gretsch/Valco, yet the amps sound quite different. Side-by-side comparison shows the Fender circuit to have been somewhat more advanced, even at that early stage in the company's existence, and the Deluxe ran its 6V6s at slightly higher voltages while giving the amp

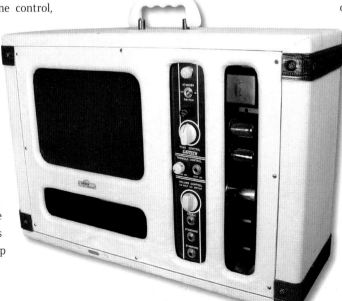

larger electrolytic capacitors in the power supply, resulting in a bigger, fatter sound. Leo had also long before abandoned cumbersome field coil speaker designs. And while we're there, dig this for a speaker configuration: the 6169 (and many of its siblings) carried two elliptical 6x11-inch speakers plus a 4-inch tweeter. Basically, it specced out like many tube gramophone units of the day.

The 6169 Electromatic Twin Western did have one thing over the early Fender amps, though—tremolo. Certain Valco-made amps had offered tremolo for a few years by the time Fender's first effects-carrying amp, the Tremolux, arrived in the summer of 1955. Of course, the Fender version had both speed and depth controls rather than the single, unspecified rate/speed control on this Gretsch's groovy yet somewhat antiquated control panel. All its shortcomings and near-obsoletisms aside, this hunk of kitschy cowboy couture really can sound damn cool when you jack in and crank up. For many players familiar with Fender's version of the sound at the heart of electric guitar music from the 1950s, plugging into a Gretsch 6169 or the near-identical 6160 or 6161 can feel like discovering one of the missing links of rock 'n' roll. It has gritty, biting highs; growling mids; round and softish (but pleasing) lows, and a slightly rubbery compression that really enhances its touch sensitivity. Addictive stuff. ●

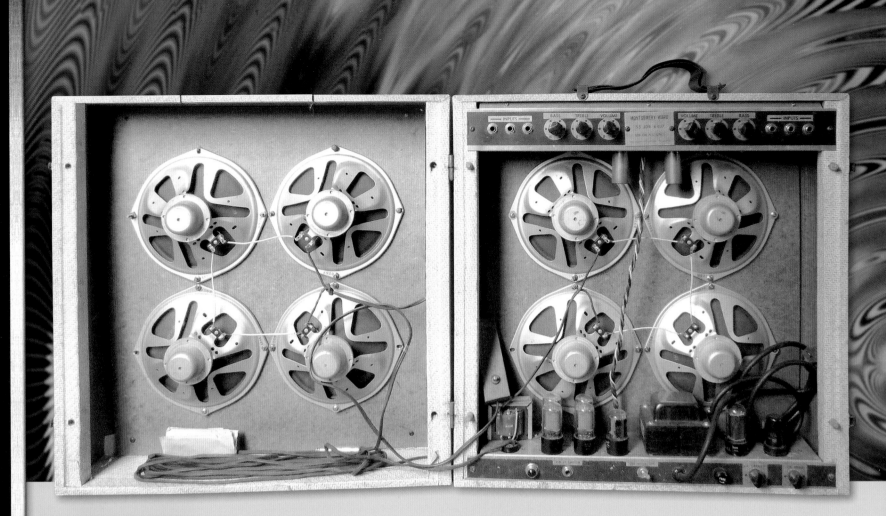

SUITCASE AMP

Freak of nature? No! This one is entirely of man's fevered imagination, and it's a head turner for sure. Known variously as the Danelectro Commando, Ward's Airline GDR-8518A, or Montgomery Ward Model 55 JDR 8437 (as pictured, with no Airline name in evidence, although that was Ward's usual amp line), this is another one of those creative alternatives some makers dreamed up in the days before the cement had dried in the template for "the guitar amplifier."

Sure, Fender's tweed Deluxe, Pro, and low-powered Twin already existed by this point in the mid 1950s, but some makers weren't ready to accept that 95 percent of the world's tube amps would one day look at least 80 percent like one of these, if you follow our thinking. So, with the benchmarks still way up in the air, why not build a combo amp that looked like a suitcase, with two halves hinged together, four 8-inch speakers in each side (eight total), and 25

feet of speaker cable to let you spread the love by separating the two halves and placing them at opposite sides of the stage? No reason at all.

The 8-inch speaker has come to be thought of as the driver of choice for small, beginner-style amps, but some manufacturers of the 1950s employed it in multiples in an effort to achieve higher fidelity for guitar, bass, and even accordion. It's an extension of the thinking that brought us Fender's 5F6-A tweed Bassman and later Ampeg's 8x10-inch SVT bass cabinet and was also applied to some other great amps, such as the Gibson-made Maestro GA-45T combo. The theory goes that spreading the amp's output and frequency range across four or eight 8-inch drivers would provide a firmer, more linear response than pushing it through one or two larger cones. In practice, however, it doesn't hold quite as much water—or tone—as it does with its multiple 10-inch embodiments, and we often find that amps like this or the Maestro sound more choked and boxy in their original guise than they do through an alternative cabinet (apologies to the spiffy Rola alnico speakers in question here). We're willing to bet that most guitarists would find this Ward's bountiful mojo even more groovesome injected into a pair of 12-inch speakers or a quad of 10s.

- Preamp tubes: Two 12AX7s, one 6SJ7 for tremolo, one 6SN7 for phase inverter
- Output tubes: Four 6V6GTs
- Rectifier: 5Y3
- Controls: Volume, Bass, Treble on each channel, vibrato Strength and Speed (shared)
- Speakers: Eight 8-inch Rola alnico
- Output: Approximately 25 watts RMS (downhill)

humble 5Y3, which would certainly squash under heavy load at high volume and be a big part of that juicy sag to which these amps succumb. The measly 315 volts DC that the power stage creates at the plates of the 6V6s, with around 300 volts on the grids, is another factor in this old suitcase's "none more brown" tone.

For all its flimsy particleboard cabinet, lightweight speakers, and relatively undersize transformers—and despite its supposed fold-and-go convenience—the 55 JDR 8437 is an awkward and surprisingly heavy amp to carry around. More often than not, you'll find them with handle busted too. Stick something reliable on there, latch it up tight, and haul it to your next blues or roots rock gig. The looks on the faces of the people in the audience—not to mention those of your own band members—will be more than worth it. It's got character aplenty and quirk to spare—and sometimes that's worth a world of fidelity and efficiency. ●

That said, it is much revered in some circles as an amp for blues harp wailers, as are many vintage amps with multiples of 8-inch speakers. Little Walter's name comes up in harp circles as a possible player of this 8x8-inch Dano/Ward model, and you can certainly imagine his sizzling, reedy tone emanating from one of these. The observation in itself highlights the fact that this is the kind of amp you play as an effect as much as an "amplifier" per se, which is what amplified harp tone is all about. Likewise, for papery, slightly ragged, gnarly, edge-of-fart-out blues guitar tone—and we mean nasty, greasy, backwater roadhouse blues—this might be your ticket after all.

Speaker configuration aside, it's an interesting amp in a number of other ways. Manufactured by Danelectro for the Montgomery Ward catalog and department store chain in the early/mid 1950s, it uses four 6V6GT output tubes to generate approximately 25 watts, where most amps would turn to a pair of 6L6GCs, which would be both simpler and more cost effective. The separate top-mounted preamp section uses a triode each from one 12AX7 for the first gain stage for each of the two channels and another 12AX7 for gain makeup after the independent Bass, Treble, and Volume controls on each. From there, an umbilical cord takes the signal down to the lower chassis (and in turn carries the B+ and filament currents up), where power and output stages are housed. A 6SJ7 (later a 6AU6) reigns over a bias-modulating tremolo circuit housed down there (called vibrato on the panel), with its own Speed and Strength controls, and a 6SN7 octal dual triode covers phase inverter duties. The rectifier is a

Elvis Presley performs in his hometown of Tupelo, Mississippi, on September 26, 1956, alongside guitarist Scotty Moore and his Ray Butts EchoSonic—set atop a folding chair to boost its volume.
Michael Ochs Archives/Getty Images

THE VOICE OF ROCKABILLY

If you want to talk star-user ratio, the Ray Butts EchoSonic has to be close to the top of the heap. Most accounts agree that fewer than seventy of these amps were ever made, yet owners included Chet Atkins, Luther Perkins, Roy Orbison, Paul Yandell, Carl Perkins, and, the most celebrated in EchoSonic lore, Elvis Presley guitarist Scotty Moore. In short, Butts' baby made *the* sound of rock 'n' roll—rockabilly in particular—and for a brief time in the mid 1950s, anyone who wanted to achieve it went to Ray Butts to get it.

The EchoSonic featured here, serial number 24, was originally sold to Paul Yandell, who played with the Louvin Brothers, Chet Atkins, Kitty Wells, and

Jerry Reed. Scotty Moore bought it in the late 1980s or early 1990s as a backup for his original EchoSonic and sold it only recently to touring guitarist Deke Dickerson, who still owns and uses it today. An illustrious history for one small brown combo, but the EchoSonic's lineage takes us even deeper into the beating heart of rock 'n' roll.

Even before the first EchoSonic was born on Butts' workbench, slapback echo was a key element of the rock 'n' roll sound—and the early 1950s guitar sound in general—but prior to the creation of this amp, the sound was produced as a studio effect, and one not easily transported to the performance stage.

Butts, who owned a music store and repair shop in Cairo, Illinois, built the first EchoSonic amp for a local named Bill Gwaltney, who wanted to replicate Les Paul's slapback sound in live performance. Using an existing 15-watt

CIRCA 1956 RAY BUTTS ECHOSONIC

- Preamp tubes: Four 12AU7s, two 12AY7s, one 12AX7 (sub for original 12AD7), one 6C4
- Output tubes: Two 6L6s
- Rectifier: 5V4GA (or sub 5AR4 or 5U4)
- Controls: Mic Level, Instrument Level (dry volume), Echo Level (echo volume), Echo Decay (repeats), Echo Input Level, Tone
- Speaker: One University UC-121 12-inch speaker
- Output: Approximately 25 watts RMS

Gibson amp based around a pair of 6V6 output tubes as a springboard for the design, Butts labored over various methods for achieving built-in echo units, finally abandoning a noisy wire recorder for a tape-loop design. Gwaltney's amp was completed, and successfully used, by 1953, and Butts had an inkling he was on to something.

He built a second EchoSonic, packed it in the car, and headed to Nashville, where he hoped to audition it for the premier name in electric guitar at that time. As Butts told Dave Kyle in an interview for *Vintage Guitar* magazine in 1994, he simply looked up Chet Atkins in the phone book and gave him a call.

"He answered the phone and I told him what I had," Butts told Kyle. "He seemed kind of interested and told me he would be rehearsing for the Opry at the radio station and if I wanted, I could bring the amp there and he'd try it out. I did, and a bunch of them gathered around, they'd never heard anything like this before." Pretty soon, however, they, and others, were hearing it plenty.

Atkins used the amp at the Grand Ole Opry the very next night and decided to buy it. Butts sold it to him the day after that for his newly established list price of $495, minus $100 for a Fender combo that Atkins gave him on trade-in. This was a hefty price at the time, given that the new Fender Twin sold for $239 in 1954, but the fact that EchoSonics carried the highly desirable built-in echo effect and were made one at a time by hand by Butts himself puts it all into better perspective.

Atkins began using the amp straight away, employing the echo on several prominent recordings—his famous rendition of "Mister Sandman" among them—and the hip new cat in town was swiftly crawling out of the bag.

As reported on the very informative ScottyMoore.net, Moore heard an Atkins instrumental on the radio and chased down the source by way of achieving on stage the slapback that Sam Phillips had been giving his guitar in the studio. Moore ordered

his own EchoSonic early in 1955 and took delivery in May of that year. In July of 1955, this most famous of EchoSonics hit the studio with Moore, Elvis, and company, where it was used on the groundbreaking recording of "Mystery Train," among others.

The EchoSonic continued to be used on every recording Moore made with Presley, up to and including the legendary 1968 *Comeback Special* on NBC TV (originally entitled *Elvis, Starring Elvis Presley*). There it can be heard and can occasionally be seen behind Moore's right leg during the seated, in-the-round performances.

Like some tube-fired chain reaction worthy of the Old Testament, Moore's purchase and prolific use of his EchoSonic—serial number 8 (though often reported as being the third one built)—continued to send waves of desire for the new sound rippling through the Nashville scene. Chet's playing begat Scotty's desire. Scotty's playing begat Luther's desire, and Carl's desire, and Roy's desire . . .

In time, Butts' work naturally begat a little desire on the part of the industry, too, and the design of the tape-echo unit mounted in the bottom of the combo cab was eventually adapted for use in the short-lived Rickenbacker Ek-O-Sound and the far-longer-lived Maestro Echoplex. Another Butts design brought Gretsch a humbucking pickup, the Filter 'Tron, which nearly beat out Gibson at the patent office. It was developed after Chet Atkins requested a pickup that produced less bass than the DeArmond Model 100 while also canceling hum.

As reported by Deke Dickerson, the current owner of number 24, these amps aren't short of quirks. The delay time of the slapback echo is fixed and is longer than the current concept of "rockabilly slapback" (and longer still when you first switch on the amp, until the capstan motor has warmed up for five to ten minutes), but, says Dickerson, "that is the EchoSonic sound."

As for the amplifier itself, it is also something of a one-trick pony. It doesn't have much punch, even for a 25-watter (by the time of Moore's first amp, Butts had changed from 6V6s to 6L6s), but that too is part of the mystique. "These amps have a magic sound," Dickerson declares. "They are not very loud, and they break up really easily, and it really only does one thing with the nonadjustable echo. In that regard, it's not a very versatile amp at all. But the one thing that it does has not been captured by any other amplifier before or since. Nothing has that sound but an Echosonic! This amp I own still works great today and still has that awesome 'Scotty Moore sound.'"

Ideally sized for the recording studio, the EchoSonic was woefully small for live use—its raison d'être—even by the time rock 'n' roll graduated from sock hop to theater stage. To that end, even before Fender designed the whopping "high-powered" Twin of 1958, and long, long before Vox and Marshall upped the ante on the AC100 and Super Lead, respectively, to help the Beatles, the Who, and other Brits overcome similar difficulties, Butts created a pair of powered 50-watt "satellite" cabs to enable Moore's lithe rockabilly riffs to be heard on stage in front of thousands of screaming Elvis fans. Otherwise, this 25-watt combo with a single 12-inch speaker and its own built-in echo effect is a quaint reminder of a time when rebellion, and groundbreaking tone, came packed into a cabi-net the size of a traveling salesman's battered suitcase. 🔊

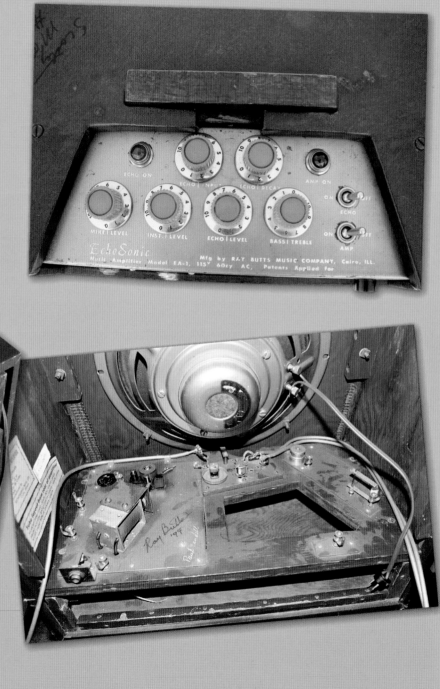

Deke Dickerson (left) and Scotty Moore with Moore's backup EchoSonic amplifier. *Rick Malkin*

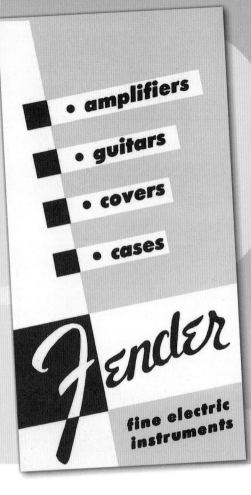

- amplifiers
- guitars
- covers
- cases

Fender

fine electric instruments

THE LITTLE AMP THAT COULD

For many players and amp-o-philes alike, the tweed Fender Champ is ground zero for vintage tube amps. The simplicity of this design and part and parcel to that, the purity of its tone make it a universal starting point for the virtues of tube amps et al for many players. As such it's a vintage amp that every guitarist should experience it at least once.

You want to hear what an electric guitar sounds like when amplified through a vacuum tube? Fender's 5F1 Champ is the way to go. With one pre-amp tube, one output tube, one rectifier tube, just a single volume control, and two signal capacitors in the circuit, this is about the most direct route from point A to point B—or from input to output—you're going to find.

When one says "purity of its tone," that doesn't mean it's a "stellar" tone in everyone's estimation. It is uncluttered, but at anything more than mid-morning on the volume dial, it will start to break up pretty fast. Crank it up and it can sound great or pure flub incarnate, depending on your tastes . . . or on your amp. That little 8-inch will lose its gusto pretty quickly too (and to think, early ones had 6-inch speakers).

For examples of small-tweed goodness, fans will rave about Eric Clapton's tone on several recordings purportedly achieved with a tweed Champ, cuts such as "Layla" (and others from Derek and the Dominos' 1970 release *Layla and Other Assorted Love Songs*). For others, though, that stuff sounds pretty boxy and ratty, like a small amp being pushed too hard—which is exactly what it is. Set your Champ's level just on the edge of breakup, though, and put a sensitive recording mic in front of it, and the raw, edgy tone that ensues will often be pure rock 'n' roll and will sit amazingly well in the right track.

Aside from any sonic virtuosity, though, these things just look so damned cute, like a Super and a Bassman got together one night after the gig and a

1957 FENDER 5F1 CHAMP

- Preamp tube: One 12AX7
- Output tube: One 6V6GT, cathode-bias
- Rectifier: 5Y3
- Control: Volume
- Speakers: One Jensen P8T or Oxford 8EV 8-inch
- Output: 4 watts RMS

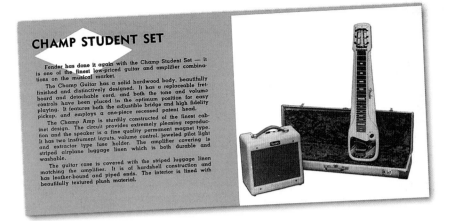

CHAMP STUDENT SET

Fender has done it again with the Champ Student Set — it is one of the finest low-priced guitar and amplifier combinations on the musical market.

The Champ Guitar has a solid hardwood body, beautifully finished and distinctively designed. It has a replaceable fretboard and detachable cord, and both the tone and volume controls have been placed in the optimum position for easy playing. It features both the adjustable bridge and high fidelity pickup, and employs a one-piece recessed patent head.

The Champ Amp is sturdily constructed of the finest cabinet design. The circuit provides extremely pleasing reproduction and the speaker is a fine quality permanent magnet type. It has two instrument inputs, volume control, jeweled pilot light and extractor type fuse holder. The amplifier covering is striped airplane luggage linen which is both durable and washable.

The guitar case is covered with the striped luggage linen matching the amplifier. It is of hardshell construction and has leather-bound and piped ends. The interior is lined with beautifully textured plush material.

sweet-looking little Champ popped out nine months later. That, and the fact that their affordability relative to the bigger tweeds makes them the one slice of Fender history that most players can aspire to, gives them plenty of desirability.

While the Fender Champ is the archetype of its breed, a similar tone and vibe are represented by single-ended models from almost every amp maker who ever put iron to solder. Aside from the potentially flabby speaker and a propensity to mush out quickly if you push them too hard, the beauty of these little beasts is their inherently, definitively class A operation. Since you are pushing just one output tube, a 6V6GT in the Champ's case, this amp has no choice but to run in pure class A, as defined by the tube amplifying the signal during the entire wave cycle. Hit it short of the freak out, and the Champ issues that chiming, harmonics-laden tone that feels so chewy and three dimensional and that so many players chase incessantly in larger amps and rarely find.

In front of that 6V6GT we get two stages from the amp's single 12AX7 twin-triode preamp tube, one for the first gain stage, another for the output driver, and fewer than ten solder joints from input to output transformer. The handful of resistors are all pulling other duties, and your signal passes through none of them after the obligatory 68k grid stopper that follows each of two input jacks. No tone control, no bright switch, no nothin'. Even the on/off switch is on the back of the volume pot.

As simple as the amp's circuit is, though, the Champ's power supply and filtering stage aren't a whole lot smaller than those of the medium-size Deluxe amp. The Champ still has three larger electrolytic (filter) capacitors to feed the OT, output tube, and preamp

tube, and the 5E1 Champ that preceded the 5F1 even had a choke—something many midsize amps still lacked at the time—although it was replaced in this iteration by a 10k dropping resistor between the first and second caps. Given the noise that high-idling single-ended circuits can be prone to, heavy filtering is often a necessary component of the design—and important if you want to rein in the fur. Also necessary, if you want anything firmer than total fart-out, is a little negative feedback around the output stage, another "big-amp ingredient" that even the 5E3 Deluxe lacked.

Stir up this simple, uncluttered stew, and, regardless of sonic nuances, the Champ is one of the most touch-sensitive amps you'll ever plug into. The 5Y3 rectifier tube sags easily but isn't strained so hard by the required voltage that it caves in entirely, and that cooking, single-ended performance lashes chocolaty goodness on every note.

This is a great platform for your avid tube taster too. Every little swap of either preamp or output tube will revoice the Champ, uncovering new and different sonic dimensions. Even plugging it into a 1x10-inch extension cab opens up its voice significantly, and a 1x12 inch or larger can be a real hoot. But the Champ is still a 4-watter, however you slice it, and for most needs that little Jensen P8T will do just fine. ◐

Fender's Champ 600 reissue harkened back to some of the company's earliest amps. *Fender Musical Instruments Corporation*

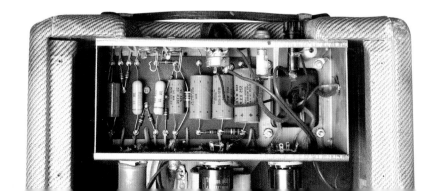

Eric Clapton performs with Derek and the Dominos during the 1970 U.S. tour, playing his Frankenstein's monster of a Stratocaster, nicknamed "Brownie." He used a Fender Champ in the studio to record the band's sole studio album, *Layla and Other Assorted Love Songs*. *Elliot Landy/Redferns/Getty Images*

DEREK IS ERIC LONDON JUNE '70

Fender's narrow-panel Champ reissue.
Fender Musical Instruments Corporation

THE TONE ALTERNATIVE

Until just a couple years ago, Fender really was the only major name in collectible vintage American-made tube guitar amplifiers. Sure, Magnatone, Standel, Danelectro/Silvertone, Supro, and the other Valco-made amps have their followers, and dealers have always been fond of selling a vintage Gibson or Gretsch guitar in a set with its corresponding amp. But for big bucks, it's Fender all the way. Even Gibson, which conversely delivered the most prized of vintage electrics in the 1958–1960 Les Paul with sunburst finish, couldn't produce an amplifier to dent the timeless desirability and escalating value of the tweed, brownface, and blackface Fenders.

Gradually, however, the underdog tubesters from the golden years of Yank-built tone are redressing the balance. Prior to the new millennium, you could have landed any early Gibson amp for way under a grand. But keen-eyed collectors and players have noticed that GA-40T Les Paul models of the mid 1950s to early 1960s have climbed steadily in price—right to the $2,500 range and

beyond for good examples—and their newfound glory has had a knock-on effect on lesser models from the same period, such as the GA-20 and GA-30, as well as other related models. Players have discovered that all of them can be hip-sounding electronic suitcases in their own way, but the 5879 pentode preamp tubes of the GA-40T push its juice factor over the top. Suddenly, the Kalamazoo amp shop haps of fifty years ago are happening, and if you want to get on the bandwagon, you'd better leap fast.

Alternatively, you could find yourself, uh, an alternative. Enter our 1957 Maestro GA-45T. Released in 1955 and manufactured by Gibson, the Maestro combo was billed as an amplifier for use with accordion and electric bass. It comes in the same cabinet as the Gibson GA-40T and looks nearly identical, except that its two-tone covering is black and luggage-grade tweed (which with wear can take on a snakeskin look) rather than the Gibson's maroon and buffalo tweed (later standard tweed) outfit, and the Maestro's control panel is chrome rather than brown enamel.

They are even more similar internally. The GA-45T uses the same tube complement and circuit as the GA-40T, except that it carries bass and treble

CIRCA 1957 MAESTRO GA-45T

- Preamp tubes: Two 5879s; 6SQ7 tremolo; 12AX7 PI
- Output tubes: Two 6V6GTs, cathode bias
- Rectifier: 5Y3
- Controls: Volume on each channel, shared Bass and Treble, tremolo Depth and Frequency
- Speakers: Four 8-inch Jensen DP-Alnico-5 Concert
- Output: 15 watts RMS

controls instead of the single tone, and both channels are intended for microphone or instrument rather than one being for mic and one for inst. Finally, the GA-45T's cab houses four 8-inch alnico Jensen speakers rather than the GA-40T's single 12-inch. This was done in the same spirit as the four 10-inch Jensens in the Fender Bassman in a bid to shelve the low fundamentals of the notes of these two bottom-heavy instruments and to avoid "farting out" the speakers. Notable but minor differences—and yes, the GA-45T can easily be reverse-engineered into a GA-40T.

The cliché "poor man's Fender" (too often completed with the word "Deluxe") gets slapped on unsuspecting Gibson combos far more often than deserved. But in this case—despite the use of a 5Y3 rectifier and a pair of 6V6GT output tubes to spew around 15 watts—you're looking at two amps that really couldn't be more different in 1957. Instead of the cathodyne (aka split-load) phase inverter in the 5E3 Deluxe, the GA-45T has a paraphase PI like tweed Fenders from earlier in the 1950s. The Maestro also carries a choke, but more significantly, those 5879 preamp tubes are simply nothing like the 12AY7 or 12AX7 found in Fenders. A little closer to the more familiar EF86 pentode than anything else, they are less microphonic than that occasionally troublesome tube of the vintage Vox AC15 and are just fat, wide, warm, and greasy sounding all at once. In short, they're the bedrock of a tone all its own.

As well as having more gain than the more common 12A-7 dual triodes, they also handle input voltage

more elegantly, which means they don't fizz up into hairy dirtballs of tone and instead pass a thick, rich frappe of a soundstage along to further stages of the amp. In addition, the EQ stages of the Fender Deluxe and Gibson/Maestro are entirely different, the latter being an odd configuration that follows the PI rather than a treble-bleed network between preamp and output stages as on the 5E3. Top it off with a very hip-sounding tremolo and you can wave farewell to Fullerton.

Aside from the differences in the speakers, the two-knob EQ seems to rein in the GA-45Ts gain just a little from that of the GA-40T, but that's not entirely a bad thing. Those 5879s are fat-sounding tubes and ramp up the gain in a big way in the first place, so it survives the two-pot journey well. If anything, you get a jot more twang than in the GA-40T, although all bets are off once you crank up either one of them past halfway.

The other disparity between the Gibson and the Maestro is, of course, the speaker configuration. The GA-45T sounds good with guitar with its stock 4x8-inch rig, but plug it into a 1x12-inch extension cab with any reputable driver and it really comes to life. A Jensen P12Q, Celestion G12H-30, or Celestion Alnico Gold produces great (if varied) results, and the amp reveals firmer lows, more aggressive and blooming mids, and much more giggable volume levels. The 22-inch (wide) x 20-inch (high) cab even allows for a 15-inch speaker if you want to cut such a baffle. Being specced for accordion, the four 8-inch speakers also work a treat for harp, of course, and the fact that blower extraordinaire Little Walter wailed on a Maestro GA-45T lends kudos to the model.

The output transformer on Gibson's GA-40T Les Paul is already a little larger than that of a 5E3 Deluxe, but many tell how, in the Maestro, they used the OT from the larger two-6L6GC-equipped Gibson GA-77. Indeed, the OT on our example is a little longer than that of a GA-40T, and it's mounted at a slight angle to fit between the rectifier and output tubes. (It's not an anomaly or an aftermarket OT—it exists on others.) That said, open-frame OTs have been seen on GA-77s, and this is an enclosed part with bell ends. However you slice it, though, this is one hairy, happening amp! ⬤

THE DEBUT OF THE QUINTESSENTIAL TWIN

The high-powered Twin undoubtedly represents the zenith of Fender amps of the 1950s. The Twin is such a legendary amp format that it has become almost a generic, like Kleenex or Band-Aid.

We've lived with its later incarnations as underappreciated house amps or dusty rec room beer holders for so long that its upholstered predecessor appears almost alien to us—but the model under the microscope here really is the first Fender Twin, for all intents and purposes. Sure, the Twin debuted as a wide-panel tweed combo of 1952, and the low-powered, narrow-panel 5E8-A Twin of 1956–1957 is more emulated by the copyists. But at around 25 and 40 watts, respectively, these early renditions are mere poor relations to the big boy that this format would grow up to be, in terms of wattage at least. In 1958, however, the 5F8 (soon 5F8-A) Twin unleashed a whopping 80 watts of output power on the unsuspecting guitar world and forever established what a Twin

should be: *muy grande* power in a relatively compact 2x12-inch grab-and-go combo package.

Or should that be "herniate and go?" Less so for the tweed-era Twins than for the gut-busting blackface and silverface Twin Reverbs, but with all the weighty iron they packed, these were still heavier than anything else to come down the pike to that point. That said, you're looking at something just a few ticks away from a Marshall JTM100 stack but roaring through a mere two Jensen P12N speakers. That's a lot of firepower in a 26x20x10 1/2-inch pine box. Let's crawl inside and look around.

The birth of the 5F8-A Twin is often pegged to the addition of another two 5881 output tubes to the pair in the 5E8-A that preceded it, but it's a very different amp in a few other crucial ways. To wit, it's actually a lot closer to being a 5F6-A Bassman with four 5881s and two 12s—which many people think is just a low-powered Twin with four 10s instead of two 12s. Have we lost you yet? Good.

1958 FENDER TWIN 5F8-A

- Preamp tubes: One 12AY7, two 12AX7s
- Output tubes: Four 5881s (6L6 equivalents), fixed-bias
- Rectifier: GZ34 (5AR4) tube
- Controls: Volume, Volume, Treble, Bass, Middle, Presence
- Speakers: Two 12-inch Jensen P12Ns
- Output: 80 watts RMS +/-

B. B. King and "Lucille" play the blues in the spotlight at the Apollo Theater in Harlem, New York, in 1964. King's Fender tweed Twin sits in the edge of light, alongside an Ampeg. *Michael Ochs Archives/Getty Images*

Danny Gatton plays his 1953 blackguard Fender Telecaster at Slim's in San Francisco on July 2, 1993, through his battered tweed Twin and a Custom Shop Fender Vibro-King. *Clayton Call/Redferns/Getty Images*

To clarify: in addition to the obvious doubling of power, the 5F8-A circuit employed a long-tailed pair phase inverter, at this time the only Fender other than the Bassman to be given this eloquent PI. This change helped minimize distortion at the inverter stage, meaning more of the full, unadulterated tonal goodness was translated to the 5881s and their bigger-output transformer.

This constitutes just a few wiring changes and half a dozen or so new resistors, and it still uses just the one tube that the 5E8-A's driver/splitter network required, but it takes an amp up to the big leagues and makes the Twin's evolution complete. From the paraphase PI and cathode-biased output stage of the original 5C8 Twin (capable of generating only 25 watts from two 6L6/5881s) to the fixed-bias output stage and cathodyne inverter of the 5E8-A to the 5F8-A's fully evolved circuit—that's a pretty big leap in just six years, and it shows how Fender was romping along and really pushing the envelope. Rock 'n' roll and electric country were getting into full swing as commercial genres, popular guitar-based music was finding its way to bigger and bigger stages, and players were demanding more volume to help them cut through. (Much is made of Jim Marshall's move to 100-watters in the mid 1960s for the same reasons, but it was happening here first, folks!)

The 5F8-A also gained a Middle control, a sturdy GZ34 (5AR4) rectifier, and firmer power filtering (20uF electrolytic capacitors in place of the 16uF caps). The latter two particularly contribute to its robust performance.

This is a good place to point out that the Twin's pair of Jensen P12N speakers really weren't up to the task if you cranked the amp up full whack. It's amazing that so many of these speakers (well, some at least) survive to this day. Their ratings changed over the years, but P12Ns of the era were nominally rated at around 30 watts RMS (the reissues claim 50 watts). Why put only 60 watts worth of speaker in an 80-watt amp? For one thing, that was one of the most robust speakers available in the day, for decent money at least. But for another, Leo Fender really wasn't intending these amps to be wound up to the max for a full-on crunchfest. He was designing for headroom, and 80 watts meant you could retain better headroom than anything else on the market with the Twin up to about 6 or 7 on the dial and putting out 60 clean watts, give or take. Push it past that point, though, and, whoa boy, this fella' really roars!

For all its impressive muscularity, the 5F8-A simply isn't going to be every player's favorite flavor of tweed Twin. Many guitarists' goal with the tweed vibe is to get to the sweet spot quickly and easily, without rupturing too many eardrums in the process. Eric Clapton and Keith Richards can get away with the full 80-watt glory, certainly, but most corner stages down at the Rusty Nut aren't going to let you fire one up on a Saturday night. For the rest of us, a Super, Pro, low-powered Twin, or even a little Deluxe will do the job beautifully. But if you ever land on a big stage where you can do justice to a 5F8-A Twin, hang on tight and enjoy the ride. 🎸

Danny Gatton's favorite amp, a tweed 1956 Fender Twin. *Steve Gorospe*

Fender's 57 Twin Amp reissue.
Fender Musical Instruments Corporation

Fender 57 Twin Amp (here with a 52 Telecaster Reissue) is made with a printed circuit board rather than being hand-wired like the originals, and includes a few other component changes, but it is largely true to the original circuit, and has been popular with players looking to acquire some vintage-style tone at more reasonable prices. *Fender Musical Instruments Corporation*

51

VIBRATO VASTNESS

When guitarists talk tremolo or vibrato, you can bet the magnificent Magnatone amps will find their way into the conversation. The watery, warbling "true vibrato" that the larger Magnatones are capable of producing is never forgotten by players fortunate enough to have experienced it.

In searching to expand the Magnatone legend, the subject is likely to come around to players who used these amps, and the pool is surprisingly small. Some might mention Lonnie Mack's formative work, which deserves credit even if a relatively small percentage of the listening public has heard his playing. And we have to stop in on Bo Diddley, who certainly moved through countless amps through the years but undoubtedly used some Magnatones early on. But inevitably we turn to the more populist Buddy Holly, who, following a range of Fender tweed amps, became a notable fan of Magnatone. So how cool is it to have the opportunity to check out Buddy Holly's *very own* 1958 Magnatone Custom 280? Unfathomably cool.

And how do we know this was Buddy Holly's own amp? Well, because Buddy told us so—by sticking his name and the date of acquisition right there on the front in gold DYMO lettering tape and by signing and dating the inside of the cabinet. That, and because Gruhn Guitars, which recently sold this amp, has Holly's ownership thoroughly documented. Oh, and of course it was also displayed at the Rock and Roll Hall of Fame for a time and has been authenticated by the curator of that museum.

Note the surprisingly good condition of this amp and be interested to learn that it was Holly's "home amp," which he kept in the apartment that he and wife Maria Elena Holly shared in New York City after purchasing it from Manny's in September 1958, just half a year before his death in February 1959. It was used to record several vibrato-heavy demos—notably "Peggy Sue Got Married"—and even the scratch tracks for many of his final studio cuts, while another amp was taken out on the road. No studio recordings of this amp were

Amp courtesy Gruhn Guitars/photos Eric C. Newell

- Preamp tubes: Three 12AX7s, three 6CG7s, one 12AH7
- Output tubes: Four 6973s, fixed-bias
- Rectifier: 5U4GB
- Controls: Loudness, Bass, and Treble for each of two channels; Vibrato Speed and Intensity, plus switches for Stereo/Normal and Remote (Instrument/foot switch)
- Speaker: Two Jensen P12Ps, plus two 5-inch tweeters
- Output: Approximately 25 watts RMS per channel

released before his death, but original takes featuring the Magnatone were uncovered for the mixes of posthumous releases such as "Love Is Strange," "Smokey Joe's Café," and "Slippin' and Slidin'" from MCA's *The Complete Buddy Holly*.

A letter written by Holly's sister, Patricia Holley Kaiter (Buddy's birth name was Charles Hardin Holley, with the extra *e*), and provided with the recent sale of the amp, indicates that she "sold the Magnatone Custom 280 'Stereo Vibrato' amplifier to Emmylou Harris on November 8, 1988" to be given as a birthday gift to Paul Kennerly, Harris' husband at the time. Rather oddly, the letter goes on to say that the amp "is one that Buddy used in his earlier years" and had been in the Holley family until that time. Buddy Holly used Fender amps earlier in his career, and the Magnatone clearly dates from 1958, so this might merely be some confusion on her part or a trick played on the memory by the haze of thirty years. Either way, this is one incomparable slice of rock 'n' roll history, although even your bog standard, no-name-ownership Magnatone Custom 280 is a pretty rare amp and an acquisition worth cooing over.

Capable not only of producing true vibrato, the Custom 280, as the late rock 'n' roller's sister informs us, is a stereo amplifier too. With the effect running on full, the vibrato's pulses and warbles alternate between each of the amp's two 12-inch speakers (each paired with a 5-inch tweeter) to create an eerie, spatial soundscape that is truly hypnotic. Magnatone dubbed this girthsome sound "vibrato vastness," as signaled by the two gold *V*s in the lower right corner of the speaker grille (and most people always thought they were birds). In addition to this tidbit, a 1957 catalog boasts: "The ultimate in modern amplifiers—the Custom 280 has a sound BIG AS ALL

OUTDOORS—the Vastness of the sky combined with MAGNATONE'S BIG 'V' Electronic True Vibrato."

To achieve said vastness, the 280 routes its preamp to a stereo vibrato circuit that feeds two entirely independent output stages consisting of two pairs of 6973 output tubes hitched to two output transformers. We see these 6973s mainly in Valco-made amplifiers—the Supro Model 24 and Gretsch 6156 Playboy among them—and they can be great-sounding tubes. Partnered with rather small OTs for the task, however, they figure as part of what many players object to in the Magnatone design: for their size, weight, and swirly potential, these amps come off as a little underpowered. Which is to say they sound phenomenal but would be mind-blowing with a little more punch, headroom, and fidelity. The P12P speakers used, for this example at least, are also among Jensen's less efficient designs, and even a P12N would throw it at you with a little more gusto.

That said, it doesn't seem like Magnatone was particularly trying to cut any corners, and these are extremely well-made amps in other regards, crafted with apparent pride by Magna Electronics Inc. in Inglewood, California. They required a full twelve tubes to achieve their vibrato-in-stereo sound and a very complex web of circuitry besides. Put it all together and it was gonna cost you $395, according to a late 1957 Magnatone catalog, quite a pretty penny considering that Fender's top models at the time, the narrow-panel tweed Bassman and Twin, both sold for $339 (and were Holly amps of choice prior to this Magnatone).

With Holly's recorded examples of Custom 280 goodness being so thin on the ground, it behooves us to turn back to our "other Magnatone artists." Lonnie Mack's first hit, the instrumental rendition of "Memphis," gets its vibrato more

from the Bigsby he installed on his 1958 Flying V, but the follow-up "Wham" swims in the this amp's swift swirl, sounding much like a Leslie rotating speaker cab. You can also hear it clearly on cuts like "The Bounce," his cover of "Suzie Q," and plenty of others. And while Bo Diddley's amps aren't always clearly documented, you can hear what you'd swear was that Magnatone bounce (from one of the larger models or another) all over much of his work from the late 1950s and into the mid 1960s.

As dramatic as the Custom 280's stereo vibe undoubtedly is, it is ultimately perhaps a little too fussy for many players to use consistently. Impressive in small doses, it can become entirely sea-sickening if overused, and that's probably why this "innovation in the world of music" didn't take over the planet. 🎱

Buddy Holly and the Crickets rock *The Ed Sullivan Show* on January 26, 1958, in New York City. From left: Joe Mauldin, Holly, and Jerry Allison. *Michael Ochs Archives/Getty Images*

November 28, 1988

Dear Paul;

I, Patricia Holley Kaiter, sister of Buddy Holly, sold the Magnatone
Custom 280 "Stereo Vibrato" amplifier to Emmylou Harris on November 8,
1988. For the purpose of her birthday gift to you, Paul Kennerely. This
amplifier is the one Buddy used in his earlier years and has been in the
Holley family until now. I certainly hope you will enjoy this gift. I
am deeply touched knowing there are still such fans as yourself.

Yours truly,

Patricia Holley Kaiter
Patricia Holley Kaiter

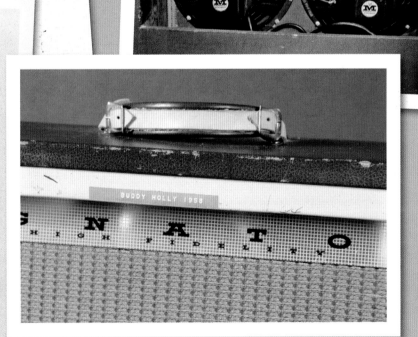

A letter attesting to the amp's authenticity from Buddy Holly's sister, Patricia Holley Kaiter.

Buddy Holly

exclusively on

THE GOLD STANDARD

The 5F6 Bassman arrived just a decade into the company's existence, but by that time the Fender Electric Instrument Company had already earned a reputation for quality and innovation, in the amplifier arena in particular.

The pinnacle model in the Bassman line was not the first one. The amp debuted in 1952 as a 1x15-inch TV-front combo with a semiclosed back to partner the Fender Precision Bass, introduced the year before. In 1955, along with the evolution to Fender's "narrow panel" tweed cabinets throughout the range, the 5E6 Bassman was given a 4x10-inch speaker configuration to help cure the single 15-inch Jensen Concert Series speaker's excessive cone flap when hit by the low E of the Fender bass. Used together, the four Jensen P10Rs suffered less from low-frequency distortion and excessive cone travel and produced a firmer bass note, even if individually they were not designed for bass reproduction. (Ampeg would expand on this thinking later for its

massive 8x10-inch SVT cabs.) The change of speakers was accompanied by circuit revisions and independent Bass, Treble, and Presence controls to update the single Tone and Volume controls of its predecessor.

This model used the cathode-follower tone stack that has been recognized as such a key ingredient of the Bassman sound and feel. It's a highly interactive EQ topology achieved with a circuit that uses an entire preamp tube to work its magic and that's attributed with a large measure of the Bassman's legendary touch sensitivity. But the 5E6 still employed a split-load (cathodyne) phase inverter, used *two* 5U4GA rectifier tubes to combat sag, and was a more primitive version of the legend in a few other respects.

A split-load PI is partly responsible for the creamy, sweet breakup of many 1950s tweed Fender amps—probably best recognized as produced by the 5E3

A 1959 Fender Bassman 5F6-A. *Dave Porter/Alamy*

1958-1960 FENDER 5F6-A BASSMAN

- Preamp tubes: 12AY7 first gain stage, 12AX7 cathode-follower tone stack, 12AX7 long-tailed pair phase inverter
- Output tubes: Two 5881s (heavy-duty 6L6 type); class AB, fixed-bias
- Rectifier: GZ34 (5AR4)
- Controls: Vol Normal, Vol Bright, Treble, Bass, Middle, Presence
- Speakers: Four Jensen P10R 10-inch drivers with alnico magnets, wired in parallel
- Output: 45 watts RMS into a 2-ohm load

Deluxe—but the amount of distortion this inverter topology contributes to the sound means it can never get the most from a pair of 6L6/5881 output tubes. Therefore it isn't really suitable in a bass amp or indeed a larger guitar amp that aspires to any degree of clean headroom.

The move to the long-tailed pair inverter in the 5F6 of late 1956 or early 1957 set a standard in big amp design and brought the market a Bassman with a circuit capable of presenting a truer, more unadulterated signal from preamp to PI to output stage than any mass-produced guitar amplifier previously available. The result was a round, open, punchy tone with more clean headroom than almost anything the guitar world had yet experienced and a toothsome grind when cranked to the point of breakup. Fender's own Twin didn't receive a long-tailed pair PI until more than a year later. By this time, the Bassman also carried a then-unprecedented Middle control and four inputs: a low- and high-gain each for the Bright and Normal channels.

In 1958 Fender further upgraded the Bassman to the 5F6-A circuit, which represents the zenith of the model's evolution and is the version that gets most guitarists drooling. A single GZ34 (5AR4) rectifier became standard, and the 1.5k "swamper resistors" between the grids of the output tubes and the PI (in line with the bias circuit, to be more precise) of previous Bassmans and other Fender amps were removed. Although this was a deletion of componentry rather than an addition, it opened up the tweed Bassman's voice to its full potential. The resistors were added in the mid 1950s to stabilize many amps, but some players and designers felt they constricted the tone somewhat, and their removal allowed the amps to breathe and sing a little more freely.

Also note that while so much fuss is made today about cathode-biased, class A amps, this tone legend is a class AB design with a fixed-bias output stage.

While we might think of any tweed amp from the 1950s as being a pretty simple affair, the 5F6-A Bassman was and remains a fairly complex and thoroughly thought-out piece of instrument amplification design. The refinements of circuitry, layout, speaker configuration, and cabinet design that Fender had achieved by 1958 represent an impressive feat of electrical engineering, and the Bassman's tonal legacy fully backs up its elegant conception and elevated construction.

Other large Fender amps of the day, such as the Bandmaster, Pro, and Super, are often mistakenly referred to as equivalents to the Bassman in all but speaker configuration and their absence of a Middle control, but each is a significantly less advanced piece of design in at least a few crucial ways. These models lack the post-1956 Bassman's long-tailed pair PI. They use smaller output transformers (capable of producing, realistically, about 28 watts, versus the Bassman OT's 45 watts) and run their 6L6s (or 5881s) on lower voltages. Each sounds different *partly* because it is driving different speakers, but you can see there's a lot more to it besides.

Of course, those four Jensen P10R alnico speakers contribute a heck of a lot to this amp's sonic signature as well. While they helped make a better bass amp than the single 15-inch driver used before them, they aren't even in the ballpark by contemporary standards of bass reproduction. But when a guitar is pumped through them, they yield a sparkling, full-frequency performance that combines shimmering highs, open and breathy mids, and firm lows. The open-backed, solid-pine tweed cabinet also adds a lot to the brew, contributing a woody resonance and broad sound dispersion, while the highly reactive "floating" speaker baffle (so called because it's attached at the top and bottom only) contributes to the multiplicity of vibrational energy going on within a cranked Bassman.

So many active elements—four speakers, cab, baffle—mean a degree of conflicting frequency reproduction and some phase cancellation from battling elements within the amp, but that's also part of the magic of the tweed mojo. When a 5F6-A Bassman works right and is sounding its best, it doesn't pay to dwell on all the reasons it *shouldn't* be sounding so good.

The 5F6-A Bassman's design footprint can be seen in more amplifiers of the past forty-five-plus years—regardless of manufacturer—than that of any other early amp. Ken Marshall and Ken Bran famously lifted the entire schematic for the original Marshall JTM45, and the design segued into the legendary Plexi Marshalls with only minor changes. Everything from the Vox AC30 Top Boost's use of a cathode follower tone stack (albeit with only two EQ controls)

to a Vox, Traynor, Mesa/Boogie, or almost any significant large amplifier's use of a long-tailed pair PI also has its roots in Leo Fender's mighty creation.

Part of the Bassman's massive appeal probably lies in the fact that it is an extremely versatile amp. With its highly interactive tone stack, a useful presence control, a preamp and PI combination that passes a gutsy and full-frequency signal along to the efficient output stage, and an output transformer capable of making the most of it, an 5F6-A Bassman can do and has done anything from Wes Montgomery–style warm jazz tone to clean Jimmy Bryant–style country to Buddy Holly–style biting rock 'n' roll to crunchy Bruce Springsteen rock. It is probably most cited and sought after as a blues amp, however, and the playing of Buddy Guy through much of his career, Jimmie Vaughan in the early days of the Fabulous Thunderbirds, or early Otis Rush—still a broad trio stylistically—typifies the sounds that today's bluesmen are seeking to achieve from this amp. That said, practically any guitarist ever tagged as a tonehound has gigged or recorded through a tweed Bassman at one point or another, along with alternative artists such as Son Volt, Pearl Jam, and Teenage Fanclub.

As often as not, contemporary guitarists play through recent Bassman reproductions—on tour, at least—rather than taking precious vintage examples out on the road—especially since passable originals have surpassed $5,000 on the collector's market. Amps such as Victoria's 45410, Clark's Piedmont, and Fender's own '59 Bassman LTD offer excellent, relatively affordable renditions of the classic tone.

However accurately built, a new amp won't sound like a forty-eight-year-old Bassman right off the shelf. A big part of a vintage amp's magic has to do with well-burned-in signal capacitors, played-in speakers, and the like. But pay your dues on a good 5F6-A repro circa 2006 and feed it the best tubes you can afford, and before long it will reveal to you a sweet spot as broad as the Grand Canyon.

Elvis Presley and trio perform in 1956, backed by a lone Fender Bassman. *Michael Ochs Archives/Getty Images*

Fender's 59 Bassman LTD reissue.
Fender Musical Instruments Corporation

Buddy Guy plays the blues through a Fender
Bassman at the Newport Folk Festival in 1960.
Michael Ochs Archives/Getty Images

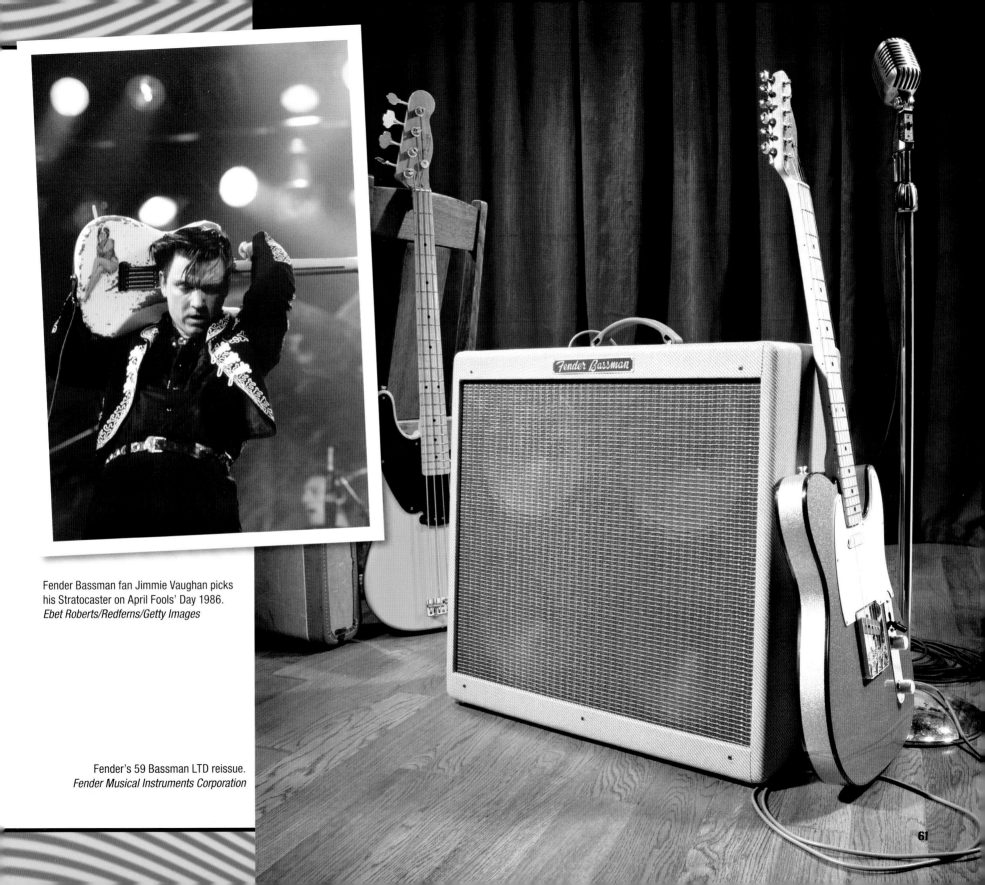

Fender Bassman fan Jimmie Vaughan picks his Stratocaster on April Fools' Day 1986. *Ebet Roberts/Redferns/Getty Images*

Fender's 59 Bassman LTD reissue. *Fender Musical Instruments Corporation*

THE CLEAN ROCK 'N' ROLL AMP

There are specific, design-based reasons Ampeg was never known as a maker of premier rock 'n' roll guitar amps.

Ampeg was one of the most successful U.S. amplifier manufacturers in the 1950s, 1960s, and 1970s. It introduced the world's first widely accepted and truly stadium-worthy bass amp for the big rock stage, as championed early on by the Rolling Stones and just about every major act since. But Ampeg never quite sat alongside Fender, Marshall, Vox, or a score of others in the lead guitar stakes. The late Ken Fischer, a former Ampeg engineer, explained that Ampeg founder Everett Hull didn't put much stock in rock 'n' roll and really held himself and his company above the genre. "Hull was saying things like, 'Rock 'n' roll doesn't swing, it never will. It's not musical, and we will not ever make anything for rock 'n' roll,'" Fischer said. Hull himself had been an accomplished

jazz pianist and bassist, and for him, jazz remained a class above. And that was the class he wanted to serve.

In the late 1940s, Ampeg was founded on the back of (and named for) an electronic pickup Hull invented for use with the upright bass. It was mounted in the peg the bass stood upon—dubbed the Amplified Peg. In 1949 Hull formalized the company name as the Ampeg Bassamp Company, and bass amplification has been its most formidable stock in trade ever since. Bass and—as many a retro-tweaked guitarist is giddy to note when enthusing over a newly bagged vintage Ampeg—accordion, the other jazz and dance band instrument of the day that was underrepresented in the amplification department. The Ampeg guitar amp's ability to produce the clean, full tones of a Barney Kessel, Herb Ellis, or Tony Mottola, with deep, hypnotic reverb as desired, has been much noted. If you want a guitar amp with loads of headroom for country, jazz, or any medium-volume playing where you get all your overdrive from pedals, by

1959 AMPEG JET 12

- Preamp tubes: Two 6SL7s
- Output tubes: Two 6V6GTs, cathode bias, with negative feedback
- Rectifier: 5Y3
- Controls: Volume, Tone, Tremolo (speed)
- Speaker: Jensen P12S

An advertisement for Ampeg's Super 800 Bassamp—the "Answer to the Bassman's Prayer."

all means seek out one of the superefficient Jet, Reverborocket, or Mercury models with firm 7591 output tubes.

But, brethren and sistern, there are vintage Ampegs that will churn it up with many of the best of the tweed-era Fenders, Gibsons, and Valcos: look for models with 6V6GT output tubes and preferably also with not totally obscure preamp tubes, such as the sweet, stylish, pre-reverb 1959 Ampeg Jet 12. Occasionally, Hull and company dabbled in designs using the 6V6, which was more at home in the small- to medium-size Fenders, and when they did, although it was never quite to their own liking, it resulted in a righteously gnarly little combo for blues, rock 'n' roll, or indie-garage stylings.

"You've got to keep in mind that Everett Hull hated rock 'n' roll, he hated distortion. . . . Amps were not to be distorted," Fischer adds. "Ampeg made [amps with 6V6s] for a short while and all the jazz guys were complaining, 'What's wrong with the new Reverborockets? They break up too early.' So Everette converted them back to 7591 tubes. But if they had marketed them as a rock 'n' roll amp, they probably would have been very successful."

Looked at tonally, this Jet 12 is not terribly far from being a poor man's tweed Fender Deluxe, with the added bonus of tremolo. (It's worth noting that late 1950s to early 1960s Jets fetch from $500 to $800, compared to a tweed Deluxe's $2,000 to $4,000.) From the perspective of some players, there's another bonus to be found in this Jet's 6SL7 preamp and phase-inverter tubes, which are accompanied by an otherwise Fenderish cathode-biased two-6V6GT output stage and a 5Y3 rectifier. The 6SL7 is a dual triode with similar gain levels to the 12AX7, but it's an octal (eight-pin-base) tube with a sound that's a little fatter, richer, and smoother than the typical 12AX7. Being a discontinued NOS tube, it can also be harder to locate, though not impossible thanks to the fact it wasn't used in many amps that are (yet) considered highly collectible. A peak around the back reveals a gold-framed Concert Series Jensen P12S speaker—a desirable chunk of alnico, steel, and paper in its own right.

It's worth mentioning, in the name of full disclosure, that there are also quite a few differences between the 1959 Jet 12 and the tweed Fender Deluxe of that era. The

Ampeg has only one channel. It has a phase inverter configured more like the self-balancing paraphase inverters of earlier 1950s Fender and Gibson amps, uses mainly .02-microfarad (uF) signal caps instead of the 5E3 Deluxe's .1-uF caps, and employs a negative feedback loop around the output stage to tighten up its performance a little. It's also worth noting that the amp's simple but effective bias-modulating tremolo has a control for speed only, none for depth. To switch it on, you stomp on a pedal that looks suspiciously like a modified doorstop.

It all adds up to make the Ampeg Jet 12 a little smoother and rounder than the king of the tweed club amps. And that's not necessarily a bad thing, because as beloved as the 5E3 Fender Deluxe is, many players strive to attain just a little more headroom from the tweed amp. In short, this Jet is an Ampeg—but an Ampeg that knows how to do rock 'n' roll with *mucho gusto*. Crank it up, whack on that tremolo, and you're in grit rock heaven. And with an Ampeg, all this alternative tone comes in a package that has been put together with more care and attention and downright roadworthiness than found in so many Valco, Danelectro, and Silvertone amps that hover in the same price range. All in all, a mightily groovy slab of vintage amplitude. ◉

Long an Ampeg fan, B. B. King rehearses backstage in 1967, playing his Gibson "Lucille" through a later Ampeg model. *Michael Ochs Archives/Getty Images*

TONE MACHINE

Ah, the glorious narrow-panel 5E3 tweed Fender Deluxe. This is such a ubiquitous design that there's almost no point detailing it. Hell, it's in our blood, part of our shared consciousness, hardwired into every guitarist's genetic memory. That may be, but it's still too delectable a morsel to resist nibbling.

In the name of added value, however, let's not just examine the tonal core of the 5E3 and discuss what makes it tick; while we're at it, let's also look at what might be done to upgrade the format a little, to give it just a little more oomph for contemporary guitarists in the recording or small-gig situation. We speak not of modifying a vintage example—no, no, no—for that would be heresy at its very root. The 5E3 circuit is probably the most popular template for homebrew amp projects, yet lots of guys building these complain that they'd like a little more headroom, punch, volume, or definition out of the amp. So let's check out the original first, then examine some upgrades.

The Deluxe name first appeared on Fender's Model 26 "woodie" amps of 1946–1948, but we usually think of the line as beginning with the TV-front tweed amp that followed. Through the 1950s, it moved from a wide- to a narrow-panel tweed cabinet, with circuit evolutions along the way, from 6SC7 octal preamp tubes and paraphase inverter to a nine-pin 12AY7 preamp tube and a 12AX7 in a split-load PI. The 5E3 circuit and narrow-panel cab arrived simultaneously in 1955, although the cab's dimensions were soon increased by 2 inches in height and 1 inch in depth, to 16.75x20x9.5 inches.

All Deluxes can be righteous little tone machines for blues and classic rock 'n' roll, or old-school country with the volume reined in, but the 5E3 has become the most beloved of all for its extra little dose of chime, cut, and clarity—although make no mistake, these little 15-watt 1x12 combos will squash like rotten tomaters when you wind them up and hit them hard.

A 1959 narrow-panel Fender Deluxe with EP-2 Echoplex and Gretsch Model 6120.

1959 FENDER DELUXE 5E3

- Preamp tubes: One 12AY7, 12AX7 PI
- Output tubes: Two 6V6GT, cathode-bias
- Rectifier: 5Y3 tube
- Controls: Independent Volumes for each channel, shared Tone
- Speaker: Jensen P12R or P12Q
- Output: 15 watts RMS +/-

If Fender back in the late 1950s had been thinking like a major amp-maker's marketing department circa 2008, it would have billed the tweed Deluxe as a "class A amp." That's essentially what it is, as far as the common use of the term goes, which is to say it's as much class A as a Vox AC15. More definitively, it's a cathode-biased 15-watt amp based on a pair of 6V6GT output tubes, with no negative feedback loop around the output stage, features that together help it sound hot, juicy, and saturated at relatively low volumes, with a pronounced yet rather compressed mid-range hump, aided by the 6V6s.

The Deluxe differs from the AC15, however, and from its big Fender siblings such as the Twin and Bassman, in its use of a split-load PI, a configuration that uses the first triode of a 12AX7 as a driver stage and the second to split the signal and invert the phase of the two legs that feed the output tubes. This was one of the most popular phase inverters for small to medium-size amps of the late 1950s. Even the larger tweed Super, Pro, and Bandmaster used this PI rather than the nobler long-tailed pair, although of course they carried 6L6s and negative feedback loops, and were fixed bias besides. The split-load PI adds its own distortion to the brew, the result being a warm, fuzzy mélange of tube overdrive that can get supercompressed and feel delightfully tactile—the perfect raw, low-volume, vintage electric blues tone, some might say. Delightful in some circumstances, but it can mush out entirely too quickly for some playing styles, and it doesn't quite hold together for well-defined twang tones or speedy picking at any kind of volume, for example.

If that's how your original 1955–1960 tweed Deluxe sounds, great. Cherish it, and plug into something else if you want more headroom. But if you're looking to build or commission your own custom-made rendition of a 5E3, as many are doing these days, you can easily get a little more cut, punch, and headroom into this circuit without losing the smooth, tweedy breakup and addictive playability of the amp at full throttle. Consider these modifications to the stock circuit:

For the rectifier, try a 5U4, 5U4GB, or 5AR4 (GZ34) in place of the standard 5Y3. Not only will one of these give you a quicker attack and less squash (though any tube rectifier will usually still induce a tasty degree of compression), each will raise the DC voltages within the amp in increasing degrees. While a standard 5E3 runs at around 340 to 350 VDC on the plates of the 6V6, get this up to about 365 to 380 VDC and you'll get a lot more headroom and clarity out of the amp.

For power filtering, add a small choke to the power-filtering stage and consider changing the first 16uF filter cap to a 30uF.

In place of the 25uF/25V bypass cap on the cathode of the output tubes (the cap in parallel with the bias resistor—which we'd make around 270 ohms instead of 250 ohms), try a 100uF/100V electrolytic cap.

Keep the original-spec 12AY7 rather than the hotter 12AX7 that so many players use to heat up the preamps of these tweed amps (or simply because they can't find good Y7s anymore). The 12AY7 won't filth up so quickly in the early stages of the amp and will pass a bolder and fuller frequency onto the output stage, where those cathode-biased 6V6s will still get plenty raw when you want them to.

Consider adding a tight/boost switch. Move the grounded end of the bypass cap on the 12AY7's cathode to an on/off mini-toggle switch (taking the other terminal to ground) to make it a boost function. Switched to off position, you'll get more headroom. (You can do the same with the PI's bypass cap for "double boost" capabilities.)

You can also use a larger output transformer—one intended for a tweed Super or Pro—to use 6L6s with this amp and still swap in 6V6s for earlier breakup.

Finally, try a Celestion G12H-30 for a bigger voice and more aggression, or any speaker you like.

Bring these little mods on board and you'll really blow the dust off the geezers at the next blues jam. ●

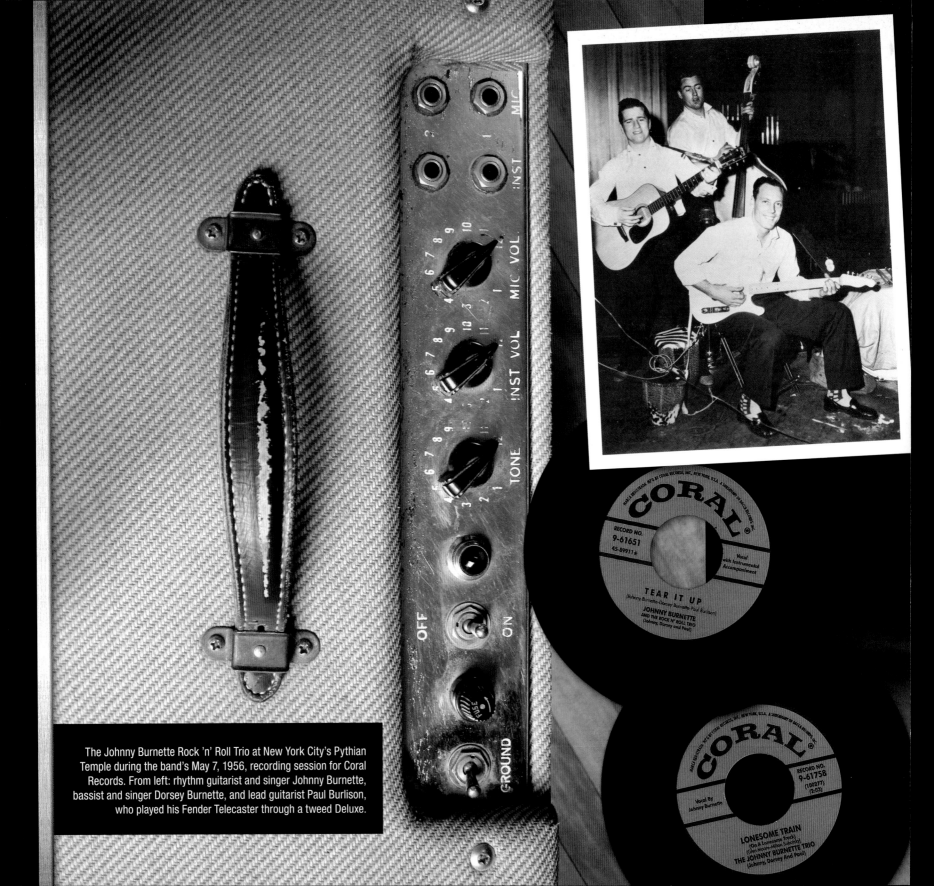

The Johnny Burnette Rock 'n' Roll Trio at New York City's Pythian Temple during the band's May 7, 1956, recording session for Coral Records. From left: rhythm guitarist and singer Johnny Burnette, bassist and singer Dorsey Burnette, and lead guitarist Paul Burlison, who played his Fender Telecaster through a tweed Deluxe.

Like the original 5E3 tweed Deluxe, Fender's current 57 Deluxe Reissue is made with a hand-wired circuit board. *Fender Musical Instruments Corporation*

TRANSITION SURVIVOR

With their transition-era specs, and cosmetics that have been revisited far less over the years than those of their tweed predecessors and blackface successors, the tan Tolex amps of the early 1960s are always fun to check out. Looking inside this early brown Fender Super amp, however, our interest level changed from mild to *wow!* This is not only a stunningly original early brownface Fender but one of the cleanest vintage Fenders of any era that you are ever likely to find, with apparently nary a part on it changed from original, including the tubes. That, and it's got a great "the one that *didn't* get away" story too.

Nashville guitarist, producer, and studio owner Vaughn Skow has worked with Keith Urban, Brad Paisley, and Garth Brooks, among others. Skow acquired the amp in 1991 while doing a two-week gig in Reno, Nevada, playing guitar with country star Tom T. Hall. Not in any position to lose money on the slots or at the poker tables, he tells us, Skow combed Reno's pawn shops

in the daylight hours during the band's downtime, looking for that cherry of a deal. One morning he walked into a shop that had just put the Super out on the floor but hadn't even priced it up yet. Skow offered $20, the pawnbroker countered with $25, and a deal was struck. Feeling dizzy yet?

After hauling the amp home to Nashville, Skow began to realize that this was not just any sweet brown Super but a very early, rare, and unusual Super. Clear outward indicators of its early status are the rough, pinkish-tan Tolex covering; the tweed-era oxblood-with-stripe grille cloth; and the reverse-order control layout, which runs bass, treble, volume. In addition, the front of the top panel of the cabinet, above the control panel, has sharp edges seen only on extremely early front-mounted amps rather than the rounded edges common from then on out.

A probe around the chassis and cab soon revealed other clues that peg this as a debutante venture into the Tolex-covered, front-mounted panel era. Although its tube chart is stamped "JC," indicating a vintage of March 1960 (there exist plenty of tweed amps dated later than that), it also carries a 5G4 circuit designation, indicating a 1950s origin, as well as a circuit that never

Amp courtesy Vaughn Skow

1959–1960 FENDER SUPER 5G4

- Preamp tubes: Five 7025s (12AX7 equivalent), including two for tremolo and one for PI
- Output tubes: Two 6L6GCs, fixed bias
- Rectifier: GZ34 tube
- Controls: Bass, Treble, Volume for each channel; tremolo Speed and Intensity for Vibrato channel; shared Presence
- Speakers: Two Jensen P10Rs
- Output: 40 watts RMS +/-

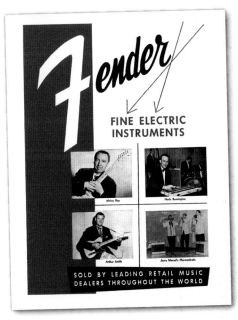

This amp also has the long-tailed pair phase inverter, which only the Bassman, the high-powered Twin, and the Tremolux had in the final evolution of tweed amps. It still includes the fixed-bias output stage, negative feedback loop, and Presence control of the 5F4, though the network for the latter is a bit more complex on the 5G4/6G4. Voltages in the output stage are also considerably higher in the early brown Super than in the tweed, contributing to its firmer response and increased volume. The 5G4/6G4 sees around 456VDC on the plates, versus 410VDC in the 5F4, although the voltages in the preamp stage are still quite a bit lower—around 170VDC—than they would be in the blackface amps. (Conversely, however, the output voltages dropped a bit, while preamp voltages increased a bit, in the 6G4-A.)

More than all of these points, though, when the discussion turns to brown-panel Fender amps, their vibrato circuits usually garner the most attention. Bestowed with Fender's short-lived "harmonic vibrato" circuit, the larger brown amps come closer to true vibrato than anything else the company ever produced. This still wasn't actually a pitch-fluctuating vibrato, as per definition—and as many fans claim—but it creates a modulated pulse that can give the aural impression of pitch fluctuation. It's probably still most accurately described as tremolo, but what a tremolo! It's a sound unto itself, and it took Fender two whole preamp tubes (four triode stages) to accomplish it, a complement increased to two and a half tubes in the 6G4-A. This amp, along with several other early brownfaces, also has a plugged and never-used hole in the back panel marked with the enigmatic "Pulse Adjust" legend. The attention was, apparently, to offer a trim pot for adjusting the pulse amplitude of the vibrato, but the feature was dropped *after* the printing up of several back panels, which the company must not have wanted to waste.

As for the sonic results of all this analog archeology, Skow pronounces it, "Very sweet! This is actually a perfect gigging amp, although she hasn't been out of the studio for about a dozen years or so. Like its predecessors, it's quite woody and warm, but it has a very usable amount of clean headroom as well. It also breaks up just the way a vintage Fender should: Not as early as a lot of tweeds, but not as late as a lot of later Fenders either." ◉

"officially" existed. (The first digit indicates the decade of the design's origination, the letter the design evolution, and the second digit the model.) Furthermore, none of the coded components used on or inside the chassis can be dated to later than October 1959. Even the two Jensen P10R alnico speakers, rare on a brownface amp, are dated to the twenty-seventh and thirty-fourth weeks of 1959.

No specific schematic seems to be available for the 5G4, but circuit-wise it appears to be similar to the 6G4 that followed later in 1960. These amps are often considered a way station on the road from tweed to blackface, but actually they have more characteristics of the latter than the former, even though their earlier transformers and other components—including the sweet yellow Astron signal caps—make them look pretty tweedy inside the chassis. When compared to a 5F4 tweed Super, however, with a cathode-follower tone stack and split-phase inverter, the extent to which this 5G4 has evolved becomes apparent.

Like the blackface Super Reverb that followed, this brown Super has the tone stack for each channel sandwiched between the first gain stage (V1B, one side of the first 7025/12AX7) and a gain makeup stage comprised of the second half of that preamp tube, with the channel volume positioned after the tone controls in the circuit itself, as well as on the panel. The component values, and layout, are somewhat different than those in the blackface tone stacks, and even in the 6G4-A brown Super that arrived in 1961, but it still shows that Fender was already looking for a little more clarity and definition out of the front end.

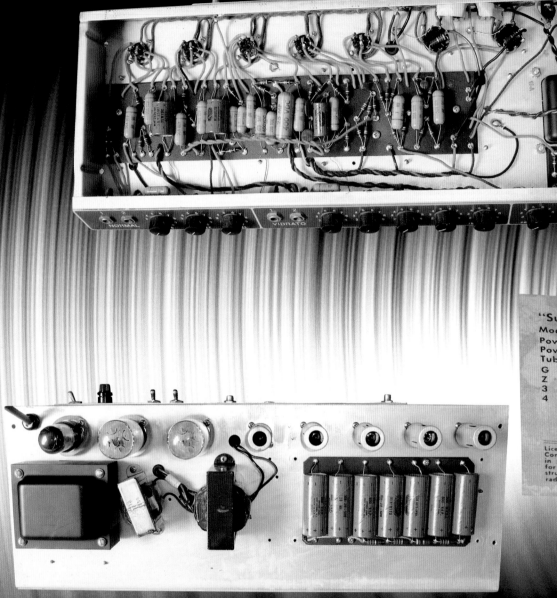

"Super-Amp" Amplifier

Model 5G4   Production

Power Supply 110 volts, 50/60 cycles AC.

Power Consumption 200 watts.

Tube locations left to right at rear:

G	6	6	7	7	12	7	7
Z	L	L	0	0	A	0	0
3	6	6	2	2	X	2	2
4	GC	GC	5	5	7	5	5

FENDER ELECTRIC INSTRUMENT MFG. CO.
Fullerton, California

Licensed under U. S. patents of American Telephone and Telegraph Company and Western Electric Company, Incorporated, for use only in public address systems, phonograph distribution systems, systems for distribution from radio broadcast receiving sets or musical instruments, and in speech input systems and monitoring systems of radiotelephone broadcasting stations.

LIVING IN THE SHADOW

The Vox AC30 grabbed most of the headlines for years, but many tonehounds have come to appreciate the sweet, juicy glories of the smaller AC15, particularly in the wake of contemporary attitudes about smaller amps' abilities to hit the sonic sweet spot at more ear- and mic-friendly volumes.

Designed by Dick Denney in 1957, the AC15 was the flagship of Tom Jennings' Vox guitar amplifier line at the time, and it served as the building block for bigger things to come. When popular British bands of the late 1950s such as the Shadows needed more powerful amps to help them be heard in the bigger and bigger venues they were playing, Denney doubled the power of the AC15 and coupled its preamp to the new AC30/4, with four EL84 output tubes and a firmer GZ34 rectifier. In 1960, however, he modified

the larger amp's preamp and tone stack, leaving the AC15 back in a tonal territory all its own.

Any player even vaguely familiar with this great British amp company will recognize some of the main ingredients of the "Vox sound" in the AC15. The amp uses a pair of EL84 tubes in cathode bias with no negative feedback to produce 18 watts from an output stage that is commonly labeled class A—a term often misrepresented among amp makers today but arguably more accurately rendered by this little combo designed fifty years ago. Rather than being just "half an AC30," however, the AC15 includes a number of key ingredients that give it its own sonic signature.

While the AC30's gutsy Top Boost tone circuit (a variation of a cathode-follower tone stack) was considered Vox's hot feature from the early 1960s onward and even into the boutique era of the past fifteen years or so, the AC15's Normal (or Brilliant) channel carried a powerful EF86 pentode tube that made this an even hotter preamp circuit. Coupled with the aforementioned

Amp courtesy Jim Elyea/photo Jennifer Cheung/Steve Nilsson

CIRCA 1960 VOX AC15

- Preamp tubes: One EF86, three 12AX7s (one for PI), one 12AU7
- Output tubes: Two EL84s in class A, cathode-bias
- Rectifier: EZ81
- Controls: Speed, Vib-Trem (switch), channel 1 Volume, channel 2 Volume, Brilliance, Top Cut
- Speakers: One or two 15-watt Celestion G12 drivers with alnico magnets
- Output: 18 watts RMS

EL84s in class A and a power supply that included both an EZ81 tube rectifier and a quality choke, the EF86 helped make for an amplifier that was extremely fat, rich, tactile, and touch sensitive, yet detailed and chiming as well, and even the aluminum chassis that it was all rigged up in helped make it a lively, breathy performer.

The Vib/Trem channel was built around a more common 12AX7 (ECC83) preamp tube, with another 12AX7 and a 12AU7 (ECC81) to perform vibrato and tremolo duties (legend has it that Denney discovered by a slip of the soldering iron that the tremolo circuit could easily be converted to vibrato; he adapted his design to make the two sounds switchable). The amp's top panel carried a Speed control and a switch for Vib/Trem selection, but the depth was preset and could be altered only by accessing a trim pot on the circuit boards inside the chassis. Neither channel carried any tone controls as such, although there was a Brilliance (bright) switch for the Normal channel—on a rotary switch with a chickenhead knob, so it appears to be another control—and a Top Cut control for both channels, a very useful feature that dials out excessive highs in the output stage.

To further make the AC15 feel and sound like a big amp in a small package, Denney gave it a phase inverter circuit that has come to be known as the long-tailed pair. The topology, in fact, originates from an applications manual published by British valve manufacturer

Mullard, and most other amp makers of the day (most notably Fender) reserved this elegant but more complex PI for their larger amps, using the more distortion-prone split-load inverter on anything under 35 watts. A long-tailed pair PI passes the EF86's bold signal along to the EL84s without adding more than a minimum of its own coloration and allows for a full-frequency performance from this relatively small package. All told, a rare combination of qualities that together create an amp that is virtually unparalleled in the studio and pure bliss to play cranked up in clubs and on small and medium stages.

Not that the bovine and succulent EF86 is without its problems. This tube is, by nature, prone to being microphonic, and even good NOS examples can become noisy or fail entirely when subjected to excessive vibration and physical jolts. This powerful little nine-pin pentode preamp tube appears in many tube hi-fi amps, but in that setting it is removed from speaker vibration and usually rests on a shelf for most of its operational life. Mount one in a guitar combo that's tossed in and out of the van between sessions of high-decibel rocking, and it can suffer. Matchless was one of the few major amp makers to use the tube in the postvintage era, to power the high-gain channel in the C30 series. Dr. Z's Mike Zaite took up the cause a few years ago with the Route 66 and Z-28 models (which use the EF86 in a preamp design that is less prone to microphony), and more recently with the Stang Ray, which is based on the Normal channel of an early Vox AC30/4 owned by Brad Paisley. Otherwise, makers mostly steered clear for fear of trouble—until recently.

Over the past couple of years, the EF86 has come back into favor—particularly as used in the great AC15 circa 1960—and outstanding new amps such as 65amps' London 18, TopHat's Supreme 16, and Gabriël's Voxer 18 all pay homage in their own way to this Vox classic. And given the ever-escalating prices of original AC15s (it's not unusual to see prices pushing $7,500), one of these newer hand-wired creations is, for many players, the best means of attaining a glimpse of that sound and feel without the risk of battering their pension to splinters on the road.

The AC15 was originally a 1x12-inch combo. A 2x12-inch Twin version was offered later in the decade. As with the AC30, the speakers played a huge part in the great sound. Early Voxes sometimes had speakers from Goodmans or Fane, but circa 1960, AC15s and AC30s settled in with the legendary Celestion G12, dubbed the Vox Blue when rebadged by Vox and often referred to today as the Alnico Blue (the name also used for Celestion's fine reissue of the model). This efficient and aggressive speaker really helps these great amps to sing, and together they're a tone template made in heaven. ●

A 1962 fawn-tolex Vox AC15. *Oliver Leiber Collection/Rick Gould*

THE LITTLE BIG AMP

Most amp nuts are utterly fascinated by Fender's rapid evolution from archaic to modern design through the course of the 1950s. Within that arc, the transitional moments are often among the most interesting, and the amp models that represent these moments provide curious little gems of discovery.

The final version of the tweed Tremolux, fascinating in and of itself, is also worthy of study for the many transitional-elements of Fender circuitry that it displays. In a nutshell, this is the small to medium-size amp getting (for the first time) the big-amp treatment, and it represents a very real bridge to the ubiquitous Deluxe Reverb of the mid 1960s.

The late 1950s Tremolux is an unsung tweed amp that has nevertheless been appreciated by players who had the good fortune to encounter one in good condition. Our example here would be noteworthy for its vintage alone. With an original Jensen P12Q dating from the second week of 1960, pots from early 1960, and a tube chart stamped "JE," denoting May 1960, it's certainly from among the last batches of tweed amps made shortly before Fender gave over to blond and tan Tolex (aside from retaining a tweed-covered Champ for some years).

- Preamp tubes: One 12AY7, two 12AX7s for tremolo and PI
- Output tubes: Two 6V6GTs, fixed-bias
- Rectifier: 5U4GB tube
- Controls: Independent Volumes for each channel; shared Tone, Speed, Depth
- Speaker: Jensen P12Q
- Output: 18 watts RMS

Mickey "Guitar" Baker was a great fan of the Tremolux. He poses for a promotional portrait with Sylvia Vanderpool Robinson in 1956. *Gilles Petard/Redferns/Getty Images*

Given this, it's surprising to see that the tube chart also carries the 5E9-A model designation, that of the penultimate rendition of the tweed Tremolux, when all aspects of this amplifier's circuitry and appointments denote it as the final evolution of the tweed Tremolux, the 5G9 (which also makes us wonder if Fender applied 5G9 tube charts to any Tremoluxes, if not to this late an example). The clues that lead to the 5G9 are precisely the same big-amp elements Fender was applying to a sub-20-watt amp for the first time here, so let's proceed by checking off those ingredients.

The tweed Tremolux, in all its forms, is often referred to as "a 5E3 Deluxe with tremolo," and for earlier incarnations—any real 5E9-A or the 5E9 before it, for example—that was true enough. For such an innovative company, Fender was slow to bring tremolo to the table, and when its first tremolo-equipped amp came out in 1955, it really just added an extra tube and a tremolo circuit to the Deluxe—voilà, the Tremolux.

A look inside the 5E9-A displays 5E3-related elements such as a split-phase (cathodyne) inverter, cathode-biased 6V6s, a 5Y3 rectifier, those three 16uF filter caps on the left of the eyelet board, and more. The early Tremolux's bias-modulating tremolo sounded great but presented a potential instability in the bias circuit. By way of improving the robustness of the model, Fender introduced a number of major changes to the 5G9 of 1957, essentially making it a big amp in a midsize package.

Here's where the 5G9 Tremolux reveals itself as a sleeper—and a major footnote in amp history as well. We generally think of all Fender 6V6 amps prior to the Tolex years as having split-phase inverters and cathode-biased output stages. But the 5G9 Tremolux graduated beyond these and several other small-amp elements to take on circuitry that only the tweed Bassman and high-powered Twin were blessed with at the time. Hell, even the Pro, Super, Bandmaster, and low-powered Twin of the late 1950s retained the split-phase inverter. But this Tremolux was long-tailed pair all the way. Serious big-amp stuff. On top of that, it was Fender's first 6V6-based amp to be given fixed bias in the output stage. Between them, these two upgrades enabled the Tremolux to retain the deep, lush, bias-modulating tremolo circuit without risks to output-tube stability.

More? Sure, there's plenty. The 5G9's rectifier tube was boosted from 5Y3 to 5U4GB. It was also given a choke in the filtering stage, another first for a push-pull 6V6-loaded Fender (if we discount the short-lived 5E4-A Super with 6V6s).

A look at the circuit board also reveals a surprise. Where did the big filter caps go? Even the amps in that quartet of medium-large tweed models—the Pro, Super, Bandmaster, and low-powered Twin—had their big 16uF caps on the board. But the 5G9 Tremolux? This privileged fellow has had his big electrolytics moved to the underside of the chassis and hidden beneath a "cap can" to give the tremolo circuitry and upgraded filtering enough room to coexist in the same amp. This is something seen only on the Bassman and high-powered Twin at this time, but it's a treatment the Deluxe and Deluxe Reverb would receive in the Tolex amps of the 1960s.

In addition to the circuit changes, the Tremolux had a bigger cab than other 6V6 amps from 1956 onward—the same cab as the 1x15-inch Pro combo, in fact, although this 18-watter retained its 12-inch speaker. This and the above upgrades help make the Tremolux more than just a big amp in a medium amp's guise on paper; the 5E9 sounds bigger too.

Our general impression is that this 1960 Tremolux, with its fixed bias, choke, and long-tailed pair PI, sounds somewhat like a Bassman in a lower-output/1x12-inch package. At low to medium volumes, it has the relative tightness, liveliness, and fidelity to punch out the twang. When it starts to break up at noon or beyond (give or take, depending on the guitar you pair it with), it has a bold, well-defined growl without quite the brown, compressed implosion of a cranked 5E3 Deluxe. The groovy part is that it offers all this at pub and club volumes, with a rich, throbbing tremolo besides.

Add it all up and it might just be plenty of players' vision of the ultimate medium-size Fender tweed amp—even if they don't know it. In the Tolex years, the Tremolux graduated to 6L6s after a brief, quirky segue via 6BQ5 (EL84) output tubes, but you could argue that as a smaller member of the large amp line, the model never quite achieved the tonal splendors it had offered as a larger member of the small amp line. ⬤

TELECASTER GUITAR
The original of the solid body guitars and the proven favorite of countless players. The Telecaster guitar features a fine hardwood body in beautiful blond finish, white maple neck with adjustable truss rod, white pickguard, two adjustable pickups, tone and volume controls and a three-position tone switch. Two way adjustable Fender bridge insures perfect intonation and fast, easy action. The Telecaster guitar is noted for its wide tone range and is equally adaptable for fast "take-off" playing as it is for rhythm.

TELECASTER GUITAR and TREMOLUX AMP

Amp Size
Height ....20"
Width ....22"
Depth ....10"

TREMOLUX AMP
A great new Fender amplifier incorporating the latest type electronic tremolo circuit. This tremolo circuit should not be confused with others of the past. The Fender tremolo provides greater ranges of both speed and depth than any previous type.
Features include the beautiful and durable case and covering found on all Fender amplifiers, 12" heavy duty Jensen speaker. Wide range tone, excellent power vs. distortion characteristics, chrome plated top mounted chassis, on-and-off switch, tremolo depth and speed controls, tone control, two volume controls and four input jacks. Comes complete with tremolo foot control switch, 15 Watts output.

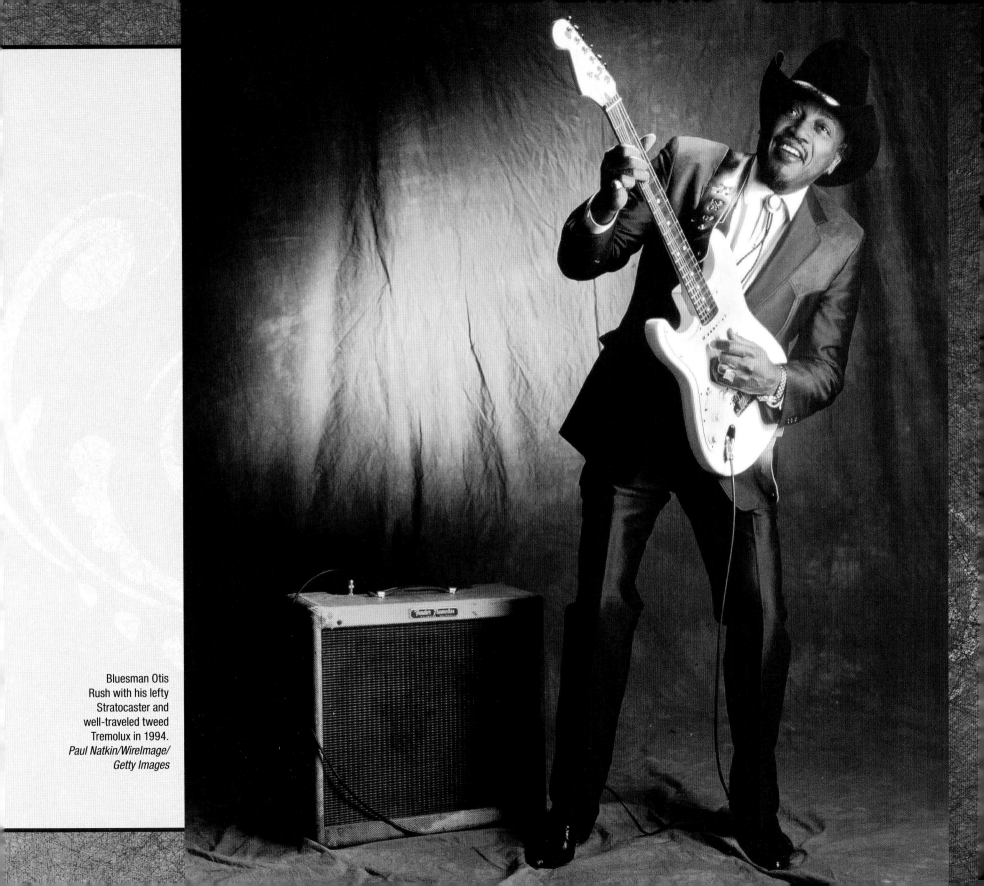

Bluesman Otis
Rush with his lefty
Stratocaster and
well-traveled tweed
Tremolux in 1994.
*Paul Natkin/WireImage/
Getty Images*

TONE GODDESS

Few vintage tube amps have attained the gilded reverence heaped upon the Vox AC30. Certainly, the late 1950s Fender tweeds and Marshall's JTM45 and Plexi amps are equally lust-worthy in the eyes and ears of many players and collectors, but JMI's creation is often discussed with an added catch in the breath, an excited charge in the air. There are vintage tone monsters and then there's the tone goddess—the AC30. That being understood, a 1960 AC30/4 is queen of the goddesses.

As with many other vintage amps, much of the AC30's thing happens when it is pushed beyond spec and starts to break up. Although the whole class A designation of many amps is often debatable (which is to say it's not debatable according to the category as defined: most by definition are not class A amps),

this breaking up is nevertheless the origin of "The Legend of the Class-A Tone." The truth behind this is that the cathode biasing and lack of negative feedback loop in the amp's output stage, and the way these work with the general characteristics of four EL84s in push/pull, as used in this particular circuit, squeeze out an extremely toothsome harmonic brew when pushed into distortion. Hit them with the EF86 pentode channel, and they give up that distortion early. Hit them with a cranked ECC83 (12AX7) channel, and they surrender it a bit later, but fully and fatly. Either way, it's a heavenly concoction that has turned guitarists' heads for fifty years.

Our featured example comes courtesy of Mike Tamposi, who acquired it some time ago from the late Vox enthusiast and collector Barry Henderson. If JMI-era AC30s of any stripe are rare, this one is the proverbial hen's tooth. According to Jim Elyea, author of *Vox Amplifiers: The JMI Years*, the total number of TV-cab AC30/4s ever built falls between 49 and 146, and of those, fewer

The Shadows in 1961 with three Vox AC30 TV-front twins for a television show. From left: Bruce Welch, Cliff Richard, Jet Harris, Tony Meehan, and Hank Marvin. *Pictorial Press Ltd./Alamy*

ESDF 1355

F.B.I.
MIDNIGHT
MAN OF MYSTERY
THE STRANGER

THE SHADOWS

Columbia

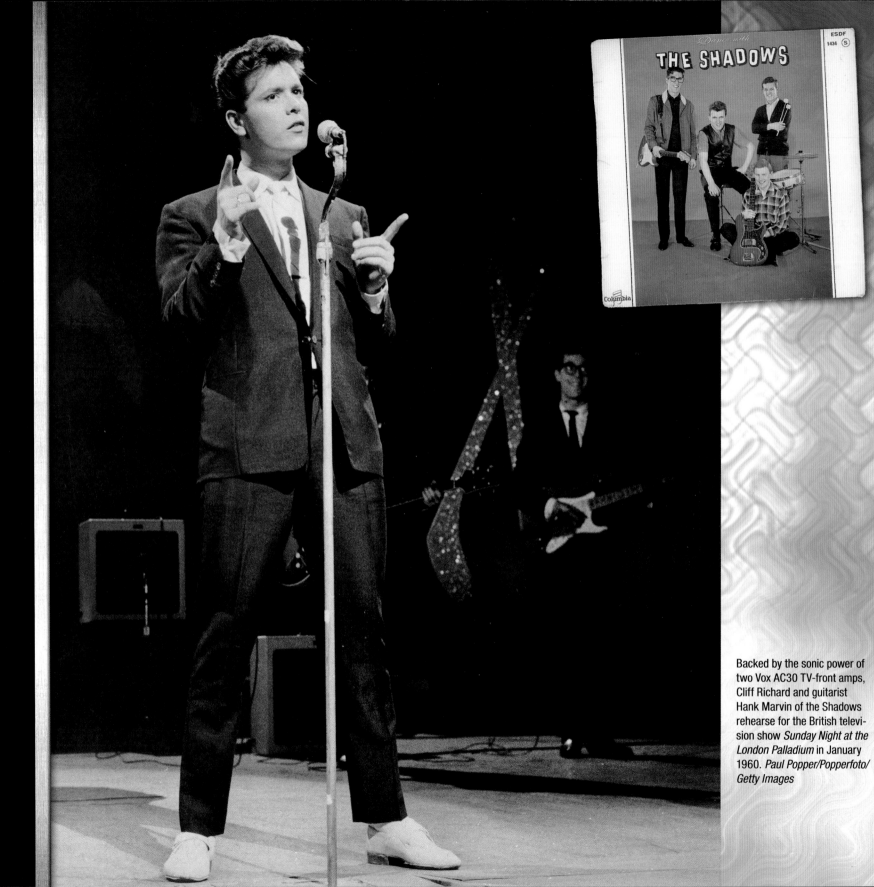

THE SHADOWS

Backed by the sonic power of
two Vox AC30 TV-front amps,
Cliff Richard and guitarist
Hank Marvin of the Shadows
rehearse for the British television show *Sunday Night at the
London Palladium* in January
1960. *Paul Popper/Popperfoto/
Getty Images*

CIRCA 1960 VOX AC30

- Preamp tubes: One EF86, three ECC83s (12AX7), one ECC82 (12AU7)
- Output tubes: Four EL84s, cathode-biased
- Rectifier: GZ34
- Controls: Speed, Vib-Trem (switch), Vib-Trem Volume, Normal Volume, Brilliance switch, Bass control (Top Cut)
- Speakers: Originally two 15-watt Celestion G12 (B025) drivers with alnico magnets
- Output: Around 35 watts RMS

The next circuit evolution of the AC30 is often referred to as the AC30/6 for its six inputs to three channels, versus this AC30/4's four inputs to two channels. And whereas that amp's Normal channel is considered by some to be its limpest offering, the Normal channel on this amp is arguably its standout feature. Like the beloved JMI AC15s, the AC30/4 carries a hot EF86 pentode preamp tube in its normal channel, a tube that really kicks out some grind and sizzle in this format. It's a tube that can be problematic in a big vibrant combo, particularly in that it's prone to microphony (not to mention all-out failure) when you rattle it too hard for too long, and it was soon dropped from the AC30 in place of two new 12AX7-based non-trem channels, normal and Brilliant, though retained in the smaller AC15. In this AC30/4, the EF86 is voiced by a two-way Brilliant switch, which offers the bright, biting tone that gives this its name or a darker, warmer sound with which, Tamposi tells us, "You can almost play death metal." But please don't.

If examples of the EF86-loaded AC30/4 are rare in the flesh (in addition to the few TV-front amps made, only some four to five hundred were made in the more standard Vox cabs that followed), we know the sound from Brad Paisley's go-to recording amp, his much-loved fawn 1960 AC30/4, and perhaps more directly from the several boutique amps inspired by its circuit. Most familiar of these is perhaps Matchless' DC30, which expands its EF86 channel with a six-way voicing switch, while TopHat, 65 Amps, Gabriél, and several others have followed suit. Notable, too, is Dr. Z's Stang-Ray, a near-clone of the Normal channel of Paisley's AC30/4.

It's difficult to imagine that Vox/JMI founder Tom Jennings and designer Dick Denney could have known quite what they were setting in motion when they doubled the AC15 into the AC30 more than five decades ago—although, given that they were doing it for major stars of the day, they might have had some inkling. The task was largely undertaken on behalf of guitarists Hank Marvin and Bruce Welch of the Shadows, who were Britain's most successful proponents of rock 'n' roll from around 1959 into the early 1960s, both as instrumental hit makers and backing band to pop singer Cliff Richard. As this new music attained bigger and bigger audiences, its performers needed bigger amps to play it through, and Vox took up the task of providing them.

While an AC30 might not seem such a large amp, in the scheme of things, to be vaunted as Britain's heavyweight contender of the day, anyone who has played a good AC30 knows that these can be loud amps by any standard. Not 200-watt Marshall Major loud, perhaps, but they'll go round for round with plenty of 50-watt half stacks, and their chime, depth, and harmonic breadth combine to give them a bigger voice than their 30-watt rating (actually closer to 35 watts) might imply. In any case, this was a revolution in the making, and the birth of a tone that, in the right hands, can still prove an utter revelation. ◉

than a dozen examples are known to have survived. Forgive us, Vox fanatics, if the following details keep you awake at night, but we proffer them in the name of posterity and not as part of any effort to further fever your addled desires. As confirmed with its current caretaker, some of the specs of this AC30 (serial number 4218) include:

- Haddon transformers
- Radio Spares choke
- typical early AC30/4 "pre list of changes" (or "pre-LOC") circuit constructed on two separate lower tag strips
- Wima signal caps
- silver Celestion B025 alnico speakers (predecessor to Celestion T.530 "Vox blues") originally, now replaced with 1960 Goodmans Axiom alnicos
- cream Rexine covering with small diamond pattern
- oxblood grille cloth with diamond pattern
- black control panel
- small brass "Jennings" badge on amp front
- single plastic handle

Although the output stage and the Vib-Trem channel on this amp are extremely similar to those on the more familiar, later, fawn-and-black AC30s, the amp differs enough in its Normal channel to be an entirely different amplifier—or at least to offer an entirely different voice.

*Amp courtesy Lee and Donna
Scaife/Vintage Tone Music*

BUILT FOR LOUD

In addition to several significant shifts in style and presentation, the transition of the late 1950s into the early 1960s represented a significant push into big-amp territory for Fender. Having introduced the 80-watt "high-powered" tweed 5F8 Twin in 1958, the rapidly expanding Fullerton, California, manufacturer sought another model to take it more forcefully into the large dance halls and theaters in which the kids were congregating in greater and greater numbers to get jiggy to the new hormone-fueled music.

Leo Fender had cut his teeth on the slightly tamer country and western scene of southern California; he needed a more bombastic test bed for this ambitious new venture. The West Coast's burgeoning surf scene proved the perfect laboratory, and there was no better test pilot than the young Dick

Dale, who was already pummeling his Strat through existing Fender creations before thousands-strong crowds at the Rendezvous Ballroom in Balboa, California, every weekend of the year. What did Dale really need to take this live music experience over the top? He needed a Showman amplifier, and Fender was ready to burn the midnight oil to give it to him.

In blending the output stage of the high-powered tweed Twin and the preamp, tone stack, and tremolo effect of Fender's first official Tolex-covered amp, the new Vibrasonic of 1959, the Showman was not *entirely* new. It was, however, Fender's first piggyback amp and therefore its first real leap from bandstand to arena stage.

The Showman also represented an intensity of research and development that was, perhaps, more intense than that required by the majority of Fender's new amplifier products, which were themselves no slouch in the R&D

1960 FENDER SHOWMAN 6G14

- Preamp tubes: Six 7025 (12AX7 types)
- Output tube: Four 6L6GC, fixed-bias
- Rectifier: Solid-state
- Controls: Normal channel: Volume, Treble, Bass; Vibrato channel: Volume, Treble, Bass, Speed, Intensity; shared: Presence
- Speaker: One Jensen P15N 15-inch driver in ported "tone ring" cabinet
- Output: 100 watts RMS

Dick Dale and His Del-Tones played music by surfers for surfers—and they wanted it loud. Armed with a piggyback Fender Showman and his trademark Fender Stratocaster, aka "the Beast," Dale and his band rocked coastal California ballrooms and school gymnasiums. Here, they play at the Rendezvous Ballroom in Balboa.

"Leo Fender gave the Fender Stratocaster along with a Fender amp to Dick Dale and told him to beat it to death and tell him what he thought of it. Dale took the guitar and started to beat it to death, and he blew up Leo Fender's amp and blew out the speaker. Dale proceeded to blow up 49 amps and speakers; they would actually catch on fire. Leo would say, 'Dick, why do you have to play so loud?' Dale would explain that he wanted to create the sound of Gene Krupa the famous jazz drummer that created the sounds of the native dancers in the jungles along with the roar of Mother Nature's creatures and the roar of the ocean.

"Leo Fender kept giving Dale amps, and Dale kept blowing them up! Till one night Leo and his right-hand man, Freddy T., went down to the Rendezvous Ballroom on the Balboa Peninsula in Balboa, California, and stood in the middle of four thousand screaming, dancing Dick Dale fans and said to Freddy, 'I now know what Dick Dale is trying to tell me.' Back to the drawing board. A special 85-watt output transformer was made that peaked 100 watts when Dale would pump up the volume of his amp. This transformer would create the sounds, along with Dale's style of playing, the kind of sounds that Dale dreamed of. But! They now needed a speaker that would handle the power and not burn up from the volume that would come from Dale's guitar.

"Leo, Freddy, and Dale went to the James B. Lansing speaker company, and they explained that they wanted a 15-inch speaker built to their specifications. That speaker would soon be known as the 15-inch JBL–D130 speaker. It made the complete package for Dale to play through and was named the Single Showman Amp. When Dale plugged his Fender Stratocaster guitar into the new Showman Amp and speaker cabinet, Dale became the first creature on earth to jump from the volume scale of a modest, quiet guitar player on a scale of four to blasting up through the volume scale to TEN!"

—DICK DALE, speaking of himself in the royal third person, on his role in the Fender Showman department. Dick Dale has frequently spoken of his role in the development of the Showman and boasts of having blown up nearly fifty amplifiers before Fender achieved a design that could take the heat. Whether or not the seminal surf guitarist exaggerates, his claims encompass the ambition of the Showman. The keys to successfully creating the bigger, stronger, and louder amp required lay primarily in two major new ingredients: a new OT and a new speaker cab design.

By the end of the tweed era of the 1950s, Fender had already moved to Schumacher transformers for many of its amplifiers. To make the Showman work, however, the company turned once again to Triad, and together they developed a super-robust OT with heavy iron for the kind of punch and tight low-end response that this new Professional Series amp demanded. Often referred to as the "Dick Dale transformer," this Triad unit (Fender part number 125A4A) helped give the new amp an abundance of girth.

The next requirement was to design a speaker cabinet that could take the wallop of four 6L6s through that mammoth OT. To do so, Fender put a lot more thought into the matter than the usual rectangular box with speaker had ever required. The result, and the original partner to the Showman amp head, was an oversize closed-back cab with a 15-inch speaker mounted on a "tone ring," a circular metal mounting ring attached to the rearmost of two wooden baffles. The system decoupled the driver from the front surface of the outer baffle slightly and served as a lens to focus and better project the sound.

A lot is made of Fender's work with JBL to develop the ultimate driver for the Showman, and Dale frequently puts in his two cents on this subject, but our example here is a very early pre-JBL Showman,

loaded with a single Jensen P15N speaker. This Jensen, entirely original to this pristine amp and cab set belonging to Lee and Donna Scaife, is an early 1959 model, alongside transformers with late 1959 date codes, so it is certainly among the earliest of Showmans built.

Add it all up, and you are left with the slightly alarming fact of a speaker that isn't rated to take the full power of the amplifier coupled to it—late 1950s P15Ns being rated at around 30 watts of power handling, 50 watts at most. But the enclosed cab does provide the speaker with some cushioning air suspension, which could arguably help keep it ticking.

That said, this might just be one of the lucky amps that was spared the usual implosion wrought by Dick Dale's pounding surf riffage and an exception to the rule that led Fender resolutely toward JBL. Available with two different JBL speaker sizes in the early years, as the Showman 12 and Showman 15, the amp would eventually go the whole hog and receive a speaker cab that could really sustain the fury. Around the time of the transition from brownface to blackface designs, Fender created a mammoth cab with two 15-inch JBL D130F speakers, a rig that would be known as the Dual Showman by 1963.

But let's backtrack and examine this early 1960 Showman a little more closely. The impressive lineup of six preamp tubes along the back of the chassis tells us that this Showman includes the beloved "harmonic vibrato," a near-as-dammit emulation of true vibrato rather than mere amplitude-modulating tremolo, achieved by a circuit powered by two and a half preamp tubes (only one triode of the middle tube is used). It also retains the Presence control that would vanish by 1963.

A look inside the chassis of this amp—which is every bit as pristine as its outside views—shows us a mix of the

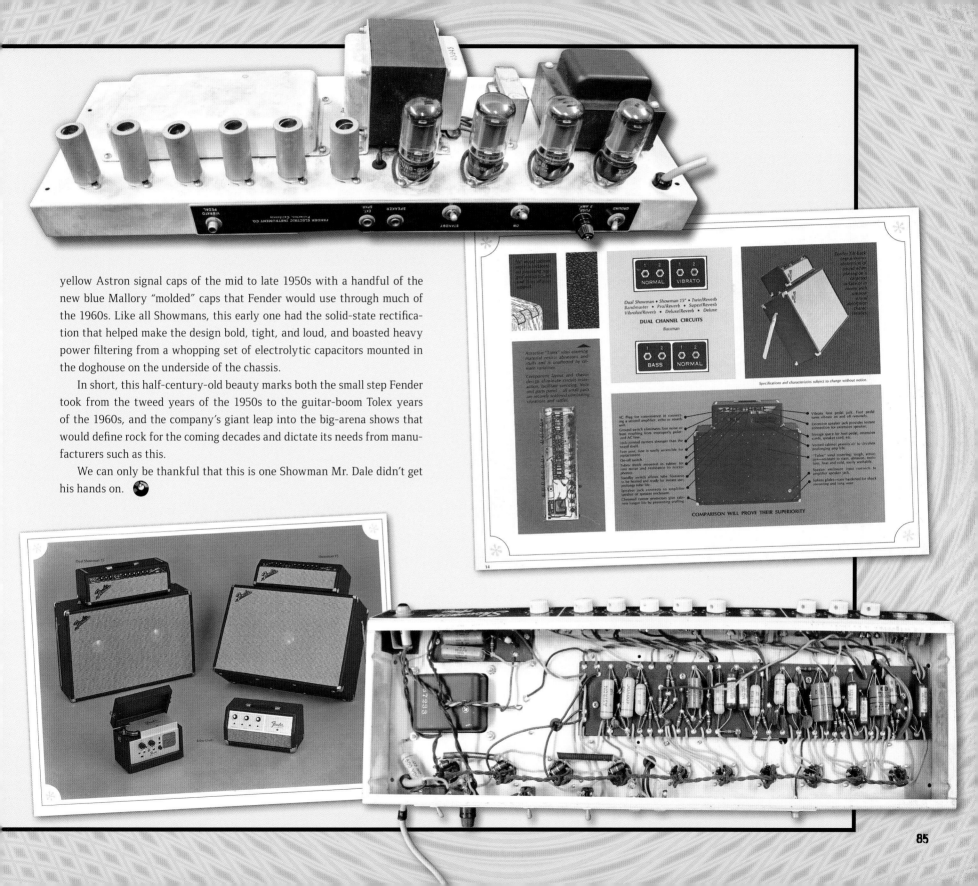

yellow Astron signal caps of the mid to late 1950s with a handful of the new blue Mallory "molded" caps that Fender would use through much of the 1960s. Like all Showmans, this early one had the solid-state rectification that helped make the design bold, tight, and loud, and boasted heavy power filtering from a whopping set of electrolytic capacitors mounted in the doghouse on the underside of the chassis.

In short, this half-century-old beauty marks both the small step Fender took from the tweed years of the 1950s to the guitar-boom Tolex years of the 1960s, and the company's giant leap into the big-arena shows that would define rock for the coming decades and dictate its needs from manufacturers such as this.

We can only be thankful that this is one Showman Mr. Dale didn't get his hands on.

THE BEAUTIFUL FREAK

I bought my first electric guitar in the mid 1970s—a used import no-brand with a pickup so microphonic you could sing through it and an unprecedented amount of skyline between its strings and fingerboard. After I'd handed over my $50 worth of lawn-mowing cash, the seller said, "Hey, there's an amp that goes with it." He fetched from the basement a mid 1950s Gibson GA-30. It was a little dusty, but its Jensen 12- and 8-inch speakers were punchy, and it made a sound that I'd later come to identify as tonus maximus. Delighted? Of course not. I sold it to get a solid-state Kasino stack with 8x10 cabs and controls on the front, "like a Marshall."

If this was anything unusual, it might be a reminiscence over which to shed the occasional tear, but Gibson amps never got much respect anyway,

and while the adolescent me would have gone entirely hormonal over the mere sight of a Les Paul, the same logo on an old brown-and-tan amp did nothing for me. The dude threw it in for free because that's about what it was worth at the time. If it had been a tweed Fender of the same year, he would have known better and asked for another fifty bucks.

Given that the costliest vintage Gibson guitars way outstrip the most desirable of Fenders, it might seem odd that vintage Gibson amps have historically fetched only a fraction of the dirty green that tweed and even tan and blackface Fender amps have commanded for years. But it makes some sense: Leo Fender was an amp designer first and foremost, and there was a studied progression of the Fender line that displayed the coexistence of relative consistency within a careful and logical evolution of the designs.

For Gibson, on the other hand, you get the feeling amps were an afterthought and that the R&D and marketing processes involved a lot of flailing in a dark

CIRCA 1961 GIBSON GA-79RVT

- Preamp/effects tubes: Three 6EU7s, one 7199, 12AU7 PI
- Output tubes: Four 6BQ5s (EL34), cathode-biased
- Rectifier: Solid-state diodes
- Controls: Channel 1: Volume, Bass, Treble; Reverb; Tremolo Depth and Frequency (speed); channel 2: Volume, Bass, Treble
- Speakers: Two 10-inch P12Qs
- Output: 2x15 watts RMS

basement in Kalamazoo. The 1950s coughed up some truly excellent models, but the specs, tube complements, cabinet designs and coverings, and other details hopped around wildly. The GA-40 Les Paul amp of the mid/late 1950s has become solidly collectible, and the knock-on effect has sent prices for GA-20s and GA-30s skyward too. In the mid 1960s, though, most Gibson amps took on a look, and arguably a sound, that makes them seem but a cheap half cousin to the very collectible guitars they were intended to partner, and by the 1970s—well, forget about it. There are some serviceable amps from the early/mid 1960s, but the clear standout is the incomparable, wedge-shaped GA-79RVT.

While other Gibson amps of the 1950s and early 1960s are generally billed as "poor man's Fenders" and propped by their proponents for how well they equal or surpass the sound of similarly sized tweed Fender models for significantly less outlay, the GA-79RVT is a Gibson amp entirely unto itself. In hindsight, you might even argue that Gibson amps fared best when they were tailing Fender designs, but the company's limited (though enthusiastic) support of the stereo guitar fad necessitated development of this boggle-eyed freak of a tone machine, possibly the last truly groovy amp of the golden years to wear the Big G logo.

In many ways, the GA-79RVT is a fairly simple amp. It is really more two amps in one designed to reproduce a stereo signal than an amp that produces a stereo-like

effect, like the Magnatone 260 and 280 or the Roland Jazz Chorus. Thus its features are pretty straightforward: two independent preamps with their own Volume, Bass, and Treble controls (the latter using ganged potentiometers with stacked knobs), plus Tremolo and Reverb (on channel 1 only when in stereo mode). Each channel can be linked and fed together to both of the dual output stages or fed individually to its own stage and onto its own speaker.

Whichever way the switch is thrown, each of the speakers receives a potential 15 watts of power from its own two output tubes and an independent output transformer, so the Stereo–Mono switch doesn't gang the output stage, it just feeds the two equal yet independent stages a common signal. The "stereo" aspect comes into play when a stereo guitar, such as Gibson's ES-345, is plugged into the Stereo input jack, which routes the neck pickup to one channel and the bridge pickup to the other. Otherwise, the channels can be given independent input signals from two guitars or a stereo effect unit.

Oddball factor number one is, of course, the dramatic wedge-shaped cabinet, with two Jensen P10Q speakers mounted at approximately 45 degrees to each other. The design accentuates the stereo field but also creates a sonic dead spot in the front-center of the amp until you get quite a distance away from it. Oddball factor number two is the tubes used here: three 6EU7s, a 7199 (these for preamp, reverb, and tremolo duties), a 12AU7 phase inverter, and four 6BQ5s (EL84s) in the cathode-biased output stage. Rectification is achieved with solid-state diodes. The design aims for smooth, round, clean tones at low to medium volumes, but it yields a sweetly textured crunch when cranked up. The scarcity and expense of the unusual preamp tubes, and the rarity of the amp itself, mean it's probably going to languish in collections more than shake its stuff on stage from here on out—and two 12s and larger OTs would probably do better service in a lot of gig situations—but raise a glass to the Gibson designers who dared to be different, and toast the beautiful freak.

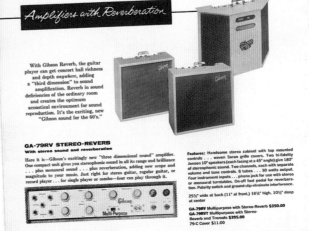

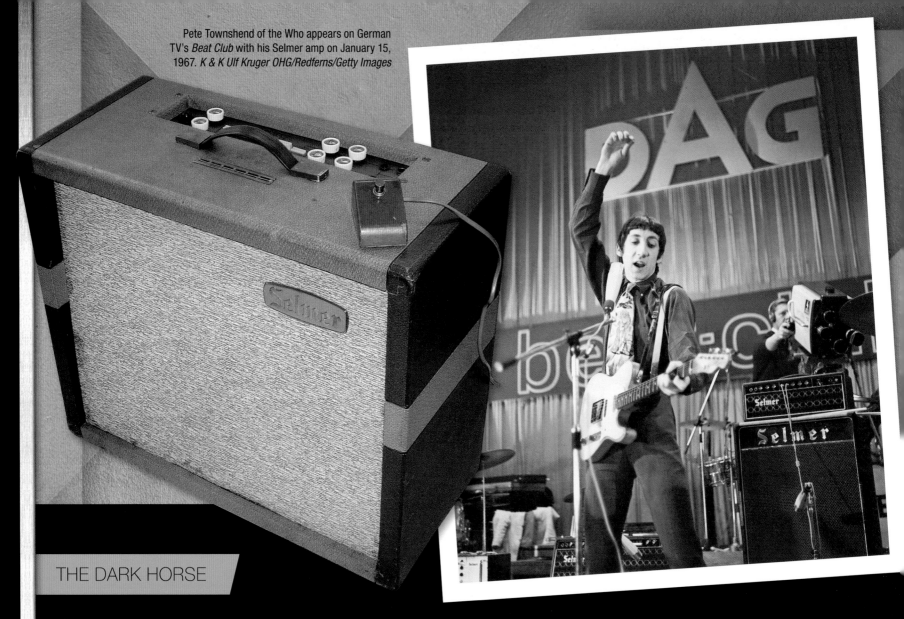

Pete Townshend of the Who appears on German TV's *Beat Club* with his Selmer amp on January 15, 1967. *K & K Ulf Kruger OHG/Redferns/Getty Images*

THE DARK HORSE

The more one digs into British amps from the formative years of tone—the late 1950s and early 1960s—the more one comes to realize that those English engineers really had it going on.

Sure, major U.S. companies like Fender and Gibson laid a lot of the groundwork, and Chicago amp maker Valco deserves a nod for its many funky models that were rebadged for other brands. But for originality of design and outright sonic virtue, it's hard to beat what the seminal Brits were cranking out pre-Plexi (and definitely pre-Hiwatt and Orange) in slightly shadowy corners behind the well-lit story of the early years of Vox or how Jim Marshall copied the 5F6-A Fender Bassman circuit. Contemplate briefly, if you will, the exotic wonders of Watkins, WEM, Elpico, Fenton-Weill, and the glorious Selmer.

In recent years, the Selmer brand has started to get some of the attention it deserves, partly because of skyrocketing Vox and Marshall prices and collectibility, partly in the wake of Jack White's use of a Selmer Zodiac 30 to record the White Stripes' *Elephant* album, and partly because people have finally realized just how cool these amps are. Although sometimes ghettoized as a B-list brand, Selmer is far from the Vox wannabe it is too often labeled as being. Many Selmers pack a degree of Vox jangle, crunch, and chime, certainly, while others come close to some Marshall chunk and roar, but they are an entity unto themselves. In fact, Selmer preceded original Vox manufacturer JMI in the instrument amplification business by nearly twenty years, having manufactured PA amplifiers at a premises on Charing Cross Road, London, since the

CIRCA 1961 SELMER TRUVOICE SELECTORTONE AUTOMATIC

- Preamp tubes: One ECC83, two EF86
- Output tubes: Two EL34s, cathode-bias
- Rectifier: GZ34
- Controls: Channel 1: Volume, Tone; channel 2: Volume, Tone, six pushbutton tone selections, tremolo Speed, and Depth
- Speaker: One 15-inch Goodmans
- Output: 30 watts RMS

mid 1930s (the RSA and Truvoice names were also used from the mid 1940s into the 1950s). By the mid 1950s—just as Vox was being founded and well before Marshall amps were a glimmer in a young drummer's eye—Selmer had moved firmly into guitar amplifiers and was one of the leading amplifier brands in the UK and Europe. Deservedly so, given the many rugged, efficient, and great-sounding units that survive in working order today. Before they were lured on to endorse the sexier and better-promoted Vox range, the Beatles, the Animals, and the Shadows all made much of their early noise through Selmer combos.

While models like the Thunderbird Twin 30, Zodiac 30, and Treble'n'Bass 50 are more common on the vintage market today, the '61 Truvoice Selectortone Automatic, here in its blue and gray Rexine covering, is a prime example of what Selmer's amplifier facility was achieving at the peak of the guitar boom in Great Britain. It's a quality piece of workmanship by any standards, a clever and versatile design, and sounds fantastic for a wide range of playing styles. Rather than the four EL84s that Vox elected to use in the AC30, Selmer employed a pair of EL34s, perhaps a more obvious choice, which produced about 30 watts in this model.

The output tubes are cathode biased with no negative feedback, so they produce that classically rich, harmonically resplendent tone commonly referred to as class A, but they do it a little differently than the archetypal AC30 template, given the EL34's low-end raunch and high-end sizzle and the wide,

full bark of the big ceramic 15-inch Goodmans speaker. All in all, it's its own puppy—looks, tone, and design-wise—and a sweet and funky little growler for anything from blues to classic Brit rock to cranked roots rock in a small/midsize club. It carries a great, sweeping, broad tremolo effect and screams alternative mojo from every angle.

A glance at the control panel tells you right off the bat that this is something different, the six pushbuttons in channel 2 that inspired the Selectortone name being the most alien feature. A look inside the back of the amp further emphasizes its unusualness. If anything, it's reminiscent of some late 1940s/early 1950s American-made amps that had separate preamp and power amp sections (positioned at the top and bottom of the cab, respectively), but the similarity ends there. The preamp section carries an ECC83 (aka 12AX7) and two EF86 pentodes in a circuit that uses one of the ECC83's two triodes as the first gain stage for each of its two channels, with an EF86 for gain makeup after the tone stage in each channel. Channel 1 has a fairly traditional treble-bleed tone pot, which is also an option in channel 2's unusual EQ stage (the pushbutton labeled "Rotary Control"), but alongside it are pushbuttons for High Treble, Treble, Medium, Bass, and Contra Bass, which tap a range of capacitors in series with a small choke to provide preset Vari-Tone-like voicing options.

In addition to the duet of EL34s, the power amp section carries another ECC83 (half of which is employed as phase inverter, the other half as tremolo oscillator) and a GZ34 rectifier tube. Although it's a cathode-biased output stage, it's worth noting that the rectifier is feeding a robust 445 volts DC to the grids of the EL34s, give or take a few volts, which makes for a punchy, firm sound and for more potential volume than many contemporary cathode-biased two-EL34 designs, which often tend to run the tubes at a softer and slightly browner 350 to 400 volts. Also, the rugged Partridge output transformer, a make most famous for its use in the classic Hiwatt designs, helps make the most of this potential wattage, being a "firmer" and somewhat more high-fidelity OT than those used in the majority of guitar amps. Be aware that early Selmers weren't wired for U.S. voltages.

Blistering volume, class A chime and dimension, great touch sensitivity, and thoroughly original features and styling: the Selmer Truvoice Selectortone Automatic—a real dark horse of a scream machine. ◉

Amp and photos courtesy Michael Tamposi

SWING AND BOP MEETS GRIT AND GRIND

With founder Everett Hull's close ties to the New York jazz community, and with the propensity of its amps to generate more clean than mean, Ampeg always swung and bopped more than it rocked and rolled. That said, there are some sleepers amid the Big A's early roster that apply themselves beautifully to all manner of grit and grind when you wind them up far enough.

The nifty 1961 Ampeg M-15, covered in navy random-flare vinyl, is a prime example. It might have been at home sitting behind Wes Montgomery or Kenny Burrell on a small club stage—or maybe gracing accordionist Dick Contino's back line. But if you look beneath the hood, it carries a mix-and-match bundle of ingredients found in a couple variations of a highly desirable

blues and classic rock amp from another maker, so there's no logical reason this jazzer's combo can't do many of the same tricks, accordion inputs or not.

Ampeg always made sturdy, good-sounding amps, and did so with pride, and the company's founders strictly avoided jumping on any bandwagons design-wise or copping the look or sound of other makers, even when those makers were leading the field the way Fender was in the late 1950s and early 1960s. Even so, in many ways the guts of this M-15 look remarkably like a Fender amp of a good ten years before—or more accurately, a lucky dip of elements from the evolution of that amp over the course of the 1950s. One need only whisper "single-15 guitar combo" and you're thinking Fender Pro, right? Bingo! The Jensen C15Q and dual-6L6 output stage are obvious clues, but bits and pieces of what's happening inside the chassis take us even farther down that road.

By the late 1950s, the highly desirable 5E5 narrow-panel tweed Pro had become a fairly sophisticated amp (for its day at least). It was still only a

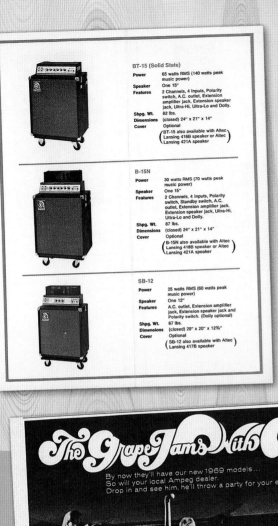

BT-15 (Solid State)

Power	65 watts RMS (140 watts peak music power)
Speaker	One 15"
Features	2 Channels, 4 Inputs, Polarity switch, A.C. outlet, Extension amplifier jack, Extension speaker jack, Ultra-Hi, Ultra-Lo and Dolly.
Shpg. Wt.	82 lbs.
Dimensions	(closed) 24" x 21" x 14"
Cover	Optional (BT-15 also available with Altec Lansing 418B speaker or Altec Lansing 421A speaker)

B-15N

Power	30 watts RMS (70 watts peak music power)
Speaker	One 15"
Features	2 Channels, 4 Inputs, Polarity switch, Standby switch, A.C. outlet, Extension amplifier jack, Extension speaker jack, Ultra-Hi, Ultra-Lo and Dolly.
Shpg. Wt.	87 lbs.
Dimensions	(closed) 24" x 21" x 14"
Cover	Optional (B-15N also available with Altec Lansing 418B speaker or Altec Lansing 421A speaker)

SB-12

Power	25 watts RMS (60 watts peak music power)
Speaker	One 12"
Features	A.C. outlet, Extension amplifier jack, Extension speaker jack and Polarity switch. (Dolly optional)
Shpg. Wt.	67 lbs.
Dimensions	(closed) 20" x 20" x 12¾"
Cover	Optional (SB-12 also available with Altec Lansing 417B speaker)

The Grape Jams With Ampeg

By now they'll have our new 1969 models...
So will your local Ampeg dealer.
Drop in and see him, he'll throw a party for your ears.

AMPEG AMPLIFIERS...
THE SHOCK TROOPS OF THE NEW WAVE IN SOUND

Bob Dylan plays his Fender Stratocaster through a later Ampeg amp while recording his album *Bringing It All Back Home* on January 14, 1965, in Columbia's Studio A in New York City.
Michael Ochs Archives/Getty Images

1961 AMPEG M-15

- Preamp tubes: Three 6SL7s
- Output tubes: Two 6L6GCs, cathode-bias, with negative feedback
- Rectifier: 5U4
- Controls: Volume and Tone for each channel, tremolo Speed and Intensity
- Speaker: Jensen Concert Series C15Q
- Output: Approximately 25 watts RMS

halfway point between Deluxe and Bassman, lacking the latter's long-tailed pair phase inverter but employing its cathode-follower tone stack, fixed bias, and a little negative feedback to tighten up the fundamentals. Earlier in the decade, the 5C5 iteration had only a simple treble-bleed tone control, a self-balancing paraphase inverter, a cathode-biased output stage, and octal 6SC7 preamp and PI tubes.

It's a little surprising, then, given the evolution of amplification technology by this point, to find a larger Ampeg from the early 1960s using a cathode-biased output stage and octal preamp tubes (6SL7s—not a mile from 6SC7s in character and performance). Also unexpected is its employment of a variation on the split-load (cathodyne) PI, much like that used in small- and medium-size Fender tweeds, a puzzling topology in this M-15 from various angles but confirmed by Mike Zaite at Dr. Z Amps.

Two of these elements—the cathode biasing and the split-load PI—will contribute to an amp that breaks up on the early side and therefore lends itself well to blues and rock 'n' roll. Despite its eight-pin socket, the 6SL7 is a dual-triode preamp tube that isn't a mile away from a 12AX7 in character. Either tube fits easily into the same basic schematic, but some players find the octal tube a little rounder and warmer sounding, while it also has slightly less gain. All told, these factors make for a full-, buoyant-sounding amp that has rich, broad, clean tones up to about ten o'clock but that breaks up with a little grit and sizzle inside its mid-range bark when you crank it up much further.

So it sounds just like a TV-front or wide-panel tweed Fender Pro? Well, not quite, and no one's entirely sure why not, except that this is more proof that a few variables in circuit and components can change the sound of an amplifier a great deal. It does get you in the ballpark, and it offers plenty of individual personality in the process, resulting in a bargain vintage find that might turn on plenty of players just as it is. But even when floored, it doesn't quite do the earlier tweed Pro's creamy, fat overdrive and addictively tactile compression. It does its own thing, and that's not bad. In the plus column, it does carry a tremolo circuit, something not available on any 6L6-based tweed Fender, which adds a major *thump-thump-thump* to the vibe when you whack it up or a subtle ripple at lower settings on the intensity dial. Each channel has its own tone control rather than the shared tone of the 5C5 Pro, and the accordion channel offers a darker, smoother voice that gives you some creative A/B options with a switching pedal.

There are a couple of notable quirks and service requirements here. For one, the electrolytic capacitors often crapped out on the early M-15s and more often than not are in need of immediate replacement. Few 1950s Fender Pros suffer the same illness, so who knows what's up with that? Not a big deal, though: caps are easy.

Also, as cool as it is to have the original Jensen speaker, this beat old C15Q is a little undergunned if you want anything other than authentic, shagged-out, forty-seven-year-old amp tone. A quality replacement such as an Eminence Legend 1518 or a Weber Vintage Alnico will help maximize the potential in those 6L6s.

The spiffy snakeskin handle here is not an original item (more's the shame), but yours should come complete with a tremolo foot switch made from an old rubber doorstop. Now that's ingenuity! ◉

Jazzman Wes Montgomery, performing here in 1964, was a confirmed fan of Ampeg amps.
David Redfern/Redferns/Getty Images

Like Fender's big boys of the early 1960s, the little 6G2 Princeton was also a fixed-bias amp, a status flagged up by the bias circuit rendered on its own little board in the upper-left corner of the chassis. The immaculate condition of this example and all those lovely blue "molded" Mallory signal caps make it a great yet affordable find for player and collector alike.

Princeton stalwart Duane Allman plays slide on his gold-top Les Paul in the studio in 1960. *Michael Ochs Archives/Getty Images*

PART TWEED, PART BLACKFACE, ALL TONE

For the past couple decades, it seemed the Fender Deluxe of the 1960s and early 1970s—in its several variants—had a firm grasp on the title "favorite small vintage combo." Lately, however, the smaller Princeton has finagled its way into that position. Whether this is a factor in the continuing decline in stage volumes tolerated at smaller venues or simply a growing recognition of the Princeton's singular sonic virtues is difficult to say. Either way, the trend behooves a look at a lesser-seen "tweeny" of a Princeton that offers a slightly alternative flavor from this popular menu.

While it isn't entirely accurate to describe the brownface, tan Tolex amps of 1960–1963 as "somewhere between a tweed and a blackface," this 1962 Princeton fits that billing rather well. In this case, though, the 6G2 Princeton circuit is perhaps closer to the 5E3 Deluxe in several ways, in tone as much as anything, than it is to its single-ended tweed forebear—or it would be if not for its rather underpowered 10-inch speaker.

In 1960 the Princeton model went from being the larger of the beginner's bedroom amps in the Fender lineup to being the smaller of the performance amps. With two 6V6GT output tubes in push-pull, fixed bias, for a robust 12 watts, it was suddenly too loud for the average kid's bedroom but graduated successfully to the basement or garage, where it could hit the sweet spot perfectly with a couple of pals from down the road on drums and bass. This is the status the brown Princeton maintained for many years—underrated as a performance amp compared to the versatile Princeton Reverb, long a studio favorite of many pros—and it's a situation for which any player likely to have acquired one lately can be thankful.

Like our example here, many 6G2 Princetons exist in outstanding original condition, having seen only light duty for a few years, then a quiet life in the closet, awaiting eventual rediscovery and a second coming as an unassuming little tone monster. And that she is. While the 6G2 packs plenty of snappy chime and twang at lower settings on the Volume dial, anything in the noon to

1962 FENDER PRINCETON 6G2

- Preamp tubes: One 7025, one 12AX7
- Output tubes: Two 6V6GTs; fixed-bias
- Rectifier: 5Y3
- Controls: Volume, Tone, Speed, Intensity
- Speaker: One 10-inch Oxford 10J4
- Output: Approximately 12 watts RMS

two o'clock region reveals toothsome growl and snarl, and settings up into late afternoon unveil a surprisingly gutsy roar.

The 6G2 Princeton's fixed-bias output stage takes it out of the nominal class A camp of the cathode-biased tweed Deluxe and the like, but its cathodyne inverter (aka split-phase inverter) puts it in a sort of "two steps forward, one step back" situation. With this PI configuration, it will never have the clarity and fidelity to be merely "a smaller brown 6G3 Deluxe," a definition its specs might otherwise imply, but will instead offer a certain grit and swagger in its tonal signature, even at cleaner settings, with some voices that do at least tip the hat toward the 5E3.

The 6G2's 5Y3 rectifier tube also keeps this amp tweedily brown, providing just around 315V DC on the plates of the 6V6s, though often a little more with today's higher domestic AC line voltages. That, coupled with readings of around 135V DC on the plates of the first triode of the 7025 (aka 12AX7) in the front end, the lone gain stage in the Princeton's preamp if you exclude the front half of the PI, makes for a chewy, tactile playing feel that can come off as being a lot more touch sensitive than that of many larger brown amps and later blackface amps. A leap to the top of the ladder in the rectifier stakes would give the blackface AA964 Princeton a GZ34 rectifier and a whopping 420V DC on the plates of the 6V6s (a 5U4GB and 410V DC in the AA1164 Princeton Reverb), and while the cathodyne PI meant these models retained some signature bite, they were also a little crisper and more aggressive too.

It might be surprising that Fender went to fixed bias at all for the 6G2, but one of this amp's other standout features offers a clue to the thinking behind this move. Other than the first-generation tweed Tremolux, the 5G9 and 5G9-A, Fender always preferred to mount its bias-modulated tremolo circuit on a fixed-bias output stage.

This was for reasons of output tube stability, perhaps, although other designs have functioned smoothly with bias-wiggle tremolo acting on cathode-biased output tubes. Either way, this preference saw the Princeton upgraded to fixed bias, and other than the single-ended Champ, there was no longer a cathode-biased amp in the Fender lineup.

Whatever the thinking, this tremolo is an utter joy, and we can thank Leo for doing it this way. While players often rave about the lush, deep "harmonic vibrato" of the bigger early brown amps, such as the 6G4 Super, the tremolo on the 6G2 Princeton is achieved with just half a 12AX7 and a mere handful of caps and resistors. As simple as it is, however, it modulates the output tubes in a smooth, organic manner that sounds utterly dreamy, providing what is, for our money, one of the most evocative tremolo effects available. (As regards the bigger brown amp's effect, sure, it is impressive, but sometimes you want a rich-sounding but *true* tremolo rather than the watery pseudovibrato these amps produce.) As with many bias-modulated tremolos, it's a very playable effect: hit the strings hard and it steps aside, so your note attack pops out proudly—allowing you to solo successfully without switching out the effect— then it makes itself known again as it throbs back into action on the decay of the note.

All in all, with its bumped-up specs and gutsier tone, the 6G2 Princeton can still find itself stuck between two stools. Is it a club amp with an underpowered speaker or a practice amp with an overpowered output stage? Make one simple change and it can be neither, and both, if you catch our drift. As sweet as the original 10-inch Oxford 10J4 speaker can sound in this amp, a decent 12-inch (or even a more robust 10) makes a big difference. If you want that bigger driver right in the amp, please don't hack a bigger hole in the original baffle; good and authentic-looking replacement baffles with 12-inch cutouts are readily available. Alternatively, use this little sweetie as a "head" perched on top of the 8-ohm cab of your choice to reduce the inherent boxiness in the smaller combo cab.

Bedroom amp? Hah! They won't be laughing for long.

Fender's 65 Princeton Reverb reissue.
Fender Musical Instruments Corporation

Amp courtesy Rick Batey

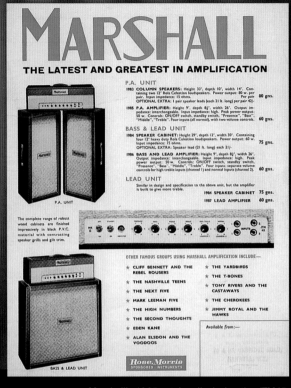

Marshall's 1965 catalog displaying the JTM45.

BIRTH OF THE BRITISH STACK

It's enlightening to recall that Marshall amplifiers and the larger Fender amps, embodying the tonal archetypes of opposite sides of the Atlantic and having come to represent very different musical voices, were born from the same root.

Or more precisely, Jim Marshall's amp line was ultimately ripped from the belly of the late 1950s Fender 5F6-A Bassman. What often proves even more fascinating is an examination of the minor differences between the Bassman and the JTM45 of 1962–1963 and of the significant difference they make to the sounds of the two amplifiers.

A ban on U.S. imports from 1951 to 1559 rendered Fender guitars and amps virtually unobtainable in Britain through the 1950s and meant they were very rare and extremely expensive in the years following. The popularity of American pop, blues, and rock 'n' roll acts in Britain nevertheless made the Fender name iconic, and figures in the English music trade who occasionally had the chance to examine the Fender gear of touring American musicians quickly discovered that it was sturdy and efficient too. Jim Marshall, a jazz drummer and owner of a music store in Hanwell, West London, was selling all the Fender amps he could get his hands on. Marshall recognized the power and versatility of the Bassman design in particular. Inspired by the revelation that it would be easier to meet the growing demand for powerful guitar amps (and just plain cheaper) if he made his own, he set about cloning the 5F6-A circuit—with a few British twists.

In 1962 Jim Marshall, repairman Ken Bran, and shop assistant Dudley Craven built an amp in Marshall's workshop using the 5F6-A as a template but employing readily available components. The Marshall line was born.

You can virtually superimpose Fender's 5F6-A schematic onto the inside of the chassis of an early JTM45 with nary a wire or component falling out

CIRCA 1962 MARSHALL JTM45

- Preamp tubes: Three ECC83s (12AX7) for first gain stage, cathode-follower tone stack, and long-tailed pair phase inverter
- Output tubes: Initially two 5881s, then two KT66s; class A/B, fixed-bias
- Rectifier: GZ34
- Controls: Volume Normal, Volume Bright, Treble, Bass, Middle, Presence
- Speakers: Initially four 15-watt Celestion G12 drivers with alnico magnets; later four 20-watt Celestion G12M-20 "Greenbacks" wired in series parallel
- Output: 45 watts RMS into a 16-ohm load

of place. Their control panels are likewise the same, knob for knob. Inside, the same values of resistors and signal capacitors form the same cathode-follower tone stacks and long-tailed pair phase inverters. Marshall employed firmer filtering in a few places through some slightly higher electrolytic capacitor values, but little else strays far from spec, and they both used GZ34 (or equivalent) tube rectifiers, so sag and compression characteristics at high volumes would be similar. Although Marshall amps are largely known as a classic example of the crunchy sound of the EL34 output tube, the debut model used 5881s (a rugged 6L6GC type) just like the Bassman. When these became expensive and difficult to get, Marshall switched to the compatible KT66, until these became expensive and short of supply and Marshall switched to EL34s—but that's another chapter. Even so, the KT66s sounded just a little bolder and fatter than 5881s and took the JTM45 a step into more original tonal territory.

One of the biggest specification differences at the amp end of the young Marshall was its use of an ECC83 (a European 12AX7 equivalent) in the first gain stage rather than Bassman's 12AY7. The higher-gain tube gave the JTM45 a hotter preamp that was prone to earlier distortion, which plenty of players discovered retroactively in their tweed Fender amps when 12AY7s grew short of supply and they began commonly substituting 12AX7s. They are a totally compatible, non-mod tube swap in this position, although the X has a gain factor of around 100 versus around 40 for the Y. Still, this is largely a factor of gain and degree of breakup. So why does an original Marshall JTM45 sound so unlike a tweed Bassman?

Eric Clapton with the famous 1960 Gibson Les Paul Standard guitar and Marshall JTM45 combo amp during the *Blues Breakers* LP sessions.

We have to take issue with the question itself. The fact is, if you plug it into an open-backed 4x10-inch cab with Jensen alnico speakers, it doesn't—not broadly so anyway. Certainly, constructing the same amp from quality British and European components rather than quality American components will result in a very slightly different sonic character in the end product. The yellow Astron caps of late 1950s Fenders and the yellow "mustard caps" of 1960s Marshalls are equally revered, but aficionados will tell you they do sound ever-so-slightly different. Also, the JTM45's chassis was made from aluminum rather than steel, which interacts differently with the electromagnetic components of the amplifier—namely the transformers. But to account for their different character, you have to look closer at what messieurs Fender and Marshall plugged their amps into.

Having identified the need for a bigger amplifier to cater to the needs of the rock 'n' roll crowd—whose stars were playing bigger venues at louder volumes thanks to the popularity of the music—Marshall and crew took the premise to its natural conclusion and developed a speaker cab that could handle the full gale of 45 gusty British tube watts. The large, closed-back, slant-topped model 1960A speaker cabinet was devised as the most logical container for the number of Celestion G12 speakers required to handle the JTM45's power. These speakers—which had alnico magnets when Marshall first started using them—were rated at 15 watts (later 20) and were prone to "flapping out" on hard low notes. Putting them into teams of four gave them a chance to handle the amp's power surges, and enclosing the cab's back created a form of air-pressure suspension that limited cone travel. The result was a directional cab with thumping lows, punchy mids,

and a tapered high-end response. In short, something very different from the Bassman.

Otherwise, the JTM45 characteristics do indeed put it in the ballpark with the 5F6-A—a smoother, rounder, more succulent sound than the crunchy roar from later Marshalls. With 5881s or KT66s and a tube rectifier, the early Marshall is a stunning amp for playing almost any form of electric blues, greasy rock 'n' roll, alt-country, or other rootsier forms. The cathode-follower tone stack, tube rectification, and firm phase-inverter stage all work to make this a tactile, touch-sensitive amp that suits players with nuanced, dynamic styles.

Although the "piggyback" head and 4x12-inch cab were the first products out of the stable, the JTM45 amplifier entered the annals of tone in 1965 in the form of the model 1962 2x12-inch combo, known forever as the Bluesbreaker after Eric Clapton plugged in his Gibson Les Paul and cranked the knobs to 10 to record John Mayall and the Bluesbreakers' "Beano" album. The ceramic magnet Celestion G12Ms the amp carried at the time were barely able to withstand the maelstrom. The result has proved one of blues rock's most enduring overdriven lead tones.

Other than Clapton's use of the 1962 JTM45 combo, there are fewer enduring name-artist examples of the KT66/tube-rectified Marshall era than of the EL34/solid-state rectified Plexi era that followed it. Alongside bassist John Entwistle, Pete Townshend occasionally used a JTM45 with the Who. And even years after the model vanished from the Marshall line, players from Angus Young to Billy Gibbons to John Frusciante discovered the juicy, sweet textures of the cranked JTM45. ⚫

Pete Townshend shows his appreciation for the Marshall JTM45 at the Windsor Jazz Blues Festival in England on July 30, 1966. *Pictorial Press/Alamy*

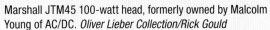

Marshall JTM45 100-watt head, formerly owned by Malcolm Young of AC/DC. *Oliver Lieber Collection/Rick Gould*

TO THE TUNE OF DIFFERENT TUBES

Certainly, most players' quests for "alternative vintage" amps stay within bounds that are less than entirely alternative. Often we seek the poor man's AC15, tweed Deluxe, or Marshall Plexi . . . insert your own desire as required.

While they wear badges that offer alternatives to the big three of the vintage amp world, the lack of originality in these "alternative" choices (meant without the least hint of the derogatory) lies in the fact that many of them use similar circuits to, or at least the same tube choices as, the more successful Deluxes, Twins, and AC30s they chased in the marketplace.

The amp makers at Gibson can rarely be accused of practicing any sort of copycat ethos. Some of us might have found life easier if they had, but the tube-fried branch of our friends from Kalamazoo were always determined to do things their own way—up into the mid 1960s at least—and Fender be damned.

With its light brown vinyl covering and golden wheat grille appearing similar if not identical to standard dress for so many Fender amps of 1960 to 1963,

the cosmetics on this 1963 Epiphone Pacemaker EA-50T might scream otherwise. But before you jump to label this 10-watt/1x10-inch combo with tremolo a poor man's Princeton, you need to peer briefly under the hood. There's not a Fender-certified tube in sight here, friends. And in the true alternatives such as this—well, that's where the fun begins.

This little Epi tube combo could perhaps be made to do the same tricks as a brownface Princeton or maybe a Vox AC10 of the same era, but that would be missing the point. Amps like this one have their own sound, and the fact that it's usually more affordable than the classic models from the big names makes it all the more enjoyable. Once you learn that chocolate, vanilla, and strawberry are not the only tasty flavors behind the counter, you're farther down the road to sounding like yourself rather than the last guy who recorded through a Champ, a Bluesbreaker, or whatever. Sure, perhaps the "tweed crunch" is a classic tone, but maybe the "Epiphone Pacemaker crunch" could be *your* classic tone.

1963 EPIPHONE EA-50T PACEMAKER

- Preamp tubes: Two 6EU7s
- Output tubes: Two 6AQ5s, cathode-bias, no negative feedback
- Rectifier: 6X4
- Controls: Loudness, Frequency (tremolo speed)
- Speaker: 10-inch Gibson Ultrasonic or similar
- Output: Approximately 10 watts RMS

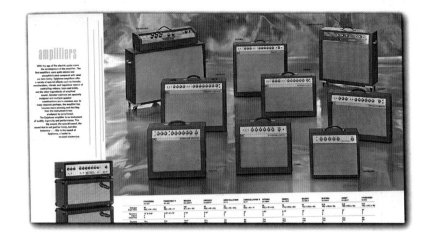

It's a little different, that's for sure. This combo produces its bold 10 watts courtesy of a pair of 6AQ5 output tubes. No, that's not a typo. These are one alphanumeric back from the American nomenclature for the classic British EL84 (6BQ5). In Euro-speak, this would be the EL90. (Its military equivalent is the 6005, not to be confused with the much bigger 6550.) The implied familial relationship of these tubes might initially encourage bargain hunters still looking for something they can hammer back into one of those familiar molds to rejig our Epi into a British EL-84-based chimer and be done with it, but the 6AQ5 is further from its cousin than the name might imply. For one thing, it fits a miniature seven-pin socket. For another, it is rated to take only around 250 volts at the plates. At this point, it performs not unlike a 6V6, but this limit means a pair is really good for only around 10 watts max. So what? It just so happens that you have discovered them inside a nifty 10-watt amp that can sound extremely groovy just as it is, so stick with it. (On the other hand, you may indeed want to find a good substitute for the original speaker, and replacing this undergunned unit with a good new 10-inch will noticeably liven up the amp.)

The happy flipside is that these tubes, being in far less demand than NOS EL-84s, are relatively cheap and in good supply. They have their own sound too (this is where we came in). If you don't push them past their limits design-wise (while feeling free to crank them up within a well-regulated design like this Pacemaker, where the pair is cathode biased, with no negative feedback), they can sound plenty gutsy, with a crispness to their overdrive that gives a sparkle to chords and single-note solos. An amp like this is clearly most useful as a recording tool, but it could handle the right kind of gigs miked up too, depending on your sound system.

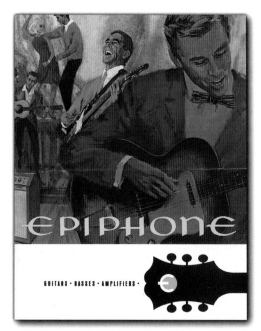

Another quirky tube lurks in the front end: a pair of 6EU7 dual triodes. These were popular with Gibson back in the day, and they cropped up in all sorts of designs. They have a gain factor similar to a 12AX7 but don't sound identical. They also have a different pin-out and heater configuration, so the two aren't interchangeable without rewiring their sockets. Gibson's use of them here is fairly straightforward; V1 provides two gain stages, so there's a simple driver stage going into the simple phase inverter formed by the first half of V2, while V2B powers a basic bias-wiggler tremolo circuit. Controls are limited to volume in the preamp (labeled "Loudness") and speed in the tremolo (labeled "Frequency"). No tone, no depth. The rectifier is a 6X4 tube, popular in other student combos and smaller audio amplifiers of the day, which offered plenty of sag when hammered.

The Pacemaker is the Epi equivalent of the Gibson GA-5T Skylark, an amp that had for some reason inherited a model designation that had previously been given to smaller, single-ended Gibson amps such as the GA-5 Les Paul Junior. Just as Casino and Sheraton guitars are dearly loved and genuinely preferred by many players, we think this little tan combo with the Epiphone badge is more fun, in its own obscure way, than its more prominent Gibson counterpart.

Shortly after this period, Gibson amp manufacture entered dark days (years even) and appeared to lose the plot, both visually and electronically. The company seemed to chase Fender's lead more doggedly while simultaneously taking the occasional stab at something radical and modern that would inevitably fall flat.

This Epiphone from the early 1960s, however, embodies an originality and overall quality of vision that makes it a virtuous little amplifier in its own right, and a fun little piece not only to collect but to play every day. And if that isn't good enough for you, you can always blur your vision and pretend it's a brownface Fender Princeton. But that would kind of be a shame. 🎱

Fender Vibroverb 6G16.

BROWN BEAUTY

It's always a little painful to write about amps that the vast majority of us are just not likely to ever get our hands on. Near the top of that list you will find the 1963 Fender Vibroverb. Even though it arrived nearly two decades after the company's inception, the brown Tolex Vibroverb has become one of the most collectible of all Fender amps, and for several good reasons.

This was the first Fender amp to carry built-in reverb, a feature that Fender—already a leader in tube guitar amp innovation—was surprisingly late to bring on board. The Vibroverb was also produced in its debutante form for less than a year. This combination of factors makes it one of the rarest and most valuable vintage amplifiers out there, according to current market prices (with original 1963 Vibroverbs hovering in the $6,900 to $9,500 range at the time of writing).

Regardless of collectibility, add to this the amp's extremely desirable feature set, including its portability, versatile size and power (small enough for clubs,

large enough for big stages), great short-lived brown-and-wheat looks, and the inclusion of sweet reverb and tremolo circuits, and the Vibroverb would very likely be many players' ideal amp even if the market was lousy with them.

The reverb circuit in the Vibroverb is much like one that would appear on several blackface models late in 1963 and into 1964, although the parallel-wired driver tube in front of the small reverb output transformer was a 12AX7 instead of a lower-gain 12AT7. Although Fender amps had survived without the effect for more than fifteen years, the inclusion of reverb would really take these combos over the top and help make Fender the market leader through the mid 1960s.

The tremolo circuit in the 1963 Vibroverb is much simpler than the "harmonic vibrato" in other large brown Fender amps of the early 1960s, but if you are looking for genuine tremolo (and despite the raves for that brownface vibrato, many players are), this is an extremely good one. The bias-wiggle tremolo circuit here is extremely similar to that used on the final iteration of the tweed Tremolux, the 5G9, and works by modulating the output tubes' fixed-bias network.

Fender's Custom Vibrolux Reverb reissue.
Fender Musical Instruments Corporation

With a slightly later blackface 1x15-inch
Vibroverb combo behind him, Stevie Ray
Vaughan "plays" his Number One Stratocaster
at the Keystone Berkeley on August 19, 1983.
Clayton Call/Redferns/Getty Images

1963 FENDER VIBROVERB 6G16

- Preamp tubes: Four 7025s, two12AX7s (roughly equivalent)
- Output tubes: Two 6L6GCs, fixed-bias
- Rectifier: GZ34 tube
- Controls: Volume, Treble, Bass for each channel; Reverb on Bright channel; Speed and Intensity for tremolo shared by both channels
- Speakers: Two Oxford 10K6s
- Output: 35 watts RMS +/-

After many years of the seeming ubiquity of the blackface-style opto-cell tremolo circuit, this bias-modulating trem has made a big comeback in popularity recently. Among the characteristics players seem to love are its smooth, watery response—with a soft edge to its rise and fall even at higher intensities—and the way it politely avoids chopping out notes as you play, the way an opto trem can do. Hit the guitar hard and the trem recedes a little, bubbling back into focus as the attack ebbs and the note begins to decay. Many find it the most musical breed of tremolo available, arguably the best type ever built into a tube amp (once again, it is a genuine tremolo effect, if you don't want to emulate a rotary speaker the way the "harmonic vibrato" circuit aims to).

Mark Knopfler remains a big fan of the Vibroverb, as well as the brown Tolex Vibrolux of the same era, which he used to record "Sultans of Swing" and several other early Dire Straits tunes. Knopfler was captured on film gigging with an actual 1963 Vibroverb in later years, although it is difficult to tell whether this amp ever surfaced on any recordings. Major differences between the two amps include, obviously, the addition of reverb on the Vibroverb, its two 10-inch speakers versus the Vibrolux's single 12-inch, and somewhat higher voltage levels on the plates of both the preamp tubes and the 6L6 output tubes. Despite virtually

identical preamp and output circuits, the latter difference gives the Vibroverb a considerably different feel (different in its nuances, anyway), with more punch and fidelity and a later onset of distortion. In fact, it is really like a marriage of the Vibrolux and the brown Super, with reverb added by stealing two preamp tubes used to create the Super's complex vibrato effect. Having said all that, we might look equally to the 1960–1963 Super or Vibrolux for tonal similarities—effects aside at least—although neither will be identical.

All this translates as increased clarity and a somewhat broader frequency range (a more "scooped" tone, perhaps) than the tweed amps of the late 1950s, but perhaps a little less glassiness than many of the bigger blackface amps that followed. The 10-inch speakers help make it a classic Tele amp, and great with a Strat, too, or a real burner when you plug in a hotter P-90 or humbucker-loaded Gibson-style guitar. Combined with the Vibroverb's light weight, these are features that define many players' ideal grab-and-go amp, a mantle that was perhaps taken up by the Vibrolux Reverb, introduced late in 1964.

The blackface Vibroverb that followed the brown Vibroverb in 1964 was a very different animal than its name might have implied, however. It carried a single 15-inch speaker, the new opto-cell tremolo circuit that acted only on one channel, and several other changes besides.

In 1990 Fender wisely reintroduced the original brown version as the 1963 Vibroverb Reissue, one of its first two vintage reissue amps (the other being the tweed Bassman). Despite a handful of changes (and a printed circuit board in place of the original's hand-wired eyelet board), the tone at least went a considerable way toward replicating that of its rare and short-lived inspiration. The reissue has remained a popular item with players, despite being deleted from the Fender lineup in 1996, semireplaced by the (arguably less popular) "Custom" Vibrolux Reverb, which was introduced in 1995.

So let us mourn the amp we shall likely never see or hear in its original form. But if old Mrs. Johnson next door ever pulls a brown Vibroverb out from behind the sofa and tells you about buying this for Junior's eighteenth birthday shortly before he shipped out to 'Nam, pay her the fair market price for it, wrap it in soft blankets, and cuddle it all the way home. ✪

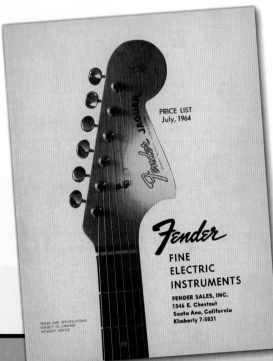

PRICE LIST
July, 1964

Fender
FINE
ELECTRIC
INSTRUMENTS

FENDER SALES, INC.
1546 E. Chestnut
Santa Ana, California
KImberly 7-5831

PRICES AND SPECIFICATIONS
SUBJECT TO CHANGE
WITHOUT NOTICE

Fender Vibroverb AB763.

Dire Straits' Mark Knopfler cut "Sultans of Swing" with the help of a brown Fender Vibrolux, an amp similar to the Vibroverb. Here, he plays live with his Suhr/Schecter guitar in 1985. *Ebet Roberts/Redferns/Getty Images*

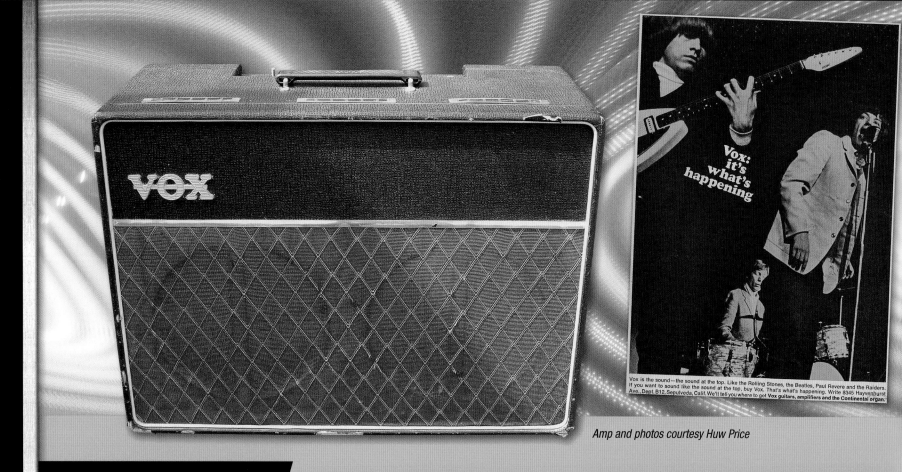

Amp and photos courtesy Huw Price

THE STUDENT'S COMBO

Anything from the 1960s bearing that sexy three-letter Vox logo will get a Beatles fan's blood pumping, though "real players" have traditionally withheld their tonal adulation from AC models below the hallowed 15.

But you can drop a nickel off that number and land in many a chime 'n' grinder's version of heaven. The humble and until recently underappreciated AC10 is one gargantuan tone machine and is arguably even more practical for many of today's gigging and recording applications than the "little" AC15 and certainly the whopping AC30. Think of it as the blackface Princeton to the AC15's blackface Deluxe (to the AC30's Pro or Super). A stock AC10 from the early 1960s is a recording tool as it stands and might survive a small gig or two as well. But, as with many—perhaps all—vintage amps, a few minor modifications can make this a much bolder and more robust music-making tool. Let's explore an overview first, though, then we'll examine a few simple ways of making this a practical everyday amp.

Hot on the heels of the early success of the AC15, Vox released the AC10 late in 1959 as a "student" model, an amp simple enough to be more affordable

than the AC15 but still big enough to keep the kids boppin' at the high school hop—or whatever the British equivalent might have been.

Originally offered as a 1x10-inch combo (in TV-front cab, then fawn), it was soon made available as the AC10 Twin, a 2x10-inch combo in black vinyl with red grille cloth and copper control panel, looking for all the world like a cute little baby AC30. In basic specs, too, the AC10 is very much just a rung down the ladder from the AC30 and AC15: its powertrain features two EL84s in cathode bias with no negative feedback, which generate approximately 12 watts to the AC15's 18 watts. The phase inverter is a big-boy's circuit, too, the elegant and sonically sturdy long-tailed pair, and rectification is achieved by an EZ81.

Notable downgrades include its slightly smaller output transformer and the flimsier—though still good-sounding—speakers that it pumps its glory through, namely a pair of 15-ohm Elacs with alnico magnets. The front end offers that powerful two-channel pairing of one chimey triode and one crunchy EF86 pentode, the latter a mainstay of the AC15 preamp and only briefly available on the early AC30/4.

In the AC10, however (and rather unusually), the EF86 is in the Vibrato channel—not unlike the configuration of the late 1950s Gibson GA-20T from the other side of the pond, which runs the tremolo on its pentode channel,

CIRCA 1963 VOX AC10

- Preamp tubes: One EF86, one ECF82, one ECC83 (12AX7)
- Output tubes: Two EL84s in class A, cathode-bias
- Rectifier: EZ81
- Controls: Amplitude, Speed, Vibrato volume, Normal volume, Tone
- Speakers: Two 10-inch Elac drivers with alnico magnets
- Output: 12 watts RMS

though in this case it uses the American 5879 preamp tube. Ah, the pentode preamp tube. We have visited the mighty EF86 on a number of occasions, and it's one of the more beloved ingredients in this amp—thick, rich, full throated, and oozing creamy drive when you crank it up.

The Normal channel hides a real oddball, though, in the form of an ECF82. This nine-pin bottle carries two independent tubes, a medium-mu triode and a sharp-cutoff pentode. The former gives a gain roughly in the range of a 12AT7 or 12AY7 or thereabouts, while the latter powers the tremolo.

Another major simplification from the specs of its big brothers lies in this "vibrato" circuit, which is actually a simple tremolo effect—that is, volume pulsation rather than pitch modulation. Much more basic than the AC15's switchable Vib/Trem, which uses two tubes (four triodes), this one employs just the pentode from the ECF82, which nevertheless serves up a warm hypnotic pulse, with Speed and haughtily named Amplitude knobs to govern its rate and depth, respectively.

Like the AC15, the AC10's single, shared Tone control is what we know more commonly as a "high cut" control, which reduces highs in the output stage, between PI and output tubes. Looked at another way, this means there's no tone control between preamp tube and PI tube to get in the way of your tone, and only one potentiometer total, the single Volume control on each channel.

Already the stock AC10 is one righteous combo; make just a few simple changes, though, and it becomes even more functional. The amp pictured here belongs to

Vox is the sound—the sound at the top. Like the Beatles, Paul Revere and the Raiders, the Rolling Stones. If you want to sound like the sound at the top, buy Vox. That's what's happening. Write: 8345 Hayvenhurst Ave., Dept. B2, Sepulveda, Calif. We'll tell you where to get Vox guitars, amplifiers and Continental organ. And how to win a movie contract in Vox's Band Battle for Stardom. See your Vox dealer for details.

UK-based recording engineer and gear writer Huw Price, the author of *Recording Guitar and Bass*, and we had the opportunity to play it in London studios both pre- and post-mod, and the post condition certainly makes it a more giggable little beastie.

First, replacing the two Elac speakers with a pair of sturdier, more efficient 10s is good sense however you look at it. If nothing else, this preserves them for the day when you might want to pass along the amp in original condition to the highest bidder. But ah, there is something else: It will simply sound much, much better (provided you choose your new 10s wisely) and will be louder, clearer, and less likely to poof out mid-solo.

Next, replacing the 220k grid resistors on the inputs with 68k resistors can instantly introduce greater tonal breadth and clarity to the amp (or replace one and keep one on each channel, as Huw has done, to provide high- and low-sensitivity inputs). Even if the change to 68k is not to your taste, it's a totally reversible mod, and extremely simple. Huw also points out that ECF82s can be problematic, noise-wise. "Finding a quiet one is almost as hard as finding a usable EF86," he said. "Play loud for any length of time, and the vibration seems to shake them loose."

Finally, if you want to get a little more invasive, you can even install a rear-mounted Top Boost in these AC10s, which makes the Normal channel notably more versatile. It's a job for a pro, unless you're handy with these things, but in terms of bloom, shimmer, and grind, the extra cathode-follower EQ stage does for the little 12-watter much what the same Top Boost mod did for its 36-watt big brother, the AC30.

Right about here is where we opine that these nifty little combos "used to go for a song" back when most players still considered them Vox Juniors. Sadly, it is no longer thus. Today a good AC10 will drag its sharp little claws through your piggy bank before you get it out the door. They were manufactured in similar numbers to early 1960s AC15s, though, and still aren't quite as desirable (or as well known), so they do remain both more plentiful and more affordable—in relative terms at least. ⊙

HEARTBREAKER

How we gearheads do dearly love that occasional epiphany—all the better, more rewarding, more enlivening when you thought you already knew the score on something.

We walked into our local guitar store a few weeks ago to buy some picks and shoot the shizzle with the owner—just a little corner-of-the-plaza place that used to stock cool B- and C-list consignment vintage back before eBay robbed our neighborhoods of that pleasure—and stepped up face to fascia with this all-original 1963 Gretsch 6156 Playboy combo sitting primly on a riser near the front desk. And tagged—we might add—at a very reasonable price, if not a total steal. Played it in the store, enjoyed it immensely (Korean guitar and the usual in-store-test alienness notwithstanding), and walked out with it under my arm fifteen minutes later.

Understand, we were already happy about it, buoyed by thoughts of sweet in-home crank potential or its possibilities as a new flavor in the studio. Its original Jensen C10R was in good shape but was certainly undergunned for its dual 6973 tubes' potential 17-watt output. It still sounded good in the third-floor home studio—and then we tried our usual new amp test, something that

proved virtually alchemical in this instance: We unsoldered the OT wires from the speaker terminals, attached a makeshift output jack, and patched it into a Matchless 1x12-inch extension cab with a Celestion G12H-30. When introduced to a 1957 Fender Esquire and floored, holy mother of mayhem, this baby screams! And the tremolo is a deep, thumping, hypnotic beauty of an effect, with a depth just right, despite its speed-only control function. A total sleeper of a fire-breathing Valco-crafted beauty, and she'll steal your heart.

From the late 1940s to the late 1960s, Valco made amps that—at various times within that period—carried the Supro, National, Harmony, Oahu, Airline, and Gretsch brand names, and a few others, and most of them shared a narrow range of the same, yet evolving, electronic templates. Certain Supro models are worshiped for their alleged studio associations with Jimmy Page and Jimi Hendrix, but if you ask me, these Gretsch renditions have the hippest looks of the bunch, entirely in keeping with the stylish guitars they partnered. They also came in cabs that were built a little more solidly than some of the others. The Electromatic range, with Detroit-inspired wraparound grilles, of the mid 1950s to around 1962, and the "tweed" versions before them, have their fans, but this simpler "box cab" version of the Playboy is still a looker, despite its simplicity. It's a little smaller than a Fender Princeton of the same era, and you couldn't fit a 12-inch speaker in here even if you wanted to, but its size belies

1963 GRETSCH 6156 PLAYBOY

- Preamp tubes: Three GE 12AX7s
- Output tubes: Two GE 6973s, cathode bias, no negative feedback
- Rectifier: 5Y3
- Controls: Volume, Tone, Tremolo (speed, with on/off switch on pot and foot switch out)
- Speaker: Jensen Special Design C10R
- Output: Approximately 17 watts RMS

a punchy—hell, powerful—drive train that really warranted a bigger cab and speaker (which the Playboy received, briefly, toward the end of its run in the mid 1960s). And, hey, it's small enough to use as a head atop your favorite extension cab.

The 6973 output tubes, cathode biased with no negative feedback, are easily mistaken for EL84s visually, if you don't check the numbers, but not only is their pin-out entirely different, they really sound nothing like that classic Brit small bottle. Apples and oranges. In general, they're a little thicker, meatier, and grittier, but still with plenty of sparkle on top and a surprisingly good low end (especially pumping through a bigger cab). As used in this Valco design, they offer a furious roar when cranked up but without the fart-out compression you'd expect from a little combo like this. What's more, they really do put out a genuine and robust 17 watts, which is more than an old Jensen C10R is going to want to see for very long at full bore.

After wailing this little beastie for half an hour or so, telling ourselves all the while, "Sure, it sounds great, but it probably couldn't hack a club gig," we plugged into a Matchless HC-30 on the half-power setting (tapping just two of its four EL84s) and ran its 12AX7 channel through the same cab at the volume setting we'd use in a hundred-seater club. Know what? It wasn't nearly as loud as the Gretsch had been running (guess we were slowly bludgeoning our hearing into submission along the way), and it didn't sound as thick and meaty as this forty-five-year-old Valco creation. Be careful what you assume in a small room.

For a little more of the "what the #@&%?" on this amp, we turned to America's own Valco authority, Terry Dobbs, known to many simply as Mr. Valco. "Although Valco used the same format for many amps, that one's got a cathodyne (split-phase) inverter," Terry revealed. "It's one of the very rare ones that did. Most of the others have the paraphase inverter, and it's a different overdrive tone." In short, to establish a familiar reference point, the paraphase PI Valcos will break up with a thick mid-range squash more reminiscent of early TV-front and wide-panel tweed Fender amps, while the Playboy, with its cathodyne PI, stays a little firmer and punchier, like a late 1950s Super or Pro, even though it has less output than those 6L6-based amps. (The 5E3 Deluxe also had a cathodyne PI, but it squashes substantially quicker than this 6156.)

We expressed how amazed we were to find this thing sounding so hot, firm, and fine after all these years, while remaining entirely original—stock GE tubes, original caps, everything—and also that it sounded so good with the plethora of little ceramic disc coupling caps that Valco used in its builds. According to Terry, though, these fellas fared a lot better over the years than bigger amps running on higher voltages. They really were built to be solid workhorses that would sound great and work long and hard with what they were born with. We're sold.

The 6793 output tubes are a revelation, too, but sadly not one that will do your own tone quest much good; functional NOS examples of these rare tubes are getting expensive and harder to find, and while Electro-Harmonix's Russian-made reissue will at least keep some old amps alive, it doesn't have quite the tonal integrity of the originals. The 6CZ5 makes a decent sub, but running them safely requires imposing a slight modification on the tube socket wiring. You'll be smitten. ◉

The excellent Gretsch reissue amplifiers from Fender, such as this G6156 Playboy Amp, are manufactured with hand-wired circuits by Victoria Amp Company in Chicago and seek to reproduce the spirit of the originals rather than the precise specs of the Valco-made Gretsch amps of the late 1950s and early 1960s. In most cases, the circuits and even the tube complements are quite different, but these are cool-looking amps with plenty of tonal mojo regardless. *Fender Musical Instruments Corporation*

Amp courtesy Elderly Instruments/photos Dave Matchette

BIG, CLEAN TWANG MACHINE

If you want to know the standard for big, clean twang, you're looking at it. Surely the blackface Fender Twin Reverb is the ultimate country amp for the big stage—the Nashville picker's live counterpoint to the Deluxe Reverb or Princeton Reverb, with which he or she most likely recorded the tracks in the studio.

Yet this classic amp is so much more: Dig Michael Bloomfield's cranked blues exploits, B. B. King's frequent use of this archetypal combo, or even the fact that Robben Ford swears by a Twin Reverb whenever his beloved Dumble isn't able to make the trip.

This 85-watt, 2x12-inch package definitely excels at rich and mammoth clean tones, and that is exactly what Leo Fender had in mind when he developed the model back in 1963. But crank it toward the max (if you're ever playing on a stage large enough to safely do so) and the Twin Reverb also issues up an ungodly sweet, trenchant, singing lead tone that more than a few great blues and rock soloists have fallen for.

For some four and a half decades, this amp was so much the standard, so omnipresent, as to have been virtually ignored. Show up at any established club that maintained its own back line, and chances were good you'd be plugging into a Twin Reverb. Check out any high school or college jazz band as it was loading back onto the bus after the state competition and there was that Twin Reverb on wheels, alongside the Bassman head and cab and the Rhodes piano that the local rep sold the school on.

The amp's reliability, versatility, and malleability—its implied genericness—have always been as much a part of its broad appeal as the superior tone it yields when you really dig in and play it the way it is begging to be played. And these humble qualities have perhaps allowed us to forget to revel in its pure tonal splendor. How many guitarists have gone through a couple dozen amps before landing an old blackface Twin Reverb and exclaiming, "Ahh . . . *this* is the tone I've been looking for!"? Plug in and this thing feels like coming home.

1963 FENDER TWIN REVERB AB763

- Preamp tubes: Four 7025/12AY7 types, two 12AT7s
- Output tubes: Four 6L6GCs, fixed-bias
- Rectifier: Solid-state
- Controls: Volume, Treble, Bass, Middle on each channel; Reverb, Speed, Intensity on Vibrato channel
- Speakers: Two 12-inch Jensen C12Ns or Oxford 12T6s
- Output: Approximately 85 watts RMS

Leo Fender's goal with the "high-powered" Twin of 1958 was to achieve more clean power and particularly greater headroom, and this was a driving force behind the evolution of the company's amp designs in general through several generations of circuits. The changes from tweed topology to blond, and from blond to blackface, all sought the same end, and it was achieved to greatest success here in the 1963–1967 Twin Reverb model AB763. (Silverface models eventually took this ethos a step further—but a step too far—and most would agree that the ultimate confluence of headroom and tone occurred in the blackface and early silverface models.)

To achieve all this, Fender adopted a multipronged attack that saw radical changes in the preamp and EQ circuits, voltage levels and filtering, and tube choices in that relatively short five-year period. By 1963 the Fender Twin was still a high-powered 2x12-inch combo, but was virtually nothing like its four-output-tubed predecessor of 1958—and that's before we even get into the reverb and tremolo.

Simply adjusting—and more to the point increasing—the voltages that both preamp and output tubes fed on helped get more oomph out of the blackface Twin Reverb. Whereas the blond Twin of 1960–1963 had around 190 VDC on the plates of the preamp tubes and 430 on the plates of the 5881 (aka 6L6) output tubes, the blackface Twin Reverb saw around 250 VDC at the preamp tubes and 458 on the 6L6GC output tubes. This created a tighter preamp and a more powerful output stage, respectively. In addition, the change from a 12AX7 in the blond's phase inverter to a lower-gain 12AT7 in the blackface hit the output tubes with a little less sonic splat and enabled them to hold firmer to higher levels on the volume dial.

A major change between tweed and Tolex preamp circuits, and tone stack designs in particular, also helped redefine the basic voice of the Twin. First seen in the blond models but further refined in the blackface, in place of the chewy, touch-sensitive, and mids-emphatic cathode-follower tone stack in the larger tweed amps, the

Tolex amps had a passive EQ network sandwiched between two gain stages in each channel. The result of this gain staging, and of the voicing of the circuitry in the middle, was a more "scooped" tonality—a firm low end and piercing highs couching a somewhat recessed mid-range.

Of course, the Twin Reverb also introduced an independent middle control on each channel, but even with that thing cranked, this big Fender was less predisposed toward mid-range crunch than the classic Marshall or Vox—or tweed Fender for that matter. The result of all this was a broad, open-sounding amp that still had plenty of richness and depth when pushed at least moderately hard, while also achieving Leo's lifelong goal of extended clarity and headroom. Ram it all through a pair of Jensen C12N or Oxford 12T6 speakers and it was an impressive sound by any standards, and still is. Or kick it through a pair of the JBL D-120F drivers that Fender offered as a factory upgrade from 1966 onward and it was not only a loud, piercing combo but a damned heavy one to boot.

As for "that's before we even get into the reverb and tremolo," well, this is about the place to get into it. While many players think the "harmonic vibrato" of the blond amps was one of the finest trem (or pseudovibrato) effects ever packaged in an amp, the photocell tremolo that replaced it in the blackface amps, introduced late in 1963, did set a new standard for clean and slightly lopsided *chop-chop-chop*. Package it with the tube-driven, long-pan spring reverb also built into this combo, and drive it all through that aforementioned broad, deep voice across a pair of robust 12-inch speakers, and you've got an impressive performance package that's primed to take on virtually any stage—or was back in the mid 1960s.

Next time you encounter one of these Twin Reverbs in good condition and are offered the privilege of plugging in, take the owner up on it. Seek his or her permission to turn it up a little. It should prove an experience that you won't soon forget.

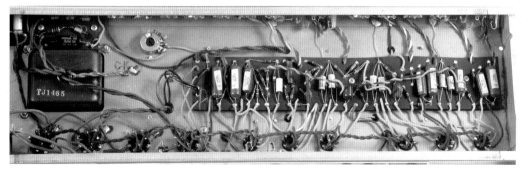

Mike Bloomfield was long a Twin reverb user on stage and in the studio. *David Redfern/Redferns/Getty Images*

FENDER VIBRASONIC AMP The design and construction of the Vibrasonic Amp features the most up to date two-channel (Normal and Vibrato) circuit. Not only does it produce tremendous distortion-free power, but it also offers exceptionally clean amplification through the use of the Lansing D-130 15 inch high-fidelity speaker. This speaker is considered to be one of the finest available for musical instrument amplification. It is capable of producing high fidelity sound at various volume levels. The Vibrasonic Amp features the convenient front panel on which are located two inputs for each channel plus separate volume, treble, bass controls for each channel; plus speed and depth and controls for vibrato settings. A presence control functions with either channel. The Vibrasonic Amp is highly recommended to those musicians desiring fine musical instrument amplification.

TUBES: 4 - 7025 (each dual purpose), 2 - 12AX7 (each dual purpose), 2 - 5881, silicon rectifiers. SPEAKER: 1 - Lansing 15" Model D-130 High Fidelity.

SIZE: Height 20", Width 26", Depth 10¼".

VIBRASONIC

Fender FINE ELECTRIC INSTRUMENTS

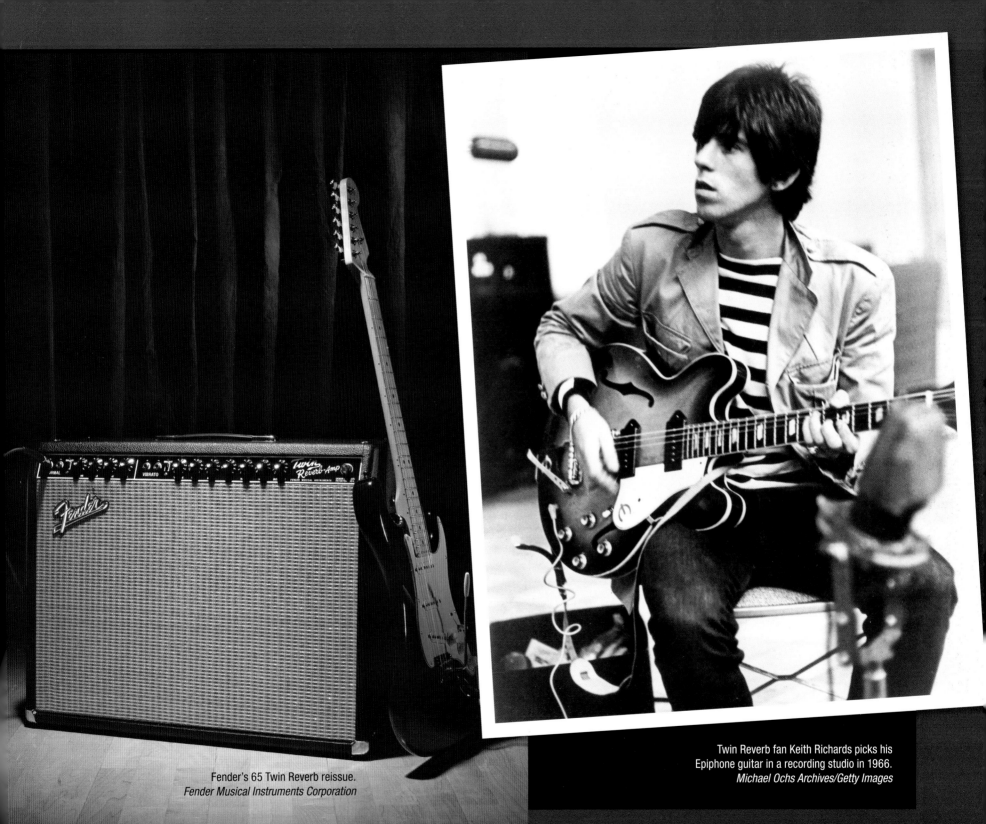

Fender's 65 Twin Reverb reissue.
Fender Musical Instruments Corporation

Twin Reverb fan Keith Richards picks his
Epiphone guitar in a recording studio in 1966.
Michael Ochs Archives/Getty Images

THE BABY AC30

Practice amps, student amps, beginner amps—call 'em what you will—in recent years, these little single-digit-output fellas have attained an elevated status that has lifted them right out of the nursery. Many players' increased awareness of the big love to be had from small wattage, tone-wise, has brought gigging amps down in size considerably over the past decade, and the size standards for recording amps have come down with them. Diminutive single-ended amps still aren't up to even the club and pub gig (if you're working with a drummer at least), but as many name players have long known, stick a studio mic in front of a little 4-watt/all-tube beauty and you're set to squeeze out some sweet juice all day long.

This little 1964 Vox AC4 is a good case in point. The "Champ" of countless aspiring young British guitarists of the early 1960s, these diminutive beauties could be had for peanuts for many years, even as prices for AC30s and AC15s

were escalating into the stratosphere. But all of a sudden they have become rare as hens' teeth, and pretty expensive when you do find one.

Although they weren't built with quite the attention to detail of the bigger Voxes (their minimalist point-to-point wiring, sans circuit board, is actually kind of frightening), they still offer a lot of tonal character, and if you're looking to nail that early/mid-period Beatles rock 'n' roll tone, this little box of tricks and a Gretsch or Rickenbacker reissue are just about all you need.

The good thing about these little entry-level vintage amps (and this applies equally to many vintage Fender Champs) is that they weren't bounced from bar to van to club over a lifetime of gigging like their bigger siblings were. They are often in remarkably pristine condition, with original tubes still going strong.

Anyone familiar with the single-ended formula will have an inkling of what's going on here, although as with most Voxes, there are a few twists lurking in the AC4's folded metal chassis. The first surprise is the EF86 pentode preamp tube that provides this circuit's single gain stage. These are deep, rich-sounding tubes, and they handle signal peaks well without introducing too much of their own distortion. Rather, they pass more of the good stuff along to the output

A 1964 Vox AC4 with 1954 Gibson ES-295.

CIRCA 1964 VOX AC4

- Preamp tubes: One EF86; one ECC83 (12AX7) for tremolo
- Output tube: One EL84
- Rectifier: EZ80
- Controls: Volume, Tone, Tremolo (speed)
- Speaker: One 8-inch Elac
- Output: 4 watts RMS (in a stiff tailwind!)

Vox amplifier warranty card.

stage, which is where most vintage-minded tonehounds want to get their mojo working anyway. The EF86 was the secret weapon in the AC15 and also in a very rare early version of the AC30. The pentode means you can drive the single EL84 pretty hard, and while you won't be hearing a whole lot of preamp distortion, you'll slide into fat output tube crunch and full-out wail pretty easily, so this is no clean machine by any means. The little 8-inch Elac alnico mag speakers (rated at an obtuse 3 ohms) aren't doing your output levels any favors either, though they do sound mean and raunchy in their own way. Patch the thing into a 2x12-inch extension cab with a pair of efficient Celestion Alnico Blues or G12H-30s, however, and the AC4 will do a mean little attenuated AC15 impersonation (the 4-ohm load resultant from two 8-ohm 12s in parallel works just fine). The speaker and tiny output transformer in this baby are hardwired, so you have to break a solder connection and attach a jack to do it, but you won't regret the minor alteration. A good AC4 pumps a pair of Alnico Blues beautifully, and the resultant tonal splendor totally belies this sweetheart's meager four watts.

One unusual thing about this amp is that the EF86, described as a "low-noise, high-gain pentode," has enough gumption to drive the output on its own, without a driver stage. An ECC83 (12AX7) is used for a basic tremolo effect and buffer stage, the tremolo created by a simple low-frequency phase-shift oscillator made up of a small network of capacitors. It isn't as lush sounding as some other tube tremolos out there, and depth is preset—with just the speed/rate controllable via the knob on the panel, on/off via a hardwired foot switch—but it sounds decent enough. AC to DC conversion is accomplished by an EZ80 full-wave rectifier tube, a close relation of the EZ81 that has come back into use in many new AC15- and 18-watt-Marshall-inspired creations.

A couple more groovy things about these little single-ended combos:

One, they are genuine class A amplification devices. There's no two- or four-tube push/pull arrangement to share the load, so the single output tube is forced to keep on chooglin' the entire time, the very definition of class A. While many other perfectly respectable push/pull amps bill themselves as class A, we know for certain only that they are cathode-biased circuits with no negative feedback—the characteristics we have come to associate with "the class A sound"—but you can't tell if they are genuinely class A in performance without putting them up on the bench and subjecting them to some fairly complicated measurements. Plug into one of these (or any one-output-tube guitar amp), and you know you're getting class A—which is not to say it's better than anything else, it's just nice to not fret the definitions now and then.

Two, these are great recording amps, not only because you can achieve sonic nirvana at less-than-deafening volume levels but because you can also use a range of totally hip microphones that are likely to freak out when exposed to higher sound pressure levels. Stick a vintage ribbon mic in front of an AC4, and anything from a fat and hairy Reslo to a sublime Coles 4038 will give you stellar results, without complaint. Or break out that sensitive Neumann tube mic that you have dared to use on only smoky-voiced chanteuses in the past. Your AC4 might not sound so big in the room, but record it right and it will sound as huge as you like on tape. What's more, it's an investment you can use. While it's really kind of painful keeping that vintage tweed Bassman or AC30 in the corner of the studio, never daring to risk taking it on the road, you can get a lot of sonic mileage, and actual professional results, from a low-watt recording amp like this. That is, if you can find one.

The Vox AC4TV reissue. *Courtesy Vox Amplification*

Vox AC4 chassis.

Amp courtesy Paul Q. Kolderie/
photos John Parker Northrup

MYSTERY MACHINE

One beauty of the obscure vintage tube amp is how some unloved, undervalued, $300 pawn shop prize can step up to the plate and become a true hero in the recording studio, knocking one out of the park in the bottom of the ninth to save the track by humbly ripping out a slamming tone that none of the big boys could muster. By doing exactly that time and time again, this early 1964 Sonola Reverb Amp 98-RT has become a fixture at one of Boston's leading recording studios, further proving that the "classic amp tone" in an artist's head isn't always best served by the classic amps on the gear closet's A list.

We were introduced to this unassuming combo at Camp Street Studios (formerly Fort Apache) by Paul Q. Kolderie, who has worked as producer, engineer, and mix artist with the likes of the Pixies, Uncle Tupelo, Dinosaur Jr., Radiohead, and others. Suffice to say, the man knows his tone tools, and a tour of the several tasty items in the house collection revealed this one as a

surprising clinch hitter. "The reverb is awesome . . . sparkly and spooky," Kolderie enthuses. "We sometimes use it all the way up, which is really swampy but sounds great. The tremolo is nice too, very smooth. This amp is a little dark, but pair it with a Tele or a Gretsch Duo Jet and it's just perfect. Turn it up all the way and it gets that singing, slightly saggy tone that makes you want to keep playing all day. It's really touch sensitive, and the reverb adds tremendous depth."

There is no consistent written history of Sonola amps, and tracing the company's lineage feels a little like playing "six degrees of Kevin Bacon." The Sonola Accordion Company of Chicago, best known for its Rivoli model, clearly needed amps to go with the line (note the "Acc." Input), but like many wholesalers and distributors, it jobbed out the work rather than making its own. These appear to have been sourced—in the early to mid 1960s at least—from the same Hoboken, New Jersey, manufacturer that made the Guild amp line, which also featured a 98-RT, but whether that was Guild itself or Ampeg in nearby Linden, New Jersey, remains unclear. Crystal clear, however, is the fact that this amp is nigh on identical to the Ampeg Reverberocket of the era, other

1964 SONOLA REVERB 98-RT

- Preamp tubes: Two 6SL7s, two 6SN7s
- Output tubes: Two 6V6GTs, cathode-biased with negative feedback
- Rectifier: 5Y3
- Controls: Volume, Tone, Reverb, (tremolo) Strength, (tremolo) Speed
- Speaker: Jensen P12R
- Output: Approximately 15 watts RMS

than in cosmetics, right down to its control panel layout, tube complement, and most of its circuitry. And considering that Ken Fischer once told us that the early 1960s Reverberockets with 6V6 output tubes were one of Everett Hull's only concessions to rock 'n' roll, this could be a good thing for owners of less plentiful but usually more affordable Sonolas.

While it's a very well-constructed amp, with a tidy hand-wired eyelet circuit board, a solidly built glued-and-screwed pine cab, and a fixed plywood baffle with a Jensen C12R speaker with magnet cover, this Sonola 98-RT uses technology that bigger-name amps had long before abandoned by this time. It is populated with octal preamp tubes that the likes of Gibson and Fender had abandoned nearly ten years before and appears to have the older-style paraphase inverter that Fender at least had left behind by 1955. The preamp, reverb, tremolo, and phase inverter employ a pair each of eight-pin 6SL7 and 6SN7 tubes between them, and a 5Y3 provides the juice. Kolderie took a meter to the 6V6s for us and found around 369 volts at the plates, which probably would have been closer to 350 VDC when the amp was made, given the lower domestic line voltages of the day. The tubes are cathode biased, like the 5E3 tweed Deluxe that's such a touchstone for all U.S. amps around this size, but are not quite as loud as the Fender, perhaps due in part to the negative feedback used around the output stage, which tightens it up a bit at lower to medium volumes.

A look inside reveals—alongside a few Mallory and "orange drop" signal caps soldered in as replacements out of necessity—a handful of those beloved Sprague "vitamin Q" coupling caps and plenty of original Ampeg-style circuitry that helps make the 98-RT's reverb and tremolo effects the beauties they are. Both are controlled via a hardwired two-button wooden foot switch, with a steel strap to hold it in place inside the cab for travel.

Of the amp's three inputs—guitar, bright, and accordion ("acc.")—Kolderie says the latter is nothing to write home about, while bright is thin sounding, but guitar is right on the money. "It's not loud enough to gig with [without miking it], but it's an absolutely killer recording amp, and it's become one of our go-to sounds." He adds: "I've had a lot of offers for this amp. One client said, 'That's what I've been trying to get my guitar to sound like my whole life!'"

Sadly, at least for those who might similarly be bitten by the Sonola 98-RT bug, these amps are fairly few and far between and are even harder to come by than the Ampeg Reverberocket (via Guild 98-RT) that inspired them, a state of affairs that the late Mr. Fischer's endorsement no doubt helped bring about. (Particularly apropos is his comment: "That amp would be a great indie rock machine. Ampeg made it for a short while and all the jazz guys were complaining, 'What's wrong with the new Reverberockets? They break up too early.'") Find a Sonola languishing with an unsuspecting seller, though, and its enigmatic name might just help you land a steal. ◉

The brown Sprague "vitamin Q" signal caps sit toward the center of the board.
John Parker Northrup

MORE THAN JUST A BLACKFACE TWEED BASSMAN

Many players affectionately consider the 4x10-inch, 40-watt Super Reverb a tweed Bassman with effects. But there's a whole lot more to the Super Reverb than that—and a little less too.

With hindsight, it seems pure insanity that Fender ever discontinued the 5F6-A Bassman, given what an enduring tone icon the amp has become. But like many manufacturers of the time, Fender was looking for more headroom and more definition—ideally housed in a more contemporary-looking package—and the entire line was progressively revamped to those ends through the course of the early 1960s. The archetypal version of the Bassman, which had arrived only in 1958, was discontinued in 1960, and for a time only the brown Tolex Concert model continued to fly the 4x10-inch flag. With solid-state rectification and many other circuit revisions, this amp is nothing like a Bassman, and aside from carrying the glorious "harmonic vibrato" circuit of the early 1960s, it's one of the least revered Fenders of the era.

Looked at outwardly, it appeared that the arrival of the Super Reverb in late 1963—which took over the 4x10-inch cab but returned to the GZ34 tube rectifier and added Fender's sweet new onboard reverb circuit and a simpler tremolo circuit to the brew—brought a modified Bassman back to the fold. But in toeing the new blackface line, it could have been from an entirely different creator.

Aside from the effects, even the uninitiated will quickly point out the independent tone controls on the Super's two channels (with a Middle control on only the Vibrato channel), its lack of a Presence control, and additional Bright switches on each channel. The latter pair of revisions provided a simpler—and cheaper—means of getting more highs into the amp when needed. The Presence control tapped the negative feedback loop around the output stage to offer a final control over brightness at the output stage. The Bright switches, however, merely introduced a high-pass cap that shunted more treble through the Volume control at lower to medium volumes to keep things cutting and sparkly (too much so when used with many single-coil Fender guitars without a severe reduction in the amp's Treble control to compensate). Other than these, though, internal

Fender's 65 Super Reverb reissue. *Fender Musical Instruments Corporation*

Jim Heath, leader of the Reverend Horton Heat, swears by his 1978 Fender Super Reverb. *Keith Martin/Yep Roc Records*

Jim Heath's 1978 Fender Super Reverb.

"I run my Gretsch 6120 through a 1978 Fender Super Reverb. That '78 Super has been the main amp on all of Reverend Horton Heat's recordings. In fact, that amp is really just as, or more, important to my sound than my guitar. I almost cannot live without that amp."

—Jim Heath of the Reverend Horton Heat

1964 FENDER SUPER REVERB

- Preamp tubes: Four 7025/12AX7s, two 12AT7s (one for PI)
- Output tubes: Two 6L6GCs in class AB, fixed-bias
- Rectifier: GZ34
- Controls: Normal: Volume, Treble, Bass; Vibrato: Volume, Treble, Bass, Middle, Reverb, Speed, Intensity
- Speakers: Four 10-inch Oxford or CTS
- Output: 40 watts RMS

differences between the Bassman and the Super commence at the first gain stage and roll through the entire circuit.

In place of the tweed amps' 12AY7, the Super used a 7025 (a more rugged 12AX7) preamp tube in the first gain stages of each channel, and it employed the tubes very differently as well. The first half of each of the first two 7025s (the first two preamp tubes at the right end of the row, as viewed from the back of the amp) comprises the first gain stage for each channel, while the second half of each is used as a gain makeup stage following the tone controls. Rather than using the cathode-follower tone stack of the Bassman and other big tweed amps, which places the tone circuits and pots after the cathode output of the amps' second preamp tube, the blackface amps sandwich their tone stacks between two more traditional grid-input/plate-output gain stages. The tone controls are placed before the Super's Volume controls rather than after.

Since the cathode-follower tone stack can be credited with a portion of the Bassman's great touch sensitivity—part of what makes it such a dynamic and "playable" amp—this is a more significant change than it might at first seem. The Super's (and other blackface amps') tone stack is effective for EQ purposes and also serves to retain a full, virtuous signal and pass it along to the next stage in the signal chain, but it doesn't interact with the amp's gain structure and overall character as much as the Bassman's does. Of course, whether this is a good or bad thing depends on your point of view and what you're looking for from an amp.

Another thing—and something you don't see with the naked eye—is that the DC voltages supplied to the first gain stage in each amp are very different. The Super Reverb gives a reading of around 230 volts on the plates of the first half of the 7025s, versus approximately 150 volts on the same pin of the Bassman's 12AY7. More than just technical mumbo jumbo, these voltages affect the sound and feel of the amp. Higher voltages here yield more of a hi-fi performance from the tube; lower voltages render it a little more interactive. Which is all to say that while a good blackface Super Reverb can undoubtedly be a touch-sensitive amp, the tweed

Bassman is—right from the drawing board—a little more tactile and more controllable according to pick attack and playing dynamics.

Staying with the voltages for a moment, the output tubes of both amps—5881s or 6L6GCs—are hit with about the same 430 volts DC or so, but other differences in the output stage throw up some variables here. Most notably, the Super and other blackface Fenders were given a 12AT7 for phase inverter duties, which, in partnership with the long-tailed pair PI (retained from the Bassman and forever after used in most Fender amps), doesn't drive the output tubes quite as hard as the former's 12AX7 and helps further achieve the goal of improved fidelity and increased headroom. To the same end, the lower-value 820-ohm resistor in the Super Reverb's negative feedback loop further tightens up the output, which of course was belted along to four 10-inch Oxford or CTS speakers—not bad drivers but not the legendary speakers of the tweed amp's 10-inch Jensen P10Qs or P10Rs.

For all these differences, input to output, the Super Reverb remains a glorious amp and ranks right alongside the tweed Bassman as an all-time favorite for blues, as well as a suitable amp for country, jazz, and indie rock styles. In good condition, these beauties churn out thumping lows, pleasantly recessed mids, and shimmering (if potentially spiky) highs. And if you're jonesin' for 40 fat watts of tube-rectified power with onboard reverb and tremolo through the classic 4x10-inch configuration—hey, there's really nowhere else to go! 🎱

Guitarist Johnny Marr of the Smiths was long a Fender Super Reverb user. From left: Andy Rourke, drummer Mike Joyce, Morrissey, and Marr on March 16, 1984. *Pete Cronin/Redferns/Getty Images*

MOCK-CROC-SKIN CHIC

An amp maker at the very heart of the British guitar boom of the late 1950s and early 1960s, Selmer was, for a time, the leader in the field, although it is all too easy to forget that today. Briefly ahead of Vox, certainly ahead of the fledgling Marshall, this was a company that had it all to lose as the new decade dawned . . . and gradually did.

By the mid 1960s, Selmer was struggling for position against a pair of strong rivals with growing international reputations, while at the same time releasing what would be its most recognized and most collectible models: the short-lived croc-skin combos of 1963 to 1965. The most popular of these, the Zodiac Twin 30 and Zodiac Twin 50, were most likely released in direct response to the Vox AC30 and Marshall Model 1962 (aka Bluesbreaker), respectively. Good efforts they were, too, but while they made some waves at the time, they ultimately failed to blow either rival out of the water, and did little across the pond to boot. In the wake of this defeat of sorts, Selmer amps, though still great

products by any standards, slid into B-list status, and started down the slippery road toward their ultimate demise.

Regardless, Selmer models of all eras have continued to appeal to players and collectors for five decades, but fans are likely to drool most profusely over the croc-skin combos like this 1964 Zodiac Twin 50. Owned by ex–Iron Maiden and Praying Mantis guitarist Rob "Angelo" Sawyer, this is a fairly rare example, certainly in this condition.

More often seen is the Zodiac 30, a combo based around a pair of cathode-biased EL34s, nominally what we refer to as "class A," as famously used by Jack White to record the White Stripe's *Elephant* album.

Changing the output stage from cathode biased to grid biased (aka "fixed biased") earned the Zodiac Twin 50, introduced in the early part of 1964, a few more watts than its class A sibling. While this increase in power might not have been tremendously obvious to the naked ear, the change in feel due to the firmer output stage and slightly increased headroom made it a different amp.

As often as these amps are compared to their above-named rivals, they have circuits that are all their own, being products from a company that prided itself on originality, was still aiming to be a leader in the field, and was

1964 SELMER ZODIAC TWIN 50

- Preamp tubes: Three ECC83, two EF86
- Output tubes: Two EL34
- Rectifier: GZ34
- Controls: Volume and Tone on each of two channels, plus six-button tone selector and tremolo depth and speed on channel 2
- Speaker: Two ceramic-magnet Goodmans 12s
- Output: Approximately 50 watts RMS

nowhere near to putting out "copies" of other British makers' products. Largely similar other than these differences in output tube bias, both Zodiac Twins have circuits that might appear quite unusual to players more familiar with the Vox, Marshall, or indeed Fender topologies, and that's a big part of their appeal.

Preamp and power amp are built on separate chassis, mounted in the top and bottom of the 2x12-inch cab, respectively. Each of two channels opens the gambit with a single ECC83 (12AX7) gain stage, without any cathode bypass cap, which keeps the tone a little tighter and lighter at this point, but the two differ considerably from there.

Channel 1, intended for a mic or a second instrument, runs through a treble-bleed tone control that's a little more involved than the average, then a volume control, then through a second gain stage comprising an EF86 pentode preamp tube, before scooting on to the octal plug that takes it south to the PI and the output stage.

Channel 2, though, is where things really get wild. After the first gain stage the signal hits a six-selection push-button tone section that offers, in addition to a "Rotary Control" option that routes it to another treble-bleed tone pot, buttons for High Treble, Treble, Medium, Bass, and Contra Bass. These are achieved by tapping a network of tone caps that shape the voice between gain stages, a circuit not unlike that of some large Gibson amps before it, or indeed the six-position rotary tone control on the lead channel of the Matchless DC30 several decades later. From here, the signal hits another EF86 pentode, then a tremolo circuit with speed and depth controls, then on to the bottom chassis via the octal plug.

In the bottom chassis, the octal plug ferried the signal to a rather unusual split-phase inverter that employed another ECC83, then on to a pair of EL34s that were pushing around 445 VDC at the plates—not a ton for these output tubes to handle, but pretty hot for the cathode-biased Zodiac Twin 30, which ran everything about the same as the 50. The alnico Celestion 12s of the Twin 30 were changed to more robust Goodmans ceramic 12s in the 50, but that's about the only other difference between the two models. Later models, however, dropped both the tube rectifier (for

solid state) and the EF86 preamp tubes (for more ECC83), making them more conventional in many respects.

Obviously, these mid 1960s Zodiacs looked very different from anything before, or after too. Their blend of mock-crocodile and black vinyde covering gave them an extremely outré look, further accentuated by the spacey green "magic eye" tremolo speed indicator on the front, which pulsed in time to the trem rate. Even if the large gold metal S-E-L-M-E-R badge on the bottom panel tied the amp to ubiquitous and less-than-hip trombone-case cosmetics, these were pretty outrageous packages, in an age and industry that was ramping up for plenty of outrage.

In addition to digging the looks (as he does those of some eight other Selmers in his collection), Rob "Angelo" Sawyer admits to an unabashed fondness for the tone of this great Zodiac Twin 50. "It has a feel and character all of it's own," he says. "The whole vibe of the amp is 'warm,' and I just love those push-button tones. The tremolo effect is great fun—pure Duane Eddy! It's not an amp that I would gig with, because it's too precious and beautiful, and because it doesn't have the heavy rock/blues tone that my band sound needs, but I really enjoy playing the Zodiac."

As cool as these amps are—and as much as you might want one now—their prices have escalated significantly over the past decade or so, to the point where they rival those of vintage AC30s. A difficult situation for the would-be buyer of a nifty Zodiac Twin 50, but it brings some measure of justice back into play to round out the history of these exquisite and unique also-rans. 🌑

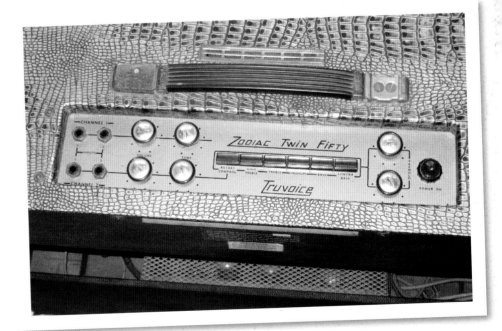

Amp and photos courtesy Rob "Angelo" Sawyer

With a solid back line of Selmer combo amps, the Who perform on German TV's *Beat Club* show on April 19, 1967. From left: John Entwistle, Roger Daltrey, and Pete Townshend. *K & K Ulf Kruger OHG/ Redferns/Getty Images*

Selmer Treble-N-Bass Fifty head and Goliath speaker cabinet with Goodman 18-inch speakers. *Rick Gould*

BRITISH INVASION

Utter the adjectives "sparkle," "chime," "shimmer," and "bloom" in the context of guitar tone, and the Vox AC30 with Top Boost is likely to come to mind before any other amplifier. In 1964 the Beatles' invasion of North America introduced Vox's class A splendor to the wider world, and for pushing fifty years now, the AC30 has been a Brit-built flagship of tonal supremacy, as well as a primo must-have of any serious amp collector. In its Top Boost configuration of the mid 1960s, this amp has inspired more boutique-grade models of the modern hand-wired era than any other single design, other than perhaps Fender's tweed Deluxe and Bassman. Makers such as Matchless, Bad Cat, Cornell, TopHat, Bruno, Trainwreck, Komet, 65amps, and plenty of others have drawn liberally from this five-decades-old British circuit, and countless smaller shops offer everything from dead-on renditions to extreme updates of the format.

Tom Jennings started his Jennings Organ Company in 1951 to sell portable organs. He founded Vox amps' original manufacturer, Jennings Musical Instruments (JMI), in 1957—releasing the AC15 soon after—with the specific intention of cashing in on the British rock 'n' roll craze. The AC30 wasn't Vox's first production model, therefore, but it was the amp that really put the name on the bigger map, thanks not only to its superb performance but also to its surprisingly wide appeal. These combos have populated the back lines of everyone from the Beatles and the Shadows to REM and Tom Petty and the Heartbreakers on the janglier side of town, while having proved themselves ballsy enough to satisfy heavier rockers like Brian May of Queen and Dave Grohl of the Foo Fighters. No surprise, really, when you consider that the amp was born out of an original new design devised specifically with the intention of making the newfangled electric guitar sound good—damned good.

This amp's cathode biasing and lack of negative feedback give plenty of sparkling and slightly unchained chime to the guitar's upper mids and highs, thanks to the way they encourage second harmonics as artifacts of distortion. This offers a flattering tonality at low and middle volume levels and a

A 1964 Vox AC30 six-input amp with 1964 Rickenbacker 360.

Mid-1960s Vox brochure.

creamy overdrive when cranked. (Note that these design elements just aren't suitable in larger amps, so you don't see them in 50- or 100-watt models.) Also, in letting the output stage run "open loop"—that is, free from any negative feedback–derived damping—Denney's design offered a rich, touch-sensitive, and therefore very playable performance when pushed. These amps' tube rectifiers also add to the touch-sensitive, slightly compressed playing feel that so many players love. While both the AC15 and AC30 are often cited as "classic class A amps" (discussed further in our coverage of the AC15), it is probably more accurate to sum up their sound as the result of these features: cathode biasing, lack of negative feedback, tube rectifier, and easily overdriven EL84 output valves.

As rock 'n' roll's appeal continued to grow, a more powerful amp was needed, so in late 1959 Denney and Jennings simply doubled the 2xEL84 output stage of the AC15 and beefed up its smaller EZ81 rectifier with a GZ34 to give birth to the AC30—a more versatile and more rocking amp all round, which is actually capable of putting out more than 35 watts in good condition. Shortly after, Vox dropped the EF86 pentode preamp from the AC30, a feature still carried by the rare TV-front 1960 AC30 also profiled in this book. The archetypal AC30, as shown here, was conceived a short while later, when the powerful active/interactive Top Boost circuit was drawn up in 1961, not so much in an effort to bring back the gain lost with the deletion of the powerful EF86 but to add the extended highs that so many players of the day were asking for. Top Boost at first came as a back-to-factory retrofit modification, which included adding the extra preamp valve required and mounting the Top Boost's Treble and Bass controls on a plate bolted to the amp's back panel. In 1964 the AC30 Top Boost model came direct from the Vox factory as an upgrade option, with the extra knobs mounted right on the main control panel. Wherever you may find it, this Top Boost EQ stage adds the extra sparkle and high-end content that bands of the day were looking for to help cut through the mix, and it is a big part of that classic Vox shimmer and chime. It is worth noting, however, that the circuit that JMI dubbed Top Boost wasn't just a treble booster but actually added active, tube-powered EQ that enabled a boosting of low frequencies as well as of high and mid-range too, depending on the relative adjustments of Bass, Treble, and Volume controls.

As much as the Top Boost circuit has always seemed to be credited as a thing unto itself, and one of the major characteristics of "Voxiness," this tone circuit is really just a variation of the cathode-follower tone stack that many tweed Fender amps of the mid 1950s and beyond were carrying, with two knobs—Treble and Bass—on models such as the Super and Pro but with a full three-knob Treble, Bass, and Middle on the larger Bassman and high-powered Twin and on the Marshall JTM45 and Plexi models that were based on them. The AC30's Top Boost appears to have been derived from a lesser-known rendition of this circuit, as pointed out in Jim Elyea's comprehensive book *Vox Amplifiers: The JMI Years*. Elyea writes that "Dick Denney came across a little-known tone control circuit that had been used on a pair of Gibson amplifiers, the GA70 'Country Western' and the GA77 'Vanguard,'" and more or less lifted it for JMI—complete with an error in the Gibson schematic (a failure to ground the far leg of the bass pot) that was corrected in Gibson production models but not in Vox Top Boost circuits. Whatever its source, Top Boost adds significant zing to the AC30 tone. It can be a somewhat fiddly tone stack to work with, given its interactive nature, and can induce a certain brittle glassiness when used unwisely, perhaps the reason many players prefer the Normal channel of their vintage AC30s.

Looks-wise, the epitome of this amp is the Top Boost model with black vinyl covering, reddish-brown grille cloth, and copper control panel—a rare combination, as reports indicate that as few as one hundred of these were ever made. By 1965 cosmetics

had evolved to the black cloth and gray panel of the mid 1960s amps, which carry a less vintage-evocative look but are identical electronically and still highly desirable.

We would be negligent to ignore a final critical component in the AC30 sound: the speakers. After hitting the ground with Goodmans drivers, the AC30 acquired its famous Celestion-made Vox Blue alnico G12 speakers around late 1960 or 1961. Players the world over agree that these are among the best-sounding speakers ever built. Their light pulp-paper cones and musical alnico magnets combine to offer a sweet, rich voice with aggressive mid-range when pushed, and their impressive efficiency offers a loud performance to boot. On paper, a Vox AC30 may not look like a powerful amp, but with a pair of these Blues, the 35-watter can rival many amps of 50 watts or more carrying less efficient speakers and often sound a lot better in the process. Many AC30s of the early and mid 1960s also carry silver Celestion alnico speakers, which are nearly identical in sound and performance but are slightly less desirable to collectors. ⚫

The Beatles jump for joy over their new Vox AC30 Twin and AC50 head. *AF archive/Alamy*

Backed by their Vox AC30 and AC50 amps, the Yardbirds perform at Wembley Studios on May 27, 1966. From left: Paul Samwell-Smith, Keith Relf, drummer Jim McCarty, and Jeff Beck. *Ivan Keeman/ Redferns/Getty Images*

Having a
Rave Up
with The
Yardbirds

Heart Full of Soul
You're a Better Man Than I
Evil Hearted You
Still I'm Sad

I'm a Man
The Train Kept A-Rollin'
Smokestack Lightning
Respectable
Here 'Tis

Rolling Stone Keith Richards takes pleasure in the sound of his Vox Mark XII guitar and Vox amp on the set of the *Ready Steady Go!* TV show at Television House, London, on June 26, 1964. *Peter Francis/Redferns/Getty Images*

VOX

VOX TEEN BEAT

THE GREATEST NAME IN SOUND

VOX: THE BRITISH SOUND INVADES U.S.A.

VOX AND THE BEATLES BRING DOWN THE HOUSE WITH THE BRITISH SOUND

Rory Gallagher celebrates the sound of his trademark Fender Stratocaster and Vox AC30 amp while performing in Copenhagen, Denmark, in 1970. *Jorgen Angel/Redferns/Getty Images*

VOX

Rory Gallagher's well-traveled Vox AC30 on stage. *Steve Lyne/Alamy*

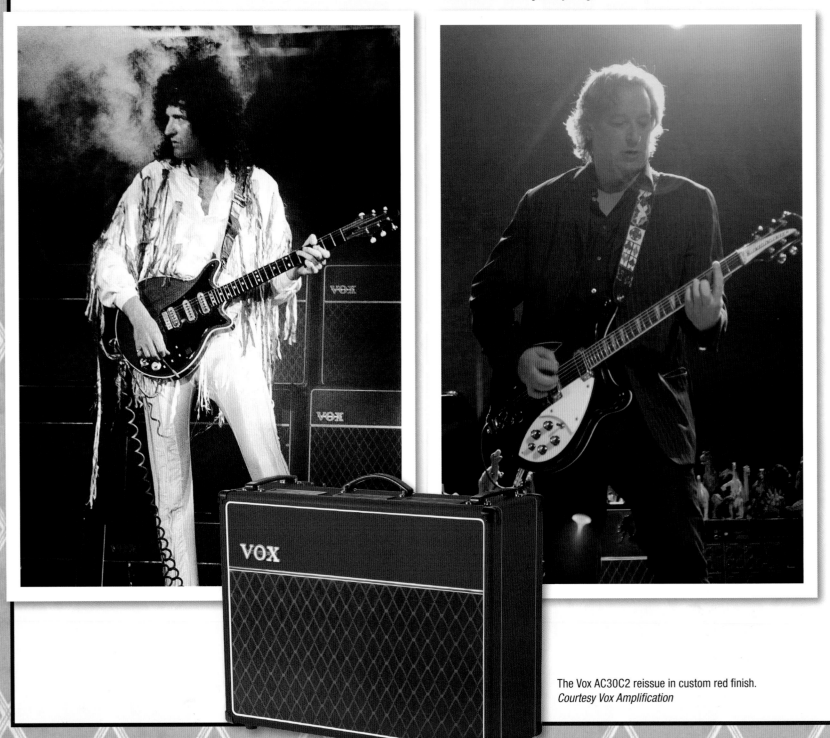

Queen's Brian May plays before a back-line wall of Vox AC30 amps. *Phil Dent/Redferns/Getty Images*

Peter Buck of REM performs with his trusty Rickenbacker guitar and Vox AC30 at Stubb's at South By Southwest on March 12, 2008 in Austin, Texas. *Paul Natkin/WireImage/Getty Images*

The Vox AC30C2 reissue in custom red finish. *Courtesy Vox Amplification*

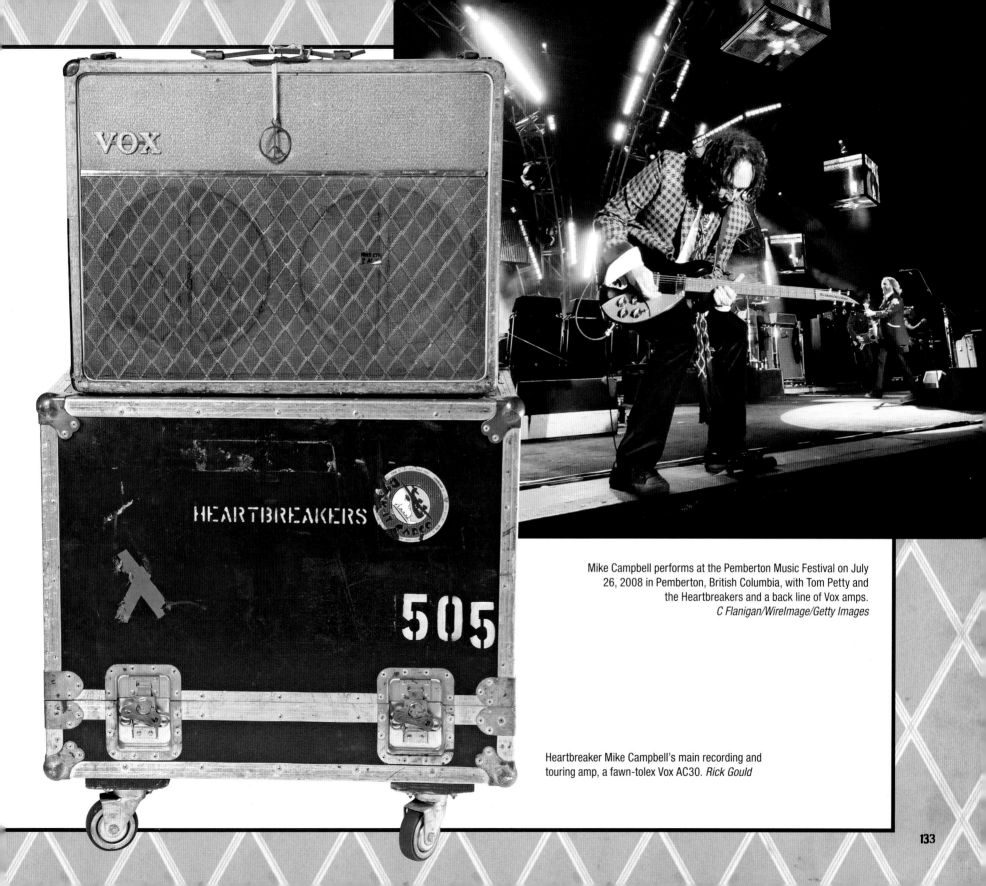

Mike Campbell performs at the Pemberton Music Festival on July 26, 2008 in Pemberton, British Columbia, with Tom Petty and the Heartbreakers and a back line of Vox amps. *C Flanigan/WireImage/Getty Images*

Heartbreaker Mike Campbell's main recording and touring amp, a fawn-tolex Vox AC30. *Rick Gould*

THE FAMED LOST JIMMY PAGE AMP?

Okay, Zep police, sound the alarm and prepare to loose the hounds—we are finally about to lift the lid on the Jimmy Page amp. Well, maybe not *the* Jimmy Page amp but almost certainly *a* Jimmy Page amp, and even this claim should be enough to get the keys clacking and the Internet forums buzzing with the vitriolic denials of naysayers and Page obsessives who have already put their money on other Supros occasionally believed to have been the source of that sweet, addictive crunch on the band's debut *Led Zeppelin* album and elsewhere. Sorry, but if the scant evidence points anywhere, it points here—given JP's difficult-to-trace yet widely accepted past statements that it was a "small, blue Supro" and a "1x12 combo"—and we say that with the firm convictions of claim-takers who understand deep down that there really is no knowing and that we could be just as wrong as we hope we are right. Which is to say, totally.

So much for the furor, because ultimately it doesn't matter anyway. Even if no name artist ever played through a sweet little mid 1960s Supro Model 24 like this one (even though he did), it's still one of the hippest-looking and coolest-sounding forty-five-year-old tube combos on the planet. Right through the years of Fender's seeming dominance of amp design in the United States, Valco designed and manufactured a broad range of amps for rebranders such as Supro, Oahu, Gretsch, and Airline that totally disregarded the Fender standard. They all did their own thing, and they did it very well. Components were largely of a slightly lesser standard, and cabinetry (which varied from brand to brand) was occasionally thinner and lighter-weight than that used by Fender and Gibson, but the circuit designs themselves are difficult to fault. They often took clever, original twists that today yield several truly stunning vintage-vibed voices that are quite different from the norm.

A look inside the chassis of the Model 24 reveals what at first glance looks like a rat's nest of wiring strung out along a series of terminal strips. Look a little closer, though, and you'll see fairly tidy workmanship and a neat logic to the design. Valco managed to fit a simple yet extremely effective circuit into a confined space and strung together a series of stages out of the tube design handbooks of the day that worked together to pump out exemplary guitar tones.

Led Zeppelin enjoy their tone while recording their second album on May 23, 1969. From left, Jimmy Page, Robert Plant, and John Paul Jones. *Charles Bonnay/Time & Life Pictures/Getty Images*

- Preamp tubes: Three GE 12AX7s
- Output tubes: Two GE 6973s, cathode-bias, no negative feedback
- Rectifier: 5Y3
- Controls: Volume and Tone on each of two channels; tremolo Speed and Intensity
- Speaker: Jensen Special Design C12Q
- Output: Approximately 18 watts RMS

One of the surprises in here is the extensive use of ceramic disk coupling caps where you'd normally see larger, more robust axial (tubular) coupling caps in amps wearing more prominent brand names. The relatively low voltages in several stages of the amp allow such caps to thrive while also giving the amp's tone a thick, chocolatey, slightly gritty character you don't hear elsewhere. At lower volumes this adds some body to the stew, and cranked up to crunch it gives the Supro's voice a meaty bite.

Another of what today's marketing men might call the "unique selling points" of this amp is its pair of 6973 output tubes. We addressed these briefly in our chapter on the Valco-made 1963 Gretsch 6156 Playboy combo, but they're worth revisiting here. This tube's nine-pin layout and tall, narrow bottle lead plenty of people to assume it "sounds like an EL84," but that's a long way from accurate. Even on paper—physical appearances aside—the 6973 is a very different tube, with maximum plate voltage ratings of around 440 volts DC compared to the EL84's 350 volts, a different pin-out, and different bias requirements. The robustness of this tube implies you can get a little more juice out of it if you try, and that's certainly the case. These tubes were favored by jukebox manufacturers of the 1950s and 1960s for their firm, bold response, although few (if any) guitar amps tapped them for all they were worth. In our Supro, they put out about 18 watts from well under 350 volts at

the plates, and they sound round, chunky, and, if slightly dark, crisply and pleasantly so. And how's this for a 6973 versus EL84 A/B test?

Curious about this tube after digging that little Gretsch 6156 a while back, we decided to try something funky: having just completed a home-brewed amp designed along the lines of a modified/slightly hot-rodded AC15—a project that was sounding stellar just as it stood with its pair of EL84s—we decided to take a leap of faith and rewire and rebias the output stage for 6973s. The result? The amp was instantly louder, chunkier, and just bigger sounding, with firmer lows and a meaty if not overcooked midrange. Different tubes, different sound.

The Supro Model 24 is likewise capable of pumping out a surprising amount of volume for its size. Anyone with a recently acquired original example that seems wimpy or anemic in that department should look to the tubes, filter caps, or speaker and should expect the amp, in good condition, to have a bolder voice than the average tweed Deluxe, for example. And its thin 5/8-inch pine cab makes it extremely lively and resonant.

Where some smaller Valcos carrying similar circuitry have scaled-back tremolos, governed by a speed knob only, and an extremely deep, choppy effect as a result, the Model 24 has both speed and intensity and can be made to sound superb at a wide range of settings, from gentle pulse to swampy throb. Each of two similar channels carries an independent tone knob (the usual simple treble-bleed circuit, but effective), along with inputs marked "Treble" and "Bass." Counterintuitive though it might seem, the Bass input sounds better for most guitar applications, tapping the full voice of the amp, while the Treble option is a bit thin and anemic.

And lest we ignore one superficial but significant factor—man, what a looker! Our featured example, courtesy of Elderly Instruments' repair tech Steve Olson, is resplendent in calypso blue vinyl (which matched the finish on many Supro Super Seven guitars and other models). It was also available in red and at other times the more familiar gray. The single Jensen C12Q sounds just right with this amp, or you can Brit it up some, and add a little volume and low end in the process, with something like a Celestion G12H-30 or an Austin Speaker Works KTS-70 (be sure to box up the original for safekeeping). Come to think of it, we wish Jimmy Page hadn't played this amp. Then there would probably be more of them around, for less money, for the rest of us to snatch up.

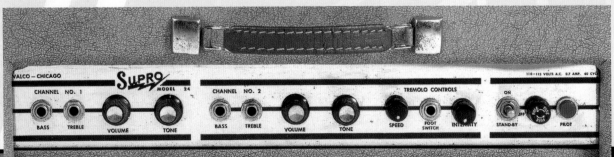

Amp courtesy Steve Olson/photos Dave Matchette/Elderly Instruments

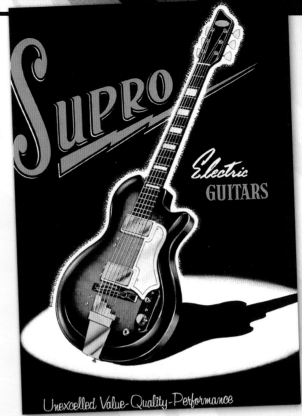

Supro's powerful 1x15-inch Thunderbolt amp was also long rumored to be Jimmy Page's "mystery" amp for Led Zeppelin recording sessions. *Oliver Leiber Collection/Rick Gould*

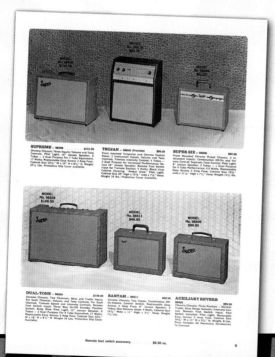

VINTAGE DEPARTMENT STORE MOJO

Ah, the glories of the 1960s department store tube amplifier. Wouldn't it be sweet if we could pick up American-made amps with this much mojo from the likes of Sears or Walmart today?

This one, from Montgomery Ward's Airline range, was manufactured by Danelectro, which also manufactured the Silvertone range for Sears. Meanwhile, Valco also built many Airline amps for Ward. In fact, it was pretty much just one big catalog-brand/amp-jobber lovefest throughout the 1950s and 1960s. But we're not complaining.

As tends to be the case, there's very little documentation available on this amp—the Airline Model 62-9015A, according to the stamp on its chassis—but given the features and circuit traits, we're guessing it hails from the mid 1960s. And what's a year or two either way, between friends?

As far as C-list/catalog-grade guitar gear goes, this would be considered one of the big-boy amps of the Airline range. With a full complement

of reverb, vibrato, two channels, and a dual-6L6 output stage through two 12-inch Jensen C12Q speakers, the 62-9015A would be gunning at both Fender's Deluxe Reverb and its Pro Reverb, and it likely landed at a retail price a little lower than the former.

Danelectro, Airline, Silvertone, and the like certainly sold a lot of amplifiers to players who couldn't afford Fenders, Gibsons, or Ampegs, but Danelectro founder Nat Daniel never was one to copy the circuits of bigger names. However, as much as his clients' marketing men might have wanted to ape the general look of the market leaders—witness the front-mounted control panel, black vinyl covering, and silver grille cloth—the circuits that made the amps tick were resolutely original affairs. It's no surprise either, considering Daniel was building instrument amplifiers for major retailers back in New York City years before Leo Fender even started poking around in the guts of tube radio sets in his one-room workshop in a boomtown out west. So, despite the seeming wannabe status that Danelectro-made amps had attained by the mid 1960s, there was no copying going on under the hood.

Amp and photos courtesy Travis Indgjer/GearHead Music

CIRCA 1965 AIRLINE
MODEL 62-9015A

- Preamp tubes: Two 12AX7s, one 6CG7 for reverb, one 6AU6 for tremolo
- Output tubes: Two 6L6GCs, cathode-biased
- Rectifier: 5Y3
- Controls: Volume, Bass, Treble on each channel, Reverb on channel A, vibrato Strength and Speed (shared)
- Speakers: Two Jensen Special Design ceramic C12Qs
- Output: Approximately 20 watts RMS

Although the main output and preamp/inverter tubes (the latter 12AX7s) are entirely conventional, the 62-9015A heads down the path less taken in its use of a 6CG7 for the reverb and a 6AU6 for the vibrato (tremolo, really). And, hey, there are plenty more tubes under the sun other than the ubiquitous 12AX7 and its cousins, so why not use a variety of them in your designs? Well, as Leo Fender had figured out by the mid 1950s, the more similar tubes you use throughout a circuit, the easier it is to make substitutions on the fly, in the field, without needing to carry a dedicated replacement for each position on the tube chart. In other words, the easier it is to keep your customers (and their repairmen) happy.

But never mind all that. It's fun to see a little variation from the norm now and then, and both of these tubes were in plentiful supply back in the day (and are still fairly easy to find). The 6CG7 is a relatively low-gain dual triode in a standard nine-pin bottle and was more common in radio and TV reception applications. This Airline uses one side as reverb driver and the other as recovery, in a simple transformerless circuit. No lush watery depth from this reverb, but it functions. The 6AU6 is a miniature seven-pin pentode used in many tremolo circuits in Dano-made amps. It also appeared in some Gibsons and Ampegs, and it suits its purpose perfectly well.

One of the biggest surprises here, however, comes not from any unconventional tube but from the juxtaposition of two old friends. The 6L6s are fed by the voltage supplied by a 5Y3 rectifier, which delivers around 325 measly DC volts. Pah! That might sound like a waste of a potentially powerful tube—and certainly you could use 6V6s in this amp, impedance mismatch aside (a tweed Fender Deluxe runs around 350 volts DC on the plates of its 6V6s)—but the intention here is an easy-going, low-voltage amp and a moderate output. This is no 440-volt DC Pro Reverb or Super Reverb, and with this rectifier, its cathode-biased output stage (with a little negative feedback to tighten things up), and other considerations, it is probably only going to put out around 20 watts at best.

What the 6L6s do for us in this circuit is add headroom, add a little more firmness in the low end, and provide tube longevity—you're not going to burn out a pair of RCA or GE 6L6s in a hurry at those voltages. As a result, you still find plenty of these amps with their original tubes. (That said, good 6V6s would be fairly long lasting in this design too.) Other budget-minded aspects of this amp's construction include its folded chassis made from light-gauge steel, the mostly nondescript components within, its rudimentary cabinet construction and second-rate materials, and the minimal effort toward styling and aesthetics.

There isn't a lot of gain on tap here either, and the two-knob tone stack in each channel runs straight to the driver stage in front of its split-phase inverter without any tube-gain makeup stage like Fender was using at the time to recover signal loss in the EQ circuit.

But forget all that. This homely fellow is one supercool amp on so many levels, and it can sound damn hip in the right setting. It offers crisp, slightly spongy cleans, with edgy, gritty, bluesy dirt when turned up higher or hit with a booster pedal, all at volumes that shouldn't rattle the foundations of smaller venues, despite the 2x12-inch/two-6L6 format. The reverb (channel one only) isn't much to write home about, but it adds a little texture when needed, and it certainly excels at thin, splashy, retro, garage band sproingage. The tremolo, on the other hand, isn't half bad. In all, there's no shortage of fun on tap, and there's plenty of grungy snarl when you find the sweet spot. Hard to fault for the modest prices these are fetching—if you can find one. 🎱

1965 FENDER DELUXE REVERB

THE GREAT ALL-ROUNDER

If guitarists were to vote for the one "best amp for all occasions," Fender's Deluxe Reverb would very likely earn a majority decision, especially if you're talking the original 1960s blackface version.

It's small enough to crank up into tone territory for recording, rehearsal, or bar gigs yet loud enough to fill a room and be heard above the drummer in a medium-size club with just a vocal PA. Of course, put it on a big stage with full sound support and a comprehensive monitor mix and the sky's the limit. To top it off, the DR has great-sounding reverb and tremolo. You want to run out and buy one right now, don't you? A lot of players felt the same way when Fender introduced the new model in 1963, and the combo has enjoyed deserved popularity ever since.

Although Fender sort of danced sideways toward the blackface amps during the brownface and tan Tolex years of 1960–1963, the new line represented the culmination of many considerable design upgrades. The Deluxe Reverb in particular was a completely different amp from the tweed Deluxe of just three years before. It carried the same pair of 6V6 output tubes and single 12-inch speaker complement as the 5E3, the final evolution of the tweed Deluxe, but the circuit of the AA763 Deluxe Reverb is otherwise entirely different—even leaving aside the addition of reverb and tremolo (which Fender persisted in calling vibrato). In short, this was Fender taking one of its larger small amps—a student amp, really—and converting it into a "small big amp," with all the circuit upgrades that were afforded the Twin Reverb, Super Reverb, and so forth.

One of many changes was that the AA763 (and the tan Deluxe before it) was no longer cathode biased like the 5E3 but was fixed biased like the bigger amps. It also had a negative feedback loop added around the output stage to tighten up the sound (in short, it was now a class AB amp rather than a class A amp). Its split-load phase inverter was replaced with the more advanced long-tailed pair PI, another bid to gain a little more headroom from the 6V6s, and a choke was added to the power-filtering stage.

1965 FENDER DELUXE REVERB

- Preamp Tubes: Four 7025/12AX7s, two 12AT7s (one for PI)
- Output Tubes: Two 6V6GTs in class AB, fixed-bias
- Rectifier: GZ34
- Controls: Normal channel: Volume, Treble, Bass; Vibrato channel: Volume, Treble, Bass, Reverb, Speed, Intensity
- Speaker: 12-inch Oxford, Utah, or CTS
- Output: 22 watts RMS

In addition, the single treble-bleed Tone control was replaced with a more interactive EQ section comprising a Treble and Bass pot configured between the first gain stage and a gain makeup stage, the two triodes in each channel's preamp tube, respectively. The move to this configuration from the cathode-follower tone stack of the bigger tweed models is often said to have robbed amps like the Bassman, Twin, and Super of a little of the legendary touch sensitivity they possessed in the 1950s. But in the Deluxe Reverb, most players considered it a step up. Besides, it's a hotter, more dynamic, and "on the edge" amp than most bigger Fenders anyway, so while these changes succeeded in giving the DR more focus and headroom, it retained a deliciously tactile playing feel.

The new version's power output was also raised from around 15 watts to approximately 22 watts. To achieve this, Fender ran the 6V6s close to the limits of their DC voltage tolerance (and even beyond it, technically, according to many tube manufacturers' specs for "the V"). The plates of the output tubes now saw a whopping 415 volts versus the 350 or so volts applied by the 5E3 circuit. Fortunately, the amp arrived in an era when great U.S.- and European-made 6V6GTs were plentiful and could handle the job. The AA763 Deluxe Reverb and variations that followed responded by belting out a crisp yet sizzling tone, packed with definition and dynamics. As good NOS 6V6s became harder to find in years to come, however, Deluxe Reverbs became notorious for burning up flimsier Soviet and Chinese variants (though the recent Russian-made Electro-Harmonix version of the tube has been proving more reliable of late).

For most players, the grooviest and most obvious upgrade of all was, of course, the new complement of onboard effects—reverb and tremolo. These were about the only means of messing with the straight sound of an electric guitar through an amp in the early and mid 1960s anyway, and Fender's versions of both largely set the standard for other manufacturers to follow. Many Gibson and Maestro amps offered a deep, lush tremolo, and Ampeg was famed for the richness of its reverb. But through the course of the decade, both were heard more as rendered by Fender amps than by the products of any other manufacturer. Fender used a relatively simple but good-sounding bias-modulating tremolo in the 1950s and briefly included a gorgeous true vibrato in some of the larger blond and tan amps of the early 1960s, but this was an extremely complex circuit that required a full two and a half preamp tubes to execute at the pinnacle of the design.

With the blackface amps, Fender introduced a new tremolo circuit that used a single preamp tube and a light-dependent resistor (LDR; also called optocoupler or opto cell) to produce a very effective and wide-ranging on/off pulsing of the signal level prior to the phase inverter. The reverb circuit used a 12AT7 really as an output tube into a small output transformer that drove a set of springs rather than a speaker, and half of a 7025 (a ruggedized 12AX7) as a recovery stage, all of which yielded a smooth and very appealing short delay sound. And because the Vibrato (effects) channel ran through the leftover half of the 7025 preamp tube, this channel sounded a little brighter and a hair hotter than the Normal channel, even with the reverb off. It's worth noting that the Oxford, Utah, and CTS speakers used in these amps were not the best-sounding drivers in Fender history. Many players upgrade their Deluxe Reverbs with a better-sounding speaker.

The Deluxe Reverb is a great amp for anything from blues to country to rock 'n' roll and even jazz. Consequently, it has long been a go-to combo for countless first-call Nashville and L.A. session players. Given the amp's all-around appeal, blackface examples have become extremely collectible; prices for good originals have recently been crashing the $2,500 and $3,000 barriers. Silverface Deluxe Reverbs can still be great-sounding amps, and examples from the late 1960s and early 1970s in particular can be converted to blackface specs by a good tech with just a few minor circuit changes.

Model "DELUXE REVERB-AMP. AB763"

Production #4

Power Supply 117 volts, 50-60 cycles AC.

Power Consumption 120 watts.

Tube locations left to right at rear:

FENDER ELECTRIC INSTRUMENT CO.
Fullerton, California

Fender's 65 Deluxe Reverb reissue.
Fender Musical Instruments Corporation

PLEXI IN A SMALL PACKAGE

In the heyday of rock 'n' roll, many amplifier builders were on a continual quest for volume. In a shift most would deem fortunate, many guitarists have since awakened to the near-universal truth that bigger is not always better. Put another way, louder is not always more toneful. The impressive high-volume monsters designed some forty to fifty years ago to take the electric guitar from roadhouses and bandstands into concert halls and sports arenas got all the headlines in guitardom, but any manufacturer with a dram of foresight also saw the benefit of marketing smaller beginner/"student" amps.

Ironically, while student players buying the small amps dreamed of graduating to the big stacks their guitar heroes played onstage, the heroes themselves—already hip to the tip—were often recording with the succulent, responsive smaller amps. Once the rest of us discovered the secret (and sound reinforcement caught up with amp development), these little belters became the gems of Tonesville.

The "less is more" phenomenon made amps like Fender's Deluxe Reverb and Vox's AC15 into prized pieces. However, in recent years especially, Marshall's 18-watt amps of 1965 to 1967—models 1958, 1973, and 1974—have attained a position very near the top of this hallowed club-combo heap. Consequently, while you could have any of these little fellas for a whistle twenty-five years ago, when humbuckerheads across two continents were paying all they could scrape together for JTM100 full stacks, an 18-watter in good condition can command more than five times more per watt on the vintage market today than its mighty EL34-powered big brothers.

Does a cranked 1965 18-watter sound just like a cranked JTM45 or JTM50 Plexi, but at a lower volume? No, not really. For some applications, it might even sound better, though some will miss the bigger amps' gut-thumping low-end kick and tangible mid-range punch. But positioned in front of the creamy, rich, and tactile delivery of a Marshall 18-watter, most guitarists lucky enough to have an opportunity discover this world of rarified playability and expression. That, and the marvelous absence of that nagging ringing in the ears for the next day or two.

Tube-wise, the 1958 (and its brethren) looked much the same as the flagship JTM45 with which it shared the catalog in 1965, only smaller (the model numbers have nothing to do with the years amps were released). The 18-watt platform carried three ECC83 (aka 12AX7) preamp tubes, two EL84 output tubes, and an EZ81 rectifier—the latter a tall, narrow, nine-pin tube that looks something like an EL84. The preamp tubes in the 18-watters, however, perform somewhat different duties. Whereas the JTM45 and JTM50's (and others') relatively advanced three-knob, cathode-follower tone stack uses an entire tube to work its magic, the 1958 uses only a single, passive, treble-roll-off-style Tone control in each of its two channels and uses half of one of these dual-triode preamp tubes to drive a tremolo circuit (with Speed and Depth controls). Both inputs in the Tremolo channel go into the other half of that ECC83, while each channel of the Normal channel gets its own triode. The two are voiced a little differently too—the Normal being a little chunkier, with more gain.

Although EL84s are sometimes referred to as the EL34's little brother, that's a little misleading. They do represent the lower-powered rank of classic Brit-toned amps—while the EL34 represents the higher-powered—but these popular nine-pin output tubes have a sound and character all their own. Hit with lower gain levels, they can be shimmering and sparkly, with a multidimensional harmonic performance and decently firm lows. Pumped a little harder, they surrender to breakup smoothly and evenly (especially in the 18-watter's cathode-biased output

stage) and can help a low-watt amp achieve a surprisingly broad, full-throated sound stage. The EZ81 is a rectifier unto itself, too, character-wise, and was unavailable for years until Electro-Harmonix reissued the tube. It's an excellent match for EL84s voltage-wise and gives into a gentle but delightfully toothsome squash when hit hard, but usually without going too floppily spongy. Put it all together, pump it through a venerable Radiospares output transformer, and you have one remarkably expressive little amp for club gigs and recording—or anything at all really if you mic it.

The two 10-inch ceramic Celestions in the 1958 combo are less typically Marshall-esque than the 1974's single 12-inch greenback or the 1973's two 12s. The models carrying 12s offer greater oomph in the mid-range, but the 10-inch Celestions provide a dash more articulation and a full, well-rounded voice. All three combos came in open-backed cabs, so they were also less directional and produced less characteristically thumping lows (even with all power disparities aside) than the closed-back Marshall cabs the bigger amps used. This arguably helps make them more versatile too, and a little sweeter sounding overall.

In 1967 Marshall revised the design of its small amp, and the 18-watter was thereby replaced—after sales of only a few hundred units—by the 20-watter, which still employed the 1958, 1973, and 1974 model numbers but was joined by the 1917 PA Head, 2019 Bass Head, 2022 Lead Head, and a few other variations. As much to simplify the construction of these amps as to increase the power, one suspects, Marshall dropped the EZ81 tube rectifier for solid-state rectification. The diodes hit the EL84 with 360 to 370 DC volts compared to the EZ81's 325VDC (give or take a dozen volts) to generate a couple more watts of power and a tighter response. Also, the tremolo effect was no longer standard, so the 20-watters required only two ECC83s instead of three to power two identical channels with volume and tone, and the phase inverter. They're still great-sounding little amps, and prized collector's pieces, but most players agree that they don't have quite the magic of the 18-watters they replaced. The 20-watter itself vanished from the Marshall roster in 1974.

The "cult of the 18-watter" has seen not only a major spike in the values of vintage originals in recent years—alongside Marshall's own reissue, the 1974X Handwired model—but a proliferation of homages to the design from boutique makers, embodied by models from 65amps, Gabriel Sound Garage, Bacino, Retro-King, and others. The rarity of the originals has also brought out a major DIY drive from tone-hungry players, supported most ably by websites like 18watt.com.

Student, schmudent: Crank up that little sucker and get ready to rock! ●

Marshall's 1966 catalog showing the Model 1961 and 1958 amps.

145

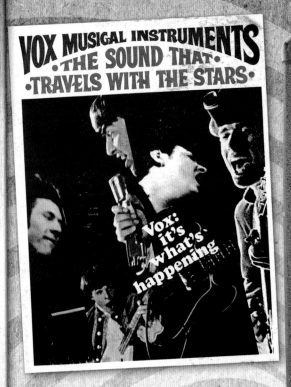

SHEEP IN WOLF'S CLOTHING

No doubt the mere appearance of that Vox logo and the diamond grille cloth beneath it has already set your heart palpitating. Let us add that this is indeed a genuine Vox combo from 1965, with two EL84 output tubes and an EZ81 rectifier, then top it off with the news that we found this amplifier for sale in excellent, all-original condition at one of our favorite local hole-in-the-wall guitar stores with a price tag listing $499. Ready for the defibrillator yet? But before we charge up the paddles and shout "Clear!" we can probably bring you back down to earth with the addendum that this is not in fact the British-made Vox AC15 over which you were already beginning to salivate mentally but a U.S.-made Vox Pacemaker V-3, manufactured by Thomas Organ in California. And although that price is perhaps toward the bargain end of the spectrum for these amps, it is still well within the expected range.

The Vox logo's transition from British glory to Californian infamy is still something of a mystery to many amp-o-philes, and the real story tells a rather tragic tale. After signing a mutual distribution deal with Vox manufacturer

JMI in 1964, Thomas Organ soon found itself—in the wake of the Beatles' massive success—unable to meet the enormous demand for British JMI-made Vox amplifiers. Early in 1965, to speed the flow, JMI started shipping only parts of amps (namely completed chassis and speakers) to Thomas Organ rather than complete amps. Even then the California company couldn't meet demand. It began sourcing its own parts to assemble its own renditions of the "British" amps. As the snowball tumbled farther, there ensued what amounted to virtually a hostile takeover of Vox/JMI by Thomas Organ. JMI founder Tom Jennings had sold his controlling interest in the company the previous year to meet the need for breakneck expansion. When Thomas Organ asked for the rights to use the Vox name in North America, Jennings, despite his vehement objections, was unable to stop the deal from going through. The result was a range of amps like this late 1965 Pacemaker, a sheep in wolf's clothing, with no real connection to the grand roots of the brand other than the name and the grille cloth.

For all that, this is still a rare amp and a piece of rock 'n' roll history. The Pacemaker segued through several variations from its introduction in 1965 until its demise around 1971, but the tube version—as we have here—was

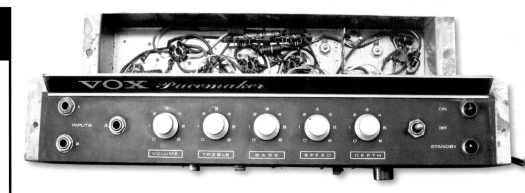

1965 VOX PACEMAKER V-3

- Preamp tubes: Three Mullard ECC83s (12AX7)
- Output tubes: Two Mullard EL84s, cathode-biased, no negative feedback
- Rectifier: Mullard EZ81
- Controls: Volume, Treble, Bass, Speed, Depth
- Speaker: Gold 10-inch Oxford Vox Bulldog
- Output: Approximately 17 watts RMS

produced only in 1965 and perhaps into early 1966. The first rendition was fitted with 10-inch Celestion speakers, which were initially sold to Thomas Organ by JMI, then purchased directly from Celestion once the Californians figured out it would be cheaper to bypass the middleman. Our rendition of the amp from later in the year had the gold Vox Bulldog 10-inch speaker made by Oxford in Chicago, which also supplied Fender and several other manufacturers.

We can already see it's a smaller amp than the JMI-built AC15—a 1x10-inch combo rather than a 1x12 or 2x12 inch—and other than the 2xEL84 and EZ81 output tube and rectifier complement, the Pacemaker is different in just about every way. It has three inputs but only one channel, powered by half an ECC83 dual triode (aka 12AX7) rather than the EF86 pentode that served as the beating heart of the British classic.

The Pacemaker does benefit from an active cathode-follower tone stack that's not unlike the Top Boost circuit of the AC30, with Treble and Bass controls, powered by a second ECC83. But it uses a much cruder phase inverter circuit, the cathodyne, or split-phase, inverter more familiar from many small and midsize tweed Fender amps and requiring only half a tube rather than the elegant long-tailed pair of the AC15 and most large amps post-1960. Another ECC83 powers its tremolo effect, with Speed and Depth controls.

One surprise bonus, though: our Pacemaker stands replete with a full set of Mullard tubes, the bottles it was born with (Thomas Organ must have bought a *big* box of these and was still feeding off them). Bonus number two: it really sounds pretty damn good, even if it's no AC15 (and would sound significantly better through a decent 12-inch speaker).

Despite Tom Jennings' objections to Thomas Organ taking over the manufacturing reins themselves, it transpires—according to

Jim Elyea—that Thomas sent prototypes of these tube models to JMI for evaluation by British engineers and modified them according to notes supplied after such testing. Furthermore, chief JMI engineer Dick Denney even visited Thomas Organ's Sepulveda, California, factory to test the post-modification Pacemaker and others and to offer further comments and final approval. (Kind of like dancing on your own grave, eh?) That said, the guts of this Pacemaker look nothing like the inside of a JMI chassis of the same era. Built up rather minimally, almost crudely, on a series of scattered individual tag strips, the Pacemaker looks more like the work of several other C-list brands. Yet it functions just fine.

The Pacemaker's bigger sibling from Thomas Organ, the Cambridge Reverb V-3, has a very similar circuit and tube complement but uses the more virtuous long-tailed pair PI for greater headroom and fidelity (thanks to Voxshowroom.com for that tidbit). In the course of 1966, Thomas Organ replaced the all-tube V-3 with the all-transistor V-1021 Pacemaker, one of the solid-state amps that led thousands of young Beatle wannabes in the United States to exclaim, "Why the $#!& don't I sound like George and John through this thing?" Nevertheless, the transistorized 1966 Pacemaker cost a full $20 more than its tube predecessor of 1965, at $149.95, adding insult to injury.

Crank up the Pacemaker V-3, though, and it has that crisp, slightly glassy EL84 sizzle and crunch that does at least hint at an AC15 (as virtually every 2xEL84-based amp does at times), and plenty of juicy sag when you push it. With the right guitar and right attitude, it can almost tease out an accurate "Day Tripper," "I'm Down," or "Ticket to Ride" tone—or at least something better than your buddy in the garage down the road is getting with his 1966 model.

SHINY CHROME AND BIG TONE

We guitarists just love gear that looks like it was salvaged from our mom's kitchen circa 1961. Give us something in high-gloss pastel, with Formica styling, gas cooker knobs, plenty of chrome, and an emblem lifted off a fridge door, and we go weak in the knees every time. As far as kitchen kitsch goes, this Supro Model S6651 Big Star amplifier from around 1966 is hard to beat. What better color for a groovin' control panel than turquoise (unless maybe it's surf green), and those chrome-centered knobs are plenty big enough to grope mid-gig with a modicum of accuracy. Now, if it sounds any good we're in business.

And being a Valco product, it naturally sounds *great*. It sounds nothing like the "poor man's Twin Reverb," which plenty of used examples have been sold as over the years, and it has little of the pristine, shimmering jangle and twang of the big, clean Fenders of the day. Instead, the Big Star has a warm, thick, slightly gnarly tone that distinguishes many of this defunct Chicago amp maker's products.

Any time a 1960s Valco-made amp raises its head these days, the sepulchral image of Jimmy Page recording early Led Zeppelin classics seems to drift up and envelop the room, but this was unlikely a piece of Page gear (he would have more likely to use a model with 6973 output tubes or something in a 1x12 inch at least). But if star associations are required, it can be said that Eric Clapton dabbled with this or a similar Supro in the studio (possibly the reverb-less Galaxy), and Joe Perry has also been seen fondling the turquoise. Although this was built to be one of Valco's larger amps in the day—being 2x12 inches with a pair of 6L6GCs in the output stage—it really isn't up to much more than club gigs or studio work, without miking through a good PA system at least. It is louder and just plain bigger-sounding than the average Valco out there, but it isn't primed for the most efficient use of its firepower. And for the tone hungry among us, we'd consider that a *good* thing.

Working from the output forward, consider that the Big Star's 6L6s are cathode biased with no negative feedback, a configuration that hadn't been seen in a 6L6-based Fender amp, for example, for more than ten years, since the 5E5 Pro of 1955. Given the relatively low voltages that these big bottles dined on, around 370V DC at the plates and 320V DC on the grids, and the rather lean-output transformers that Valco is largely known for, we're going to see only about 30 watts at best, running downhill on a freshly waxed

Amp and photos courtesy Brad Klukow

CIRCA 1966 SUPRO S6651 BIG STAR

- Preamp tubes: Four 12AX7s, one 6973 reverb driver
- Output tubes: Four 6L6GCs
- Rectifier: Solid-state
- Controls: Volume and Tone on each of two channels; Reverb, Tremolo Intensity, and Tremolo; Speed on reverb-tremolo channel
- Speakers: Two Jensen C12N ceramic
- Output: Approximately 30 watts RMS

out panache than many of the major brands exhibited at the time, we might argue, but this Supro Big Star is certainly one of the sweetest. (The original silver grille cloth on our well-gigged example appears to have been replaced with Fender-style silver grille cloth, but no matter.)

Players and collectors tend to fawn more over the early 1960s Supros, partly thanks to supposed associations with Jimmy Page and partly because . . . well, if vintage is cool, *more* vintage is generally assumed to be cooler. But these later Valco-made amps packed many of the same characteristics and offered many of the same tonal responses as earlier models with similar tube complements. Plenty of people might prefer an earlier tube-rectified model, but "solid-state" in the case of this Big Star's diode bridge shouldn't be considered any kind of sonic second rate. A little extra firmness in an amp like this is often a good thing, and you'll get all the dirty sag you need when you crank it up. Amid all the hype over the Thunderbolt or the Model 1624 of a few years earlier, pause to consider the younger siblings like the Big Star and the Galaxy—potentially great values in vintage Supros and truly fun examples of tube amps made just a few years before this great Chicago manufacturer's sad demise.

board. What this setup loses in volume, though, it makes up for in brown, gritty sonic goodness and pliant, tactile feel. It isn't overly spongy, given the solid-state rectification, but it certainly offers a compressed edge to the attack when you roll up the volume and hit it hard. The original Jensen C12N speakers the amp came with acquitted themselves well as regards crispness and sparkle, though overall the Big Star is still no twang machine.

The preamp stages in each of the two independent channels, though outwardly fairly simple, pack plenty of Valco-style quirkiness. The Standard channel is nothing unusual, though it still exhibits this maker's propensity to do things its own way, but the Reverb-Tremolo channel is masterfully odd. The unsuspecting Volume control hides a dual-ganged potentiometer that simultaneously controls the first gain stage (after the first triode in that channel's own 12AX7) and the output from a second gain stage that follows the reverb circuit and Tone control. Later examples used a 12AX7 to drive the reverb, but this one uses a 6973 output tube. Its reverb is arguably a bit fuller as a result, although none of these have a delay sound to write home about. The tremolo, however, so often a standout feature of Valco-made amps, is a real treat. It runs from soft pulse to throbbing groove.

The circuits between the amps Valco made for the many different brands it supplied were usually very similar, but the amps distinguished themselves by their looks, and models sold as Gretsch, National, and Supro always had individual styling that made each special. All looked pretty damn cool, with more out-and-

PURE LOUD

Marshall might have established the juicy, saturated, full-on valvulicious rock lead tone of the late 1960s and early 1970s, but for pure in-your-face power and punch, Hiwatt always ruled the roost; the amps helped make the Who the loudest band on the planet (official!) throughout the dawn of the arena rock era and contributed to David Gilmour's larger-than-life guitar tone in Pink Floyd shows of the 1970s. Hiwatt by name, high wattage by nature—these babies pumped a lot of air, and in 1971 there was no better way of filling a football stadium with the roar of monster-size rock guitar.

The Custom 100 DR103 was the big boy of the range, but we're going to examine the Custom 50 DR504, which uses the same circuit and is even built on the same chassis, minus two of the DR103's four EL34 output tubes. Though few players today take full advantage of a cranked 100-watt British full stack (or ever need to), the power issue bears consideration. In good condition, with a correctly biased quartet of NOS Mullard EL34s, a Custom 100 can put out well over 100 watts at full throttle, while a Custom 50 will easily push 60 watts or more. That's 60 real watts RMS, not the marketing team behind some

contemporary offshore-made PCB amp's rendering of a piece of consumer-electronics-grade amplification that will do you 38 watts in a stiff tailwind from its pair of modern-day EL34s or 6L6s.

Some players mistakenly think of Hiwatts as semicopies of Marshall stacks. They have a roughly similar look, after all, and are made in the UK, and based around EL34 output tubes. But these amps are as far from Marshall as are Fenders—farther, in many respects. Hiwatt founder Dave Reeves was working at Arbiter's Sound City ampworks in the mid 1960s when he developed the notion of building a better amp. He began prototyping the Hiwatt designs in 1967. Pete Townshend, before moving on to actual Hiwatt products, played Sound City amps that were highly modified by Reeves himself in 1967 and 1968. To achieve his goal, Reeves designed new amplifier circuits from the ground up, and despite similar-looking control panel legends, took few—if any—clues from the popular Marshall amps in the process. Instead of the succulent breakup a Marshall JMP50 introduces to the signal at almost every step of the way from input to output, the DR504 circuit is designed to pass a bold yet full-frequency signal along to the output stage, where it can be amplified to crankus extremus, as desired. There's a lot of gain in the circuit, make no mistake, but the amp handles it elegantly every step of the way, resulting in

Backed by his lineup of Hiwatt amps, Pete Townshend of the Who takes to the air alongside Roger Daltrey during the Quadrophenia Tour on November 5, 1973. *David Redfern/Redferns/Getty Images*

Pink Floyd perform at the Shelter Benefit concert on May 18, 1973. From left, David Gilmour with his Hiwatt amp, Nick Mason, Roger Waters, and Rick Wright. *Steve Morley/Redferns/Getty Images*

CIRCA 1968 HIWATT CUSTOM 50 DR504

- Preamp tubes: three ECC83 (12AX7) and one ECC81 (12AT7) for gain stages, gain make-up, and phase inverter
- Output tubes: Two EL34; Class AB, fixed-bias
- Rectifier: Solid-state (diodes)
- Controls: Normal Vol, Brill Vol (aka brilliant, bright), Bass, Treble, Middle, Presence, Master Vol
- Speakers: Four 50W Fane drivers in each 4x12 extension cab
- Output: Approximately 60 watts RMS

amplification efficiency and maximum power. It'll break up, sure, but by the time it does, it's frighteningly loud.

Also different from the Fender and Marshall template is the way the EQ shaping is achieved. Although the Bass, Treble, and Middle controls on the front panel imply a descendent of Fender's tweed Bassman, upon which Jim Marshall and company based the JTM45 and Plexi circuits, the Hiwatt tone stack's functions occur in an entirely different part of the circuit. After each channel's first gain stage, the signal hits a Volume control and then runs straight to a second gain stage, with the three-knob tone network configured between the plate (anode) of this triode and the input of yet another ECC83 (12AX7) following it, which constitutes a further two gain stages to condition the signal before passing it along to the phase inverter. This is very different from the cathode-follower tone stack of Marshall and the big tweed Fenders and a little more like the tone network of the blackface Fender amps if anything, but it's still something unto itself.

Also, like larger post-1963 Fenders, Hiwatts used a 12AT7 (an ECC81 in Euro-speak) in the PI, a tube that has less gain than a 12AX7 and is therefore likely to distort the signal less as it passes it along to the output tubes. There's more to the Hiwatt PI stage than just the tube choice, however. For an insider's look, let's turn to Victor Mason, a longtime fan of vintage Hiwatts and a man who has serviced plenty in his time.

"The magic part of the Hiwatt, and [the reason] it will produce such a powerfully clean sound, is its phase inverter," he says. "It has a bias on the grid. That bias prevents the phase inverter from shifting upward or downward, as does a typical Fender or Marshall, which gives rise to early distortion." He further confirms the robustness of the Hiwatt output stage and adds that these amps were biased to idle at a whopping 25 watts per tube—that's at idle, not when hit with a signal and working hard—simply because the Mullard EL34s could take it, and still keep cranking out the good stuff. "Few contemporary makes of EL34, if any, prove up to the task with such gusto, and few amps would dare to bias these tubes so hot."

In addition to the circuit design, these amps were just built right. Among all the vintage Fender, Marshall, Vox, Gibson, Selmer, and other golden-era amps, Hiwatts exhibit the most impressive build quality. And that's really saying something. Reeves commissioned military-specification chassis wiring from Harry Joyce, who did other high-end contract electronics work, including wiring jobs for the British Royal Navy. Military-grade components were used wherever possible, alongside rugged Partridge transformers, massive hunks of iron that also played a big part in rendering the Hiwatt sound with such enormity. To top it all off, Hiwatt often used sturdy Fane speakers rather than Celestions in its SE4123 4x12-inch cabs, a choice that carried the ethos for bold, punchy tones all the way to the cab. Look inside the chassis of a vintage Hiwatt: the board layout and wire runs are breathtakingly neat and linear. It's worth noting that, although build quality slipped considerably in the 1980s following Reeves' death in 1981, we're almost as impressed by the quality of workmanship inside the current British-made Hiwatt amps, which go a long way toward reclaiming the standards of the brand's glory years. Punch, bang, wallop—Hiwatt!

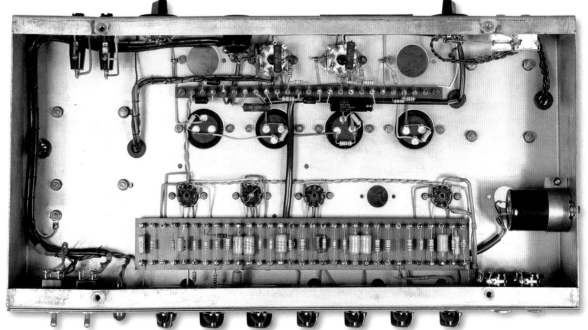

Amp and photos courtesy Victor Mason/Mojave Ampworks

John Fogerty and his Kustom amp lead Creedence Clearwater Revival on stage in London in 1970.
Michael Putland/Getty Images

TUCK-AND-ROLL BLISS

If ever a solid-state amplifier made a devoted valvehead abandon his or her beloved warm glow and soft clipping, chances are good it was a tuck-and-roll Kustom model from the mid 1960s or early 1970s. The lack of tube circuitry didn't stop many a great artist from endorsing these groovy combos and stacks, though, and the brand was a force to be reckoned with in its day. We first caught an inkling that there might be more to them than looks when guitarist Mike Campbell said in an interview in 1999, that he had acquired a

Kustom stack from the late 1960s to record some tracks on Tom Petty and the Heartbreakers' *Echo* album because he'd heard that's what John Fogerty of Credence Clearwater Revival played. In particular he wanted to achieve that deep, bold tremolo sound. John Fogerty? Mike Campbell? Sign me up!

Kustom was founded by Bud Ross in Chanute, Kansas, in 1965 and quickly began landing significant artist endorsements and making its way onto major stages. The Jackson 5, James Jamerson, a number of major funk and soul acts of the 1970s, Carl Perkins, Waylon Jennings, and much-seen Kustom advertising personalities such as Roy Clark, Leon Russell, and the Carpenters all plied their craft through groovy tuck-and-roll stacks. Johnny Cash even toured with a tuck-and-roll PA system for many years. The tuck-and-roll nomenclature is not, in fact, the schoolroom nuclear obliteration drill that it sounds like. Rather it is derived from the padded upholstery technique with which the seven available colors of Naugahyde vinyl covering were applied to the cabinets. It was a clever stylistic move on Ross' part.

- Topology: Solid-state
- Controls: Volume, Bass, Treble, Reverb, Speed, Intensity
- Speakers: Single 15-inch JBL D130Fs in a ported cab
- Output: 100 watts RMS

No doubt looks alone sold an awful lot of Kustom amps—which is not to say by any means that their sound fell short of the mark. While big fish Fender was struggling to convince players that its debut solid-state line released in the same year Kustom arrived could a) sound halfway decent, and b) survive gigging life without need of constant repair (neither of which proved attainable for Fender's trannie line), Kustom pumped out confident, on-the-money solid-state models that were built like tanks and sounded pretty darn good, even when cranked up to the point of breakup, if not far beyond. Put simply, Kustom out Leo-ed Fender when it came to solid-state by making straightforward, well-manufactured amps that were roadworthy professional tools. And to get back to where we came in, they sure as heck looked a lot hipper.

The Kustom 100 1-15L-2 was a major workhorse for the company in the late 1960s. This one is covered in a green metallic vinyl that Naugahyde called Cascade. Whereas many designers would use solid-state as an excuse to slap on an array of nifty but often boggling (and occasionally useless) features and effects, the 100 head of this era is refreshingly simple: Volume, Bass, and Treble on the left; Reverb, Speed, and Intensity on the right (the latter two for the tremolo, with foot switch connections for both effects).

Kustom called the amp the "Solid-state Energizer" (whatever that means) with "resonant treble boost circuitry" (whatever that was). And whatever they named it, the discrete solid-state circuitry sounded surprisingly fat and rich, and its effects were delightfully hypnotic. Its 100-watt output was considered enough for club and church gigs and maybe a Howard Johnson or two, considering that PAs were mostly only for vocals back in its day, but its big brothers offered outputs of 200 watts and 400 watts for players with need of big-stage sound support. The 1x15-inch speaker cab was sold with a JBL D130F driver (although the example in our photograph might be

a replacement, as it lacks the JBL's silver dome dust cover) and has a closed back and a pair of ports. It's an unusual cab to partner with a guitar amp, but the design projected well and presented plenty of low-end kick, as you might expect.

Kustom changed hands a few times in the 1970s and 1980s, while the tuck-and-roll covering technique was abandoned in the mid 1970s in favor of a more contemporary black vinyl. It was owned for a time by Baldwin, which acquired Gretsch in a buying frenzy of the late 1960s. A new company, based in Cincinnati, purchased the Kustom name in the late 1980s and worked to revive the brand, initially mainly by offering good-value ranges of affordable solid-state PA gear and practice amps; it has expanded into larger and better-equipped amplifiers over the years. None of the great, original solid-state tuck-and-roll models have yet been revived—perhaps because, rather ironically, it might be difficult to convince players today that simple, nonmodeling solid-state amps have any virtue in the professional realm, despite these being exactly how the company got its foothold forty years ago. The recent Coupé series of tube amps (ahem!) received good reviews, however, including a bevy of magazine awards. And to celebrate the company's fortieth anniversary last year, Kustom added a tuck-and-roll top panel to the Coupé and issued a limited run of its little 10-watt, solid-state Dart combos in all tuck-and-roll cabs. Worthy products, without a doubt, but hey—would the Carpenters tour in front of them?

The company has just opened a new factory in Hebron, Kentucky, in the greater Cincinnati metropolitan area. The original Chanute factory was closed in the early 1980s. Meanwhile, if you want an original Kustom 100 1-15L-2 or one of its contemporaries, you'll have to scour the usual used gear outlets, where you'll most likely find one selling for something closer to its original $545 retail price circa 1968. A pretty lofty figure, considering that a tube Fender Twin Reverb listed for $499 the same year. But, hey, we're talking cutting-edge technology after all. ●

FUZZ-TORTION MONOLITH

A major artist's endorsement of a piece of gear is often seen as a springboard to that product's success, or at least it serves as a footnote to keep the product in the history books. Having graced the U.S. tours of Led Zeppelin, the Jeff Beck Group, and Steppenwolf in the late 1960s, and Cheap Trick after, the Rickenbacker Transonic series should have had its shrine in the annals of geardom secured, yet this wild line of hulking solid-state amplifiers has all but vanished from memory. Examples exist as prized pieces

in the collections of a handful of amp-o-philes, certainly, and are still gigged out by a few dedicated enthusiasts, but the name has little to show for itself up against the Fenders, Marshalls, Voxes, and Boogies of the world, and even the solid-state Roland Jazz Choruses and Polytone Brutes.

What went wrong?

According to their designer, Bob Rissi, "They were just so expensive, most artists couldn't afford to buy them. You could buy three Fender Twin Reverbs for the price of a Rickenbacker Transonic TS200."

The fact that Jimmy Page and John Paul Jones left most of their Transonics in the United States after returning to England in 1969 at the end of the tour leads some people to assume they weren't thrilled with the Rickenbackers. No doubt, the Marshall head and cab ultimately suited Page better live, and a little Supro and others did the trick in the studio, but he had already recorded the main guitar part to "Heartbreaker" on one of his Transonics and purportedly retained another in his home collection for many years. In fact, most players who have come close enough to a rare Transonic to get their jack into one will

CIRCA 1968 RICKENBACKER TRANSONIC TS100

- Topology: Solid-state
- Output: 100 watts RMS
- Controls: Volume, Treble, Bass controls and Hollow, Mellow, and Pierce switches on each channel; Tremolo Speed and Depth, Reverb, and Fuzz-Tortion on Custom channel
- Speakers: Two 12-inch Altec 417

tell you that they sound strikingly good (occasionally with the caveat "for a transistor amp"). Truth is, the occasional dissing of these rigs is probably symbolic of the acceptance of the rock world at large of the solid-state amps that abounded in the late 1960s, which is to say the near-wholehearted *rejection* of those amps once they'd given them a whirl. Time and time again, the manufacturers stumped up a fleet of impressive-looking solid-state amps for a big tour only to have said artists declare that they "don't break up" like the tube amps they already knew and loved. In the grand scheme of things, though, Rickenbacker's Transonics were a cut above the flawed first-generation Fender and Vox efforts and others that forged the dismal early reputation for the breed. They deserve some love here.

The big amps that most of our name-checked artists toured with hail from the TS200 series of 200-watt head and cab rigs, but our subject is the lesser-seen 100-watt TS100 combo. The preamps were the same on each, and they differed only in their power amps, speakers, and cabinet configurations. Having contributed to designing Fender tube amps in the early 1960s (as well as enjoying a brief stint away to design a rare line of tube amps for Rickenbacker in 1963–1964), Rissi was in on Fender's big push toward solid-state in the mid 1960s, which resulted in the company's ill-received first run of tranny amps. These were given model names that were identical to many of their tube-loaded predecessors, which apparently Fender thought they would eventually supersede entirely. "I was unhappy with Fender marketing the solid-state amps to replace the tube amps, though," says Rissi, "because rock 'n' roll was still big, and the solid-state amps wouldn't distort well even if you turned them to 10."

Happy to seek his fortunes elsewhere, Rissi was hired for a second time by Rickenbacker's Frances Hall, but this time to work on a new type of solid-state amplifier aimed at the professional guitarist. "I wanted to make these solid-state amps sound more like tube amps. I put the transistor circuitry in similar to

the way a tube amp is made. They were not direct coupled, like most solid-state amps of the time, but were capacitively and nondirect coupled, so the circuit worked the way a tube amp circuit works. That's where the warmth and the tone came from, and that's why so many big groups liked them. They were well made too. Every so often I have to work on one, and there usually isn't much wrong with them other than needing a filter cap or something. The parts we used in those amps were real high-quality parts, usually Motorola or RCA, and we used Schumacher transformers."

Our TS100 has two channels, Standard and Custom, each with its own Volume, Treble, and Bass controls. In addition, each carries a trio of big white "Rick-O-Select" switches with different colored indicator lamps for each of three voicing modes: Pierce, Mellow, and Hollow. Just be sure to pop in those earplugs before you flip on that Pierce setting. The Custom channel also included Reverb and Tremolo, and another clear nod to tonal fashions of the times: a Fuzz-Tortion circuit. According to Rissi, the fuzz circuit wasn't something he was fond of—"I prefer natural overdrive"—but fuzz was the sexy ticket of the late 1960s, and Rickenbacker head Frances Hall wanted it in there. As it turned out, a lot of players found it an effective fuzz tone, and several even tracked down Rissi in later years to have him put the circuit in a pedal configuration. The TS200 also included a stereo preamp so that each channel could be split to a separate power amp, producing a stereo signal for Rick's "Rick-O-Sound" guitars with the use of a second powered speaker cab. The pièce de résistance topside, however, has to be the big power meter with "overload" light.

More than anything going on inside the chassis, though, the Transonics cut their dashing figures thanks to the large, top-heavy-looking trapezoidal cabinets. Made from solid pine and carrying either a pair of 12-inch Altec 417s or white-frame British-made Rolas in the TS100, or four 12 inches or two 15s and a horn in the TS200, these made for a heavy package and contributed to the hefty price tag: a whopping $1,345 for the flagship TS200 in 1973, shortly before the demise of the series.

Eager to build an amp that working guitarists could actually afford, Rissi left to start his own company, Risson Amps, where he sold mostly tube amps, but a few solid-state models too, to several major-name players—Joe Walsh, Nikki Sixx, Rick Vito, and Lita Ford among them—before sidestepping into the computer industry in the early 1980s. Now in retirement, Rissi still builds the occasional tube amp in his home just a few blocks from the site of the old Fender factory in Fullerton, and he currently offers the compact Marvell model, handmade from mostly new old-stock components that have lain in storage since his first go-round as a designer.

As for the Transonics themselves, plenty of the relatively few made are still out there, and still rockin' when called upon. ●

Bob Rissi, designer of the Rickenbacker Transonic line, poses with circuit board in hand in front of an early prototype of the model.

Jimmy Page coaxes strange sounds from his Fender Telecaster and Rickenbacker Transonic amp while performing live on TV in Copenhagen, Denmark, while on tour in March 1969. *Jan Persson/Redferns/Getty Images*

Amp designer Bob Rissi and guitarist Al Perkins meet and greet behind Jimmy Page's Rickenbacker Transonic rig.

Rickenbacker Transonic Sound Systems

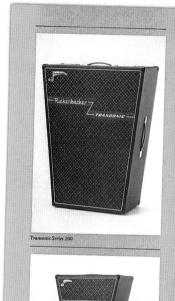

Transonic Series 100

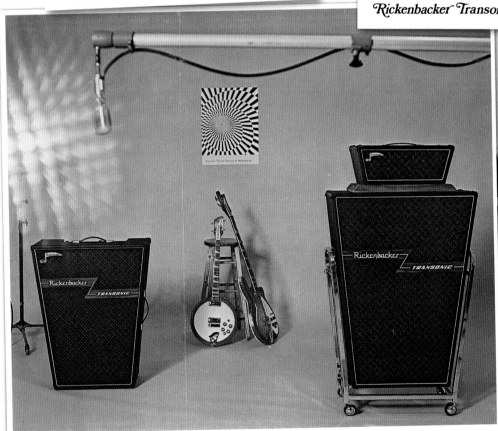

Catalog page showing the 100 and 200 Series Transonic models.

THE MIGHTY CRUNCH

Kids wanna rock? Plug into your Plexi and bow to the mighty crunch. Marshall amps of the company's first ten years are interesting for having thrown up classics of different eras—from the original JTM45 to the Plexiglas-panel JTM50/JMP50 of 1966–1969 (from whence the Plexi nickname is derived) or the metal-panel JMP50 of 1969–1972—that all bore the Model 1987 Lead Amp designation, despite some significant changes. As hallowed as the 1962–1966 Marshalls might be, and as desirable as those later metal-panel heads might still remain, the late 1960s Plexi is undoubtedly the pinnacle of Marshall amps for the rocker and typifies what we think of as "the Marshall sound" more than any other product the company has ever produced. Let's take a look at a gorgeous Plexi-panel JMP50 from around 1968, by which time the archetypal Plexi formula had been firmly established.

That's "despite some significant changes"—even if analyzed against the big picture, these changes might appear relatively slight or at least far less significant, say, than the changes wrought by Fender between the tweed Bassman of 1960 and the blond Bassman of 1960–1961, or by Gibson between the Les Paul of 1960 and the Les Paul/SG of 1961. This is mainly because, despite

being a very different looking amp, the JMP50's circuit is still a direct descendent of the circuit found in the 5F6-A tweed Fender Bassman of 1958–1960, upon which Jim Marshall based his original amp, the JTM45. The Plexi still had many significant elements that helped form the way the tweed Bassman did business, including the three-knob cathode-follower tone stack, presence control, long-tailed pair phase inverter, and a class AB output stage in fixed bias with a negative feedback loop to tighten up the performance. Poke your nose inside the chassis of the two—figuratively, please—and the component layouts are still virtually identical, aside from the mounting positions for the tubes. But the changes from JTM45 to JMP50 are certainly more impacting on this amp's performance than those from 5F6-A Bassman to JTM45, and while indeed relatively few in number, they are indeed significant.

The most obvious evolutionary trait, and the one most amp fans will point to first, is the move from the 5881/6L6/KT66 output tube types of the JTM45 (and Fender Bassman) to European EL34 tubes, bottles that became synonymous with British rock tone from 1967 onward. Not only did these tubes yield the now-famous Marshall crunch tone, the sound that helped define the genre, they could be driven at higher voltages to provide that louder amplifier that players were demanding, even in its "smaller" 50-watt version—an amp that could actually put out around 60 watts when pushed.

- Preamp tubes: Three ECC83s (12AX7) for first gain stage, cathode-follower tone stack, and long-tailed pair phase inverter
- Output tubes: Initially two EL34s; class AB, fixed-bias
- Rectifier: Solid-state diodes
- Controls: Volume Normal, Volume Bright, Treble, Bass, Middle, Presence
- Speakers: Four 20- or 25-watt Celestion G12M greenbacks, wired in series parallel, in closed-back 4x12-inch cabs
- Output: 50 to 60 watts RMS into a 16-ohm load

made the Marshall bolder and punchier and helped shape it into a better high-volume amp for rock lead playing. To further tighten up the low end, the big filter capacitors in the power supply were also upped from 22uF caps to 50uF caps, a value increase that partnered well with the move to solid-state rectification.

A less obvious alteration in the Plexi is found at the first preamp tube. Unlike the tweed Bassman and JTM45, the two triodes of the ECC83 (aka 12AX7) are now individually biased, which means each channel can be more independently voiced. The change allows Marshall to use a different bypass cap around the cathode-bias resistor of one side to create its notoriously crunchy bright channel (a .68uF cap). The spec bypass cap for the other channel is 320uF for a rounder, warmer sound. Note that Marshall had already upped the gain at this stage in the JTM45 by using the higher-gain ECC83/12AX7 instead of the mellower 12AY7 found in the Bassman. Also, because you could easily "jumper" these two channels together by running a short cord from the 2 input of the channel you'd plugged into to the 1 input of the other, you could blend the two as desired for some serious bang from this relatively simple preamp stage.

Despite the higher power, EL34s also compressed and broke up a little more quickly, and some would say more sweetly, than 6L6 types in a similar circuit. That gritty, chewy, slightly crispy-sounding EL34 grind is a standard of the heavy rock sound that was clearly established by Marshall and has been emulated by countless manufacturers ever since.

Perhaps the next most obvious change from Bassman/ JTM45 to Plexi was the move from GZ34 tube rectifier to solid-state diode rectification. Early Plexi-panel amps still wore the JTM prefix, but their rating was bumped up to 50, although for a time they simultaneously carried EL34s and a tube rectifier. In 1967, however, the company name evolved from Jim and Terry Marshall to Jim Marshall Products, and the initials on the panel were changed to reflect that.

Ramping up the DC voltages to the EL34s in a cranked Plexi requires yanking a whole lot of current through the rectifier (where AC from the power transformer is converted to the DC that lets the tubes do their thing) and would result in a lot of sag in a tube rectifier, creating a delayed note response and mushy playing feel at high volumes. Solid-state rectification took care of that, so while the rectifier isn't in the signal chain, it still contributes in a very real way to the sound and feel of the amp. This change

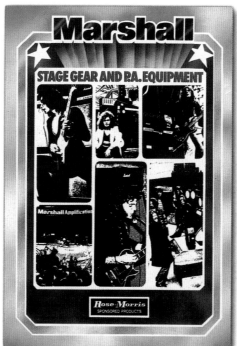

Trace a 1968 Plexi in detail and you'll find a few other minor changes, but these three outwardly simple alterations—and all the implications that go with them—are the biggies. Between them they account for what really is an entirely different amp from the Marshall flagship of two years before. Belt it all through a closed-back cab (or two) with four Celestion G12M greenbacks, or the bass-intended version of the G12H-30 that Jimi Hendrix favored, and you've got some serious rock action on tap.

This is the sound not only of Hendrix but of Jimmy Page, Paul Kossoff, Cream-era Eric Clapton, Eddie Van Halen, George Lynch, and so many others we could list them into tomorrow. Tap it, and feel which way the wind is blowing. ●

OPPOSITE LEFT. Marshall Plexi JMP50 head with a rare 1968 8x10-inch cabinet, all in custom white tolex. *Steven Seagal Collection/Rick Gould*

OPPOSITE RIGHT. Eddie Van Halen performs at London's Rainbow Theatre on October 22, 1978. *Fin Costello/Redferns/Getty Images*

AC/DC's Angus Young revels in the sound of his Marshall back line during the band's Black Ice World Tour at the Conseco Fieldhouse in Indianapolis, Indiana, on November 3, 2008. *Joey Foley/FilmMagic/Getty Images*

BRITISH PIONEER

Ah, the ones that got away—or, put more succinctly, the ones we gave away. It haunts any player and gearhound of "ahem" number of years—those of us who have had had ample opportunity to reflect on the tasty tidbits we sold or swapped in years past in the name of liquidity and have since come to regret the loss.

Some guitarists pine not for some dusty tweed box or faded, weather-checked slab of nitro-covered ash but a relatively recent piece of gear that resided briefly in our basements before taking wing to make its beautiful noise at the hands of another player.

We're talking WEM Dominator Mk III. Not the unusual and collectible wedge-shaped Watkins Dominator of the late 1950s that appears most notably in *The Tube Amp Book* by Aspen Pittman but the ungainly, uncelebrated Mk III version of this budget British tube amp that arrived after Watkins became WEM and graced so many school talent show stages around the United

Kingdom in the early 1970s. We acquired one of these in London in the late 1990s for about $150, played it in secret for a year or so, then sold it on for a small profit. It was really rather ugly, and its dusty, unkempt guts seemed a minor offense against thoughtful tube amp manufacturing everywhere. I just couldn't bring myself to love it—or to play it in public at least. Yet for all this, that amp sounded phenomenal. It was a sweetheart of chiming, crunchy, EL84-generated tone; possessed dynamics by the boat-load', and was just a killer little club/recording amp in every respect. Having fallen to reminiscing about this working-man's hero, we contacted a friend, Tim Moore, in London, whom we'd pointed toward another fine example of the Dom Mk III for his own use before moving back to the United States, to ask for a photo and an update. The photo you see before you. The update concluded, "It still sounds great, although it has taken to making odd crackling noises now and then, which might need to be seen to."

An early Watkins Dominator MK I amp. *Oliver Leiber Collection/Rick Gould*

- Preamp tubes: Three ECC83s (12AX7)
- Output tubes: Two EL84s, cathode-biased, no negative feedback
- Controls: Volume, Bass, and Treble on each of two channels, with Bright switch on channel 1
- Speaker: Single 12-inch Celestion (15-inch in Bass model)
- Output: 15 watts RMS

WEM founder Charlie Watkins was manufacturing guitar amplifiers branded with his own name even before major British players, such as Vox, and certainly Marshall, came into the game. Having started as an importer of guitars from Germany in 1954, he introduced his first Watkins amp, the 10-watt Westminster, in 1955. Despite being early on the scene, Watkins amps, and WEM amps after them, never ascended to the premier league of British-made gear. They were always satisfactory—not poorly built as such but not the most meticulously or ruggedly crafted pieces of gear either. Inspired by the success of Vox, Watkins started using the initials of his Watkins Electric Music for the bold three-letter acronym on his amps in the early 1960s. Despite considerate success in the "budget" sector of the day, the change demarcates the arrival of a less desirable amp from the collector's point of view.

But stuff all that. The Dominator Mk III, frumpy looking and rather dated though it might be (and not in a good way), is one righteous little beastie, and any semivintage combo you can bag for $250 or under that has its own distinct character is a winner in my book. Loosen the mounting screws and slide the slightly flimsy aluminum chassis out the back, and you'll discover a basic printed circuit board hand loaded with components of reasonable quality, including board-mounted preamp tube sockets (output tube sockets are chassis mounted) and even odd board-mounted potentiometers. The transformers are nothing to write home about, and the entire assemblage reeks of an effort to pinch a penny or two. But

hell, these amps came a lot cheaper than Voxes or Marshalls, or even Sound City or Selmer amps, and they made all the sounds a young rocker might desire.

The circuit is something of a blend of AC15 output stage and blackface Fender preamp. The full, independent tone stacks of each channel are sandwiched between the two gain stages provided by a dedicated ECC83 (12AX7) in each, a configuration that provides an effective EQ circuit while keeping the signal relatively taut and clear in the early stages (as compared to the gainier structure of a single treble-bleed tone control or the juicy, touch-sensitive performance of a cathode-follower tone stack). The long-tailed pair PI (with another ECC83) passes a robust signal along to two cathode-biased EL84 output tubes run at fairly low voltages, with no negative feedback, where a surprisingly toothsome tonal flurry ensues.

The Dom Mk III stays chirpy, sparkling, and well defined at lower volumes and eases into smooth, harmonically rich breakup when cranked. Close your eyes and there really is a surprising portion of the Vox AC15 magic going on here. It's different in certain nuanced ways, sure, but so is every vintage AC15 you'll ever line up. In short, it's a stunningly good, near-as-dammit, poor man's stand-in and a fun little amp in its own right.

Our own Dominator was actually a version dubbed the Dominator Bass Mk I, which we tended to forget then as now, since the aluminum plate mounted at a slant beneath the control panel, which carried both the control legends and the model name, was missing. The II used the exact same chassis and cab, and they are differentiated only by the fact that the Mk III carries a single 12 inch and the Bass Mk I a single 15 inch.

Herein lies one hip little nugget of a rub, though: the Dominator Bass Mk I carried an unusual and rather rare Rola Celestion G15M, a 15-inch speaker that wore an olive-green plastic magnet cover just like its smaller sibling and sounded for all the world like a bigger, beastlier greenback, despite its heartier 50-watt rating. Oh, brother, we're telling you—it was a holy terror with that speaker. We should have kept it for that driver alone. The Mk III version for guitar was sold with either a Rola Celestion G12M greenback or some less distinctive G12 variant. Happening stuff in either package.

Anybody out there on the other side of the pond got my old Dominator Bass Mk I? It's easy to recognize: some angry punk stripped it and spray painted it in an odd black finish—a dress befitting of its unsung tonal fury if a rather shameful abuse of a sweet little B-list beauty. ◉

Amp and photo courtesy Tim Moore

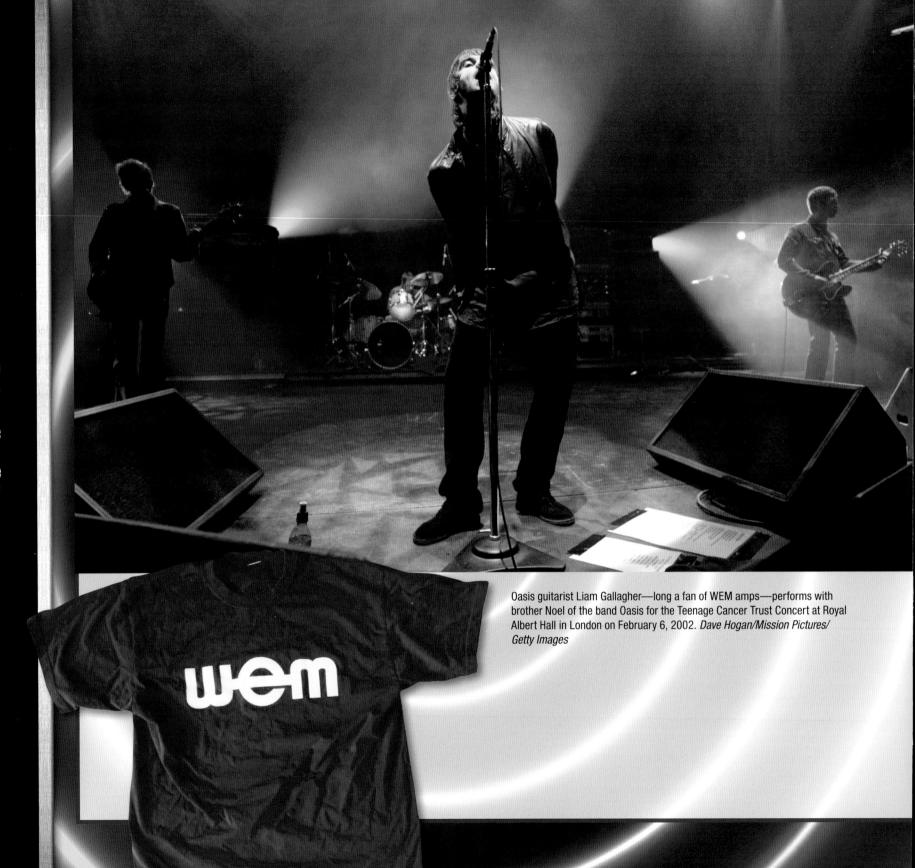

Oasis guitarist Liam Gallagher—long a fan of WEM amps—performs with brother Noel of the band Oasis for the Teenage Cancer Trust Concert at Royal Albert Hall in London on February 6, 2002. *Dave Hogan/Mission Pictures/ Getty Images*

A Watkins Joker amp with built-in Kopicat tape echo chamber. *Oliver Leiber Collection/Rick Gould*

Amp and photos courtesy Paul Moskwa/PM Blues

THE FULL STACK

Ah, the wind in your hair, the buzz in your ears, and the feel of a raging 100-watt Marshall stack in your gut. For several years the trend among guitarists was leaning toward 50-watters, the culmination of a drive to attain that desirable tube breakup at even moderately more tolerable volumes. But lately we seem to be seeing a return to the hefty 100, a new appreciation for that extra oomph the full dime gives you. It's not that a Super Lead is anything close to twice the volume of a Model 1987 JMP50—the perceived volume increase of 100 watts over 50 watts to the human ear is relatively minor. But the interaction of the larger output transformer with four EL34s, the increased body and headroom, and the way the bigger amp just breathes all combine to make a sizable impression on the player and the audience.

Circuit-wise, this Super Lead isn't much different than the 1968 JMP50 Model 1987 "Plexi" also featured in this book. Which, come to think of it, isn't *that* much different from the 1962 JTM45 featured in this book. Which isn't all that different from the late 1950s Fender 5F6-A tweed Bassman—well, you

get the picture. By the early 1970s the renowned Marshall stack seemed a very different beast from the tweed suitcase that begat it.

But from tweed Bassman to Super Lead runs what is really a fairly straight road, with just a few detours along the way for burgers and comfort stops—or voltage tweaks and tube changes anyway. Although, it has to be said, nothing along that evolutionary track looks quite like the red 1970 metal-panel Super Lead featured here, an early example from the company's much-vaunted custom color period. Not unlike Fender's custom colored Strats and Teles of the pre-CBS era, the mere fact that a cabinetmaker in the Marshall plant slapped on some red levant in place of black one day more than forty years ago means that this amp can be worth up to twice as much to the collector today. In good shape, though, they all rock supremely, whether black, red, purple, or puce.

In any case, enough of the cornerstone elements remain detectable in this Super Lead to enable us to trace a relatively straight line back through the earlier Marshalls to the tweed Bassman. Among these are its single ECC83/12AX7 gain stage (although the Bassman was specced with a mellower 12AY7), three-knob cathode-follower tone stack, long-tailed pair phase inverter, class AB output stage with a little negative feedback, and presence control. Tonally—in

Jimi Hendrix bathes in the sound of his
Marshall amp at the Bakersfield, California,
Civic Auditorium on October 26, 1968.
Michael Ochs Archives/Getty Images

- Preamp tubes: Three ECC83s (12AX7)
- Output tubes: Four EL34s, fixed-bias
- Rectifier: Solid-state
- Controls: Volume I, Volume II, Treble, Bass, Middle, Presence
- Output: Approximately 100 watts RMS (conservatively rated)

rough terms—these add up to firm lows and enough sonic tightness to cut through a loud stage mix, with lots of EQ versatility and touch sensitivity from the interactive tone stack and the retention of plenty of fidelity as the signal goes through the circuit stages.

More noticeable evolutionary changes along this road include the move to solid-state rectification (bigger, firmer, bolder), increased voltage levels at the output stage (louder, tighter), and the introduction of a High Treble channel for archetypal crispy-crunchy tones courtesy of a .68μF cathode bypass cap at the first gain stage, not to mention a wholesale move to EL34 output tubes. Enthusiasts also talk avidly of the different transformers that Marshall used over the years, raving variously about Radio Spares, Dagnall, Drake, and so forth, but the voice of these amps is primarily formed in the circuit and tubes. While different OTs might make each sound just a little different, they all sound great and characteristically "Marshall," and preferences are likely to come down to taste—and other variables—as much or more than to differences in transformer design.

Whether you were playing this through Celestion's 25-watt G12M or 30-watt G12H speakers (both green-backs in the day, thank you very much, and pre-Rolas too if they were from production earlier in the year), with 75Hz lead or 55Hz bass cone resonance according to taste, you were likely to need more than just the one 4x12 cab if you were going to crank it at all. Four speakers and a 100-watt power handling, or even 120 watts, was always taking a risk with one of these monsters wound up to full whack. Those four EL34s could hit peaks well beyond the amp's 100-watt RMS rating, taking out a speaker or two as they did. Pile up

two 4x12s for the full stack, however, and you were soaring heavenward on buoyant waves of near-tangible sonic splendiferousness.

While many players and collectors alike rave about the glories of the Plexis of 1967–1969, the aluminum-panel amps of the early 1970s were, in the long haul, responsible for just as much great music and very possibly more. Either represents what we think of as "classic Marshall"—both more so than the JTM45 that launched the brand, with its tube rectification and more American-sounding 5881 or KT66 output tubes—but these metal-fronted Super Leads are far more accessible to the average player today than their Plexiglas predecessors (when they aren't covered in an original custom color at least). Just the thought of it kinda makes you want to strap on the Les Paul and rock, doesn't it?

No matter what kind of music you play, every guitarist out there has a soft spot for a Marshall stack. In just a few years, the arrival of the printed circuit board and the master volume would demarcate the end of the vintage years for Marshall. The brand kept rocking in grand style, sure, but these early hand-wired models are the ones to jack into.

Free's Paul Kossoff supported by a back-line wall of Marshall amps in 1970. *Jan Persson/Redferns/Getty Images*

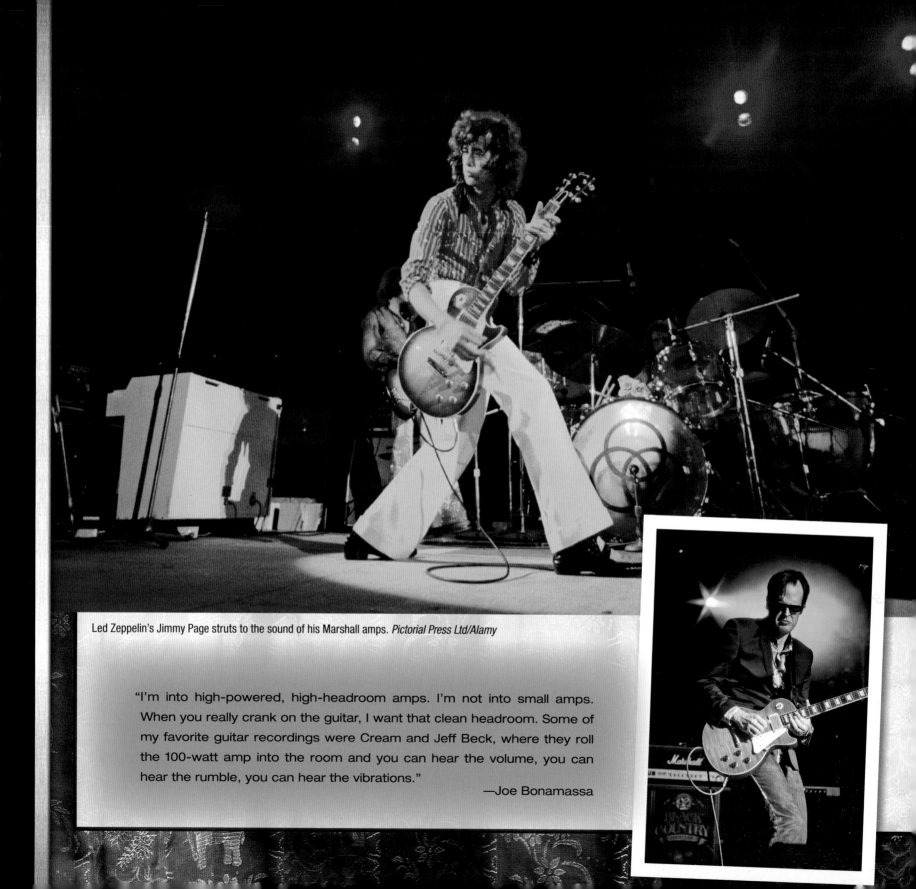

Led Zeppelin's Jimmy Page struts to the sound of his Marshall amps. *Pictorial Press Ltd/Alamy*

"I'm into high-powered, high-headroom amps. I'm not into small amps. When you really crank on the guitar, I want that clean headroom. Some of my favorite guitar recordings were Cream and Jeff Beck, where they roll the 100-watt amp into the room and you can hear the volume, you can hear the rumble, you can hear the vibrations."

—Joe Bonamassa

Backed by a wall of Marshalls, Cream plays its final show, at London's Royal Albert Hall on November 26, 1968. From left, Jack Bruce, Eric Clapton, and Ginger Baker. *Estate of Keith Morris/Redferns/Getty Images*

OPPOSITE. Marshall fanatic Joe Bonamassa.
Courtesy J & R Adventures

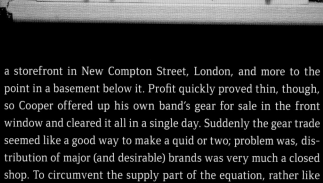

LOUD WITH A BRITISH ACCENT

Like a pendulum do? You'd better believe it. We don't recall whether the sound system in Austin Powers' E-type "Shaguar" was made by Orange, but it bloody well should have been. If any musical venture embodied England of the Swinging Sixties, it had to be Orange. And we mean the entire Orange enterprise, as ambitious as it initially was, not just the amplifiers that have carried the brand forward into the twenty-first century. In fact, when founded by musician and wannabe music producer Cliff Cooper in 1968, the Orange brand did not even span amplifier production. It encompassed music publishing, a record label, an agency, and a recording studio, all housed in a storefront in New Compton Street, London, and more to the point in a basement below it. Profit quickly proved thin, though, so Cooper offered up his own band's gear for sale in the front window and cleared it all in a single day. Suddenly the gear trade seemed like a good way to make a quid or two; problem was, distribution of major (and desirable) brands was very much a closed shop. To circumvent the supply part of the equation, rather like Jim Marshall six years before, Cooper decided, "If people want this stuff so bad, I should make it myself."

Orange amplifiers proper were born soon after and quickly made a name for themselves, their all-encompassing image making the hip new product impossible to miss. The amps were Orange, and the amps *were* orange. Or occasionally black by custom order. But the Orange esthetic extended to far more than just the color of the cabinets' vinyl covering. From the vintage computer graphic control legends to the hippie-chic logo, these things were stylized to the max—front, back, inside, and out. The odd "British Empire meets Bacchanalia" coat of arms gets the prize, though, adorned as it is with, to the left, a goat-man figure described in the company's 1970 catalog as "the god of nature and hypnotic

CIRCA 1971 ORANGE GRAPHIC OVERDRIVE GRO100

- Preamp tubes: Two ECC83s (12AX7)
- Output tubes: Four EL34s, fixed-bias
- Rectifier: Solid-state
- Controls: FAC, Bass, Treble, HF Drive, Gain
- Output: Approximately 100 watts RMS (conservatively rated)

music," with good old bare-shouldered Britannia to the right and beneath it all the "Voice of the World" motto in the musical stave banner, a hilariously ambitious declaration for a toddler of a company. While all this sounds like the story of a guy looking for any angle that would make him money in the music industry, Cooper, to his credit, sought out quality from the start, both in design and manufacture. Chassis weren't merely painted orange but were coated in baked-on enamel for a long, corrosion-free life; transformers were robust and significantly oversized; and components were of a good pedigree throughout.

Early Orange amplifiers were made by Matamp in Huddersfield in the north of England, but production was moved to a plant in the London suburb of Bexleyheath in time for the first classic original Orange models to come along in late 1970 or early 1971. The mighty Graphic Overdrive, or GRO100, is right up there among them. With four EL34 output tubes, solid-state rectification, and that hefty output transformer, this thing pounds out massive clean to crunchy tones. There are a mere two ECC83 (12AX7) tubes in the preamp, providing two gain stages and a cathodyne (split-phase) phase inverter with preceding driver stage. From the left-side inputs working to the right, the first rather enigmatic control is Orange's famed FAC (frequency analyzing control), graphically illustrated with sine waves of decreasing amplitude. It is simply a six-way tone switch not unlike Gibson's Vari-Tone or the tone switch on the EF86 channel of a Matchless DC30, but here it is placed between input and first gain stage rather than after. The other mystery knob on the front is the HF (high-frequency) drive (with a rather menacing fist

graphic), also sometimes listed as "boost," which is essentially a twist on a presence control. Otherwise, it's all pretty straightforward, with independent bass and treble controls (bass and treble clefs, respectively) and a volume control beneath the blasting speaker graphic. The jacks beneath the Swiss Alps are echo send and return—and FX loop intended for reverb or tape delay—and the lightning bolt of course indicates the power switch.

Around the back, earlier examples, such as this one, display the odd-numbered output impedance values that many British makers used, with selections for 3.75Ω, 7.5Ω, and 15Ω. There's also a slave out. The owner of this head, Nick Santore, added a standby switch on the back panel, a useful feature that wasn't original to this beast. Circuit-wise, unusual features of this design (and Orange amps that followed) are its split-phase PI, a rare topology post-1960s in any amp of this wattage, and the Baxendall tone stack, a remnant from the hi-fi world that enables just two potentiometers to craft a wide range of variation in EQ (which, some might add, is not always well applied to the guitar, although it works here).

The current caretaker of this GRO100 acquired it in 2003 from the original owner in California, who used it briefly and then literally stored it in the closet for twenty-five years. Santore tells us that he modified the preamp circuit slightly to be closer to that of the OR120 introduced in 1972, which has a gainier preamp that helped secure Orange's fame with rock players. A fairly simple alteration, the OR120 virtually flip-flops the preamp circuit of the GRO100, placing the tone and volume controls between two gain stages and the six-way FAC switch after, between preamp and PI. Otherwise, this example retains virtually all its original components and is in excellent condition, a crack in the corner of its rare early Plexiglas front panel notwithstanding. Tone-wise, Santore tells us: "Like any old-style Orange, it has a very unique sound to it. Although it's very loud, it doesn't have much headroom to speak of, and overdrive is really its forte. Being non–master volume, it transitions gradually into a wonderful 3D, tubey breakup, with a prickly, fuzzy character to it that's very pleasing to the ear. When overdriven, the amp gives the term *fat* a new meaning. The FAC knob progressively adds girth, gain, and the infamous Orange amp 'fog' as you click it left."

Orange achieved moderate success into the mid 1970s, then faded into the background and a general state of hibernation through little else than Cliff Cooper's own frustration with a changing amp market. The company's return to the fore in the 1990s, with Cooper at the helm once again, has been well received in the rock world and has brought another classic British voice back to the guitar world.

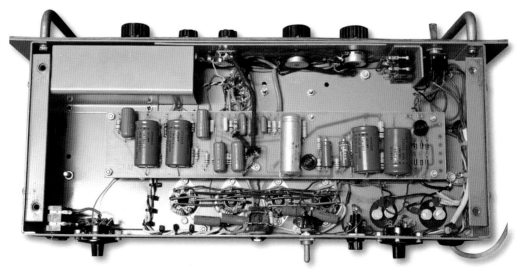

With a back line of Orange amps, Fleetwood Mac performs at the Royal Albert Hall, London, in 1969. From left: Jeremy Spencer on keyboards, Danny Kirwan, Mick Fleetwood, John McVie, and Peter Green. *Michael Putland/Getty Images*

Orange fan Marc Bolan of T. Rex in 1973. *Marty Temme/WireImage/Getty Images*

A MARSHALL BY ANOTHER NAME

For younger guitar-playing residents of the United Kingdom, the Park name mostly conjures up images of small, budget-priced, solid-state, sub-Marshall beginner's combos. In recent years, the make has survived as a stepping-on brand to the big boy of British amplification, much as Squier is to Fender or Epiphone is to Gibson. British players of a certain vintage, however, and their clued-in Yank counterparts, will already be swooning over visions of Park amps that were entirely different from the little Far Eastern–made chipboard-and-tranny boxes of today. To such guitarists, the Park name means "vintage Marshall," but with a twist.

The Park story makes an interesting sidebar to the history of Marshall. In the mid 1960s, Jim Marshall signed a fifteen-year agreement, selling exclusive distribution rights for Marshall amps to UK music industry giant Rose Morris. But to sidestep the limitations of this deal and to continue supplying amps to Birmingham music store owner Johnny Jones—who had previously distributed Marshalls in northern England—Marshall initiated the Park line. The amps were made in the same English factory as all the other Marshall amps, and early models featured circuits that were virtually identical to the Big M's main models, with variations in cabinetry, cosmetics, and control layouts to differentiate them. Very soon, though, Marshall and his engineers started to have some fun with Park amps, perhaps experimenting with a few little mods they had been considering for their main line but couldn't risk on their flagship models without testing the waters first.

The Park Lead 50 shown here doesn't look or sound quite like any particular Marshall, although it's similar to many classic models. We encountered two of them while living in London a few years ago but have never seen another and haven't even heard of one in existence in the United States. This one was in the New King's Road Vintage Guitar Emporium; the other was for sale in Chandler Guitars in Kew in southwestern London. The latter is pictured in the revised edition of Aspen Pittman's *The Tube Amp Book,* which has photographs of other extremely cool Parks, along with a little more history on the brand. Some confusion remains regarding the date of manufacture of this model; they were thought to have been made in 1972, but Marshall didn't introduce its own master volume models until 1975, so this Park is probably from closer to

- Preamp tubes: Three ECC83s (plus one for reverb)
- Output tubes: Two EL34s, fixed-bias
- Controls: Input Gain, Reverb Gain, Bass, Mid, Treble, Edge, Output Level
- Speaker: Single 12-inch Celestion
- Output: 50 watts RMS, conservatively rated

Flanked by their Park amp head, Fugazi performs at New York City's Roseland Ballroom on September 24, 1993. *Steve Eichner/Getty Images*

that period. (If you have the inside scoop, please let us know!) It's entirely possible, of course, that they were trying out the master circuit on their lesser-known Parks, and certainly other manufacturers were using master volume controls before this time.

Whatever its vintage, it's an extremely cool variation on the Marshall theme. Internally, the raw ingredients of the Lead 50 aren't a million miles from the late 1960s Marshall "Plexi." Although the topology is roughly the same, there are plenty of details that make this little screamer a different beast. For one, we're looking at a printed circuit board (PCB) design rather than the turret board format of the earlier Marshalls and Parks. The front panel controls include Input Gain (preamp gain); Reverb Gain (depth/mix); an "Equalization" section with Bass, Mid, Treble, and Edge; and Output Level. That final control is the master Volume, and you could label the Edge control Presence and it would still do the same thing. Essentially, this is the classic Fender Bassman–derived circuit with a cathode-follower tone stack, a Presence tap in the negative feedback loop, and a fixed-bias class AB output stage.

The amp uses ECC83s (aka 12AX7s) in the preamp, reverb driver, and PI stages and two EL34s in the output stage, while rectification is from solid-state diodes. But rather than use the twin triodes of the first preamp tube to feed two channels, the Lead 50 has just one channel but allows you to tap the gain stages either individually or in series—via its Low and Gain Boost inputs—to route the signal through just one triode for clean tones or through both for driving lead tones. A stereo foot switch jack on the back panel facilitates reverb on/off switching and boost switching when a standard two-button foot switch is connected.

"Aha! The JCM800 preamp!" you declare, and certainly the Lead 50's series gain stages in Gain Boost mode are not unlike the hot Marshall introduced in 1981—or indeed the

lead circuit of the Mesa/Boogie MkI of some years before. This Park has a pumped, rockin' tone to back up the theory too. We recall its sound—classic Marshall EL34 crunch tones with a juicy playability and excellent dynamics at lower/medium volumes, and sizzling neo-vintage lead voicings with the gain maxed—with a fondness seasoned with the bitter sting of loss. Yeah, we all should have bought one of the damn things, or both. At the time—just five years ago—they were selling in the £350 to £450 ballpark, which was 500 to 750 of our then healthier U.S. dollars. Ah, the gut-twisting wisdom of hindsight.

A hot, big-sounding amp, yet fairly compact for a 50-watt fire breather. The entire shebang is packaged in a closed-back 1x12-inch combo that hides a high-powered Celestion ceramic G12 behind the hip checkered grille cloth. The unusual but functional front-mounted control panel is also a new twist for a Marshall product.

While the rarity of the 1960s Parks and their similarity to highly prized Marshall "Plexi" and metal-panel models finds them commanding astronomical prices on the vintage market today, many early 1970s Parks are also priced in the stratosphere while some Marshalls from the era are relative bargains. Bigger heads go for $3,000 plus, and a little 20-watt combo from the mid 1970s recently listed for $2,799. But then again, these are Marshalls in everything but name, and a nifty detour in the history of that mighty maker to boot, so the interest is hardly surprising. Hell, a rock monster by any other name still roars as loud. ●

Park fan David Grissom performs with Joe Ely in Austin, Texas, on April 16, 2010. *Jay West/WireImage/Getty Images*

LEADING THE REVOLUTION OF CASCADING GAIN

High-gain lead tones are so commonplace today that it's difficult to recall what a revolution—and revelation—the sound was when it first came along.

Sizzling preamp-generated overdrive is stock in trade for makers like Soldano, Bogner, Rivera, Engl, VHT, and many others. Peavey's 5150 and Crate's BlueVoodoo perform similar tricks, as do plenty of models from great originators such as Fender and Marshall. Chain 'em all together and that's enough cascaded triode gain stages to go to the moon and back (or so we'd like to imagine), and they all owe a tip of the cap to the Godfather of Gainsville—the square little Mesa/Boogie combo.

Consider what was available in the late 1960s and early 1970s, when this little hot rod first came along: rock was big-stage music back in the day, and the best-sounding gig-ready amps, which at the time meant a minimum of 50 watts, had to be cranked up to deafening levels before they'd generate the

kind of creamy, sustaining, fully saturated lead tones that sizzled enough to satisfy ever more gain-hungry tastes. Then along comes this little combo in a cabinet just barely big enough to contain its 12-inch speaker. And while it can roar pretty ably alongside a Marshall half stack, it can also produce singing, sustain-for-days tone at club-volume levels. Whoa, Nelly!

The tone originally arrived in the form of approximately two hudnred modified Fender Princeton combos, into which Mesa designer and founder Randall Smith squeezed a revised circuit, seriously upgraded transformers, and a 12-inch JBL or EVM speaker. The very first, built in 1967, was done as a practical joke on a guitarist who had dropped off his little Princeton for servicing. (Oh, how they must have laughed!) As choppable Princetons ran thin, Smith decided to manufacture amps from the ground up. In 1971 or 1972, the first Boogies appeared (dubbed simply Mark I after the Mark II appeared circa 1980). They were initially covered in a faux snakeskin, then became available in black or cream Tolex or a range of polished hardwood cabinets.

Backed by his Mesa Boogie combo, Jimmie Vaughan carves out a blue note in June 1984 in New York City. *L. Busacca/Larry Busacca/WireImage/Getty Images*

CIRCA 1977 MESA/BOOGIE MARK I

- Preamp tubes: Three 12AX7s
- Output tubes: Two 6AL6s
- Rectifier: Silicon diodes
- Controls: Volume 1 (pull Mid Boost), Volume 2 (pull Bright), Master, Treble, Bass, Middle; Presence on back panel
- Speakers: One JBL D-120E
- Output: 60 watts RMS

Suddenly, everyone had to have one, and practically everyone who was anyone did. The catalog I ordered as a kid in the late 1970s, drooled over, and still possess lists among "well-known players with Boogie amplifiers" Carlos Santana, the Kinks, Frank Zappa, Waylon Jennings, Wishbone Ash, Joe Walsh, Ted Nugent, Pete Townshend, the Blue Oyster Cult, Steve Cropper, Keith Richards, Ron Wood, Jerry Garcia, Bruce Springsteen, Christopher Cross, Leo Sayer (huh?), and on and on. Only one among them has remained a notable Boogie endorsee, but it's a safe bet that they all did play through the little beastie at one time or another.

Back in 1977 or so, when the Mesa/Boogie Mark I rolled out of the workshop in Lagunitas, California, it was a hot item. When I finally saved up enough grass money (from the kind you mow) in 1981 to order my own Mark IIB straight from the factory—the only way you could get them back then—we had to wait five months for delivery, and when it finally arrived, that cream-covered beauty was the talk of the town. And man, carting it to London, we gained *mucho* respect from every studio and live-sound engineer who had the honor of miking it up, along with more than a few envious leers from British guitarists—a humbling "oversexed, overpaid, and over here" kind of vibe, for sure.

After gigging that sizzling Mark IIB for ten years, we were bitten by the vintage-toned, non-master-volume bug, as were so many players who graduated from the preamp-generated-overdrive school to the sultry pleasures of a simpler signal chain. But that's not to devalue the achievements of the Boogie template, which continues to be the preferred means to excesses of saturation for countless shred, contemporary rock, and nu-metal players. With hindsight, the route that Smith took to achieve this over-the-top gain appears obvious, even simple, but it is devilishly clever.

Where most tube guitar amps' preamp stages had one or two gain stages (the second usually to make up gain lost as the signal ran through level-sapping EQ stages), Smith gave his Mark I a walloping four gain stages between Input 1 and the phase inverter, with two Volume (gain) controls and a Master along the way, plus Treble, Bass, and Middle controls, with a Presence on the back panel. By ramping the gain up high from one stage to spill its 12AX7-generated distortion over into the following stage—a process that came to be known as cascading gain—where it could be dialed up even further, with overall volume levels finally set by the Master, placed after the fourth triode in the chain, previously unattainable degrees of overdrive could be generated right from the amp, resulting in sizzling tones and endless sustain.

While from the Mark IIs onward Boogies became famous for their seminal foot switchable lead channels, the Mark I had no foot switch. You plugged into Input 1 for the full-blast, four-stage lead preamp (with pull Mid Boost on Volume 1) or Input 2 for a more restrained, Fenderish tone generated by a mere three gain stages, with a Pull Bright switch on Volume 2. All this complex circuitry was achieved right from the start of the official production versions with a printed circuit board, although one was etched and hand-wired by Smith himself in the early days, later with help from his wife, Rayven. In many ways, Mesa Engineering deserves acknowledgment as an early force in the boutique amp market.

The fine hardwood-cab Boogie shown here is the 60-watt version, sans the optional five-band graphic EQ or reverb. These bonus features were popular, as was the 100-watt option, which came with a 60/100-watt switch on the front panel alongside the Standby and Power switches. Back panel facilities—Presence, Reverb, speaker outs, effects loop—were endearingly distinguished by stick-on DYMO labels. Boogie output ratings were always a little liberal, and these amps generally put out something closer to around 45 watts in low-power mode and 90 watts with all four 6L6s roaring, but who's counting. Also, the Boogie has often been billed as a modified 4x10-inch Fender Bassman circuit, but, in addition to the obvious cascading gain, several details make it very unlike a tweed Bassman. It doesn't have the Bassman's lauded cathode-follower tone stack but something a little more akin to a blackface tone stack placed between gain stages, and of course Boogie Mark Series amps all used solid-state rectification. But again, so what? It is what it is, and it does what it does, with bells on. 🎱

Keith Richards at his home in upstate New York in 1978 with guitar and Mesa Boogie amp. *Michael Putland/Getty Images*

As ubiquitous as the little 1x12-inch Mesa/Boogie Mark Series combo has become over the past thirty-five years—and as large and successful as the company has grown to be—it is with a hint of nostalgia that we recall a time when the world's leading guitarists had to plead their case on the phone with Randy Smith himself to jump the months-long waiting list for amps the Boogie creator was turning out one by one from his California home. Here we poke our noses into the interior of Boogie serial number A804, built in early 1977, the first of several such amps that Rolling Stone Keith Richards would purchase—that's right, purchase—and play on tour and in the studio. Currently owned by Boogie enthusiast Ian Dickey of Bangor, Maine, and generally known for posterity as Keef's El Mocambo Boogie, it's a Mark I 60/100-watt model with reverb, five-band graphic EQ, Altec speaker, and export transformer, housed in a hardwood combo cab. At the time of the Mark I (so-called only after the Mark II came

out), the Mesa/Boogie was not a channel switcher, but had two inputs to directly access different preamp configurations. Input 1 tapped the Lead channel with four stages of 12AX7-fired gain, and Input 2 tapped three stages in the Rhythm channel for a more hot-rodded Fender style tone. Foot switchable or not, as Richards, the Stones, and countless hundreds of thousands of fans could no doubt attest, this Boogie still rocked like the friggin' bejaysus.

Famous as the little club that big acts liked to play when they wanted to get real for a gig or two, Toronto's El Mocambo hosted the Rolling Stones for two nights in early March 1977. They were the first proper club dates the band had played in fourteen years and served as a recording venue for what would become side three of the album *Love You Live*, as well as a warm-up of sorts for a forthcoming arena tour. Check out any of a handful of photos of the shows that have been in circulation over the years (none of which would be released for publication by the time of going to print), and you're likely to see this hardwood-cab Boogie just over Richards' shoulder, standing on top of an unmiked Ampeg rig set up as a spare. From some angles, the characteristic cigarette burn Richards had already scorched into the cab above the Treble knob is visible. Second guitarist Ronnie Wood is also playing a Boogie—one manufactured hot on the heels of Keith's A804 Mark I. Heady times.

So how did it all unfold? According to Mesa/Boogie founder Randy Smith, it started, as so many things do, with an unexpected phone call.

"The phone rang—and at this point it was a cottage industry and I did everything—so I picked it up, and it was [Stones pianist] Ian Stewart. He said, 'We're interested in trying a Boogie amplifier.' They'd heard a lot about them and wanted to try one, and would I just send some to them. I said, 'I really can't do that. I'm just a one-person shop here. I don't give away amps.' And he said, 'We're the Rolling Stones. We don't pay for amps.'"

So our contenders were at a stalemate, it would seem, until our pioneering amp builder kicked it up a notch.

"Meanwhile, I could hear Keith in the background," Smith continues. "He was talking to Ian, telling him what to say. So I said, 'Is that Keith? Put him on, would you please?' So Keith comes on the line, and he's just the best—superfriendly guy—and he says, 'Hey man. How you doing? Yeah, I'd love to get my hands on one of your amplifiers.' We went through the same thing as with Ian, and he said, 'Well, it just doesn't seem right. We haven't paid for gear in forever. We just don't pay for gear.' And I said, 'Well, I just don't give gear away because it's all I've got. I'm basically just a starving cat here, and besides, if I was going to give gear away, wouldn't I be better off giving it to some guy—whether he's a broken-down blues player or an up-and-coming guy—who truly couldn't afford it?' And he kinda said, 'Yeah, I guess so.'

"And—I'd probably been toking up myself, so I really stepped out on the plank here—I said, 'Keith, look at it this way: you guys are just getting ready to go out on tour, and you're going to be raking in huge bucks. Now, I know the tax bracket you're

in. Pay for the amp, and if you don't like it, you've got two choices. Send it back and I'll give you a full refund. But a better option in light of your tax situation would be, people are trying to get their hands on these things, I've got a backlog that's endless, so if you don't like the amp, you'd be better off just to sell it and take the cash, which you've already written off for tour expenses, and go buy drugs with it.'

"There was a long pause, and I thought, 'Uh-oh, I might have gone a step too far.' And after this pregnant pause, he comes back and says, 'Well yeah, mate. That would be a really good idea, except I already know I want the amp. There's no doubt about that. I played Santana's when he sat in with us. I don't want just one amp, I want six of 'em.' So that amp that Ian [Dickey] has is one of that first six. Over the years, the number that the Stones have bought and paid for is up to forty-two."

After the El Mocambo dates and recordings, the Boogie was used for the *Some Girls* sessions and further live dates, then was returned to Mesa for servicing in 1992–1993 before going on Richards' X-Pensive Winos tour. Sometime during the Stones' epic Forty Licks tour of 2002–2003, the Boogie A804 was given to Stones guitar tech Pierre de Beauport, who in turn sold it to Outlaw Guitars. An investment broker purchased it from Outlaw and sold it on to Billy Penn, who hipped our current owner to its existence in 2005 and sold it to him in 2007.

Having been put through the intensive Stones CSI for authentication by Dickey and others, this Boogie's lineage leaves little to the imagination. In addition to the serial number linking it directly to the Richards purchase, we have the telltale cigarette burns, evidence of blue gaffer tape with "KR" that formerly adorned the amp's top, Smith's own "Stones" legend in faded Sharpie on the sidewall of the chassis, and several other distinguishing marks. And after all it has been through, it's still as mean and raucous as it was churning out "Honky Tonk Women," "Crackin' Up," and "Brown Sugar" on Friday, March 4, 1977, shortly after Randy Smith himself had delivered it into Keith Richards' hands in Toronto. All in all, this little box is about as formidable a chunk of rock's gear history as you're likely to stumble upon. 🎱

After taking the order for A804, Randall Smith marked both sidewalls of the chassis in Sharpie.

The serial number, stamped into the cabinet.

The bottom of the chassis of A804 has Randall Smith's initials and tube-socket designations in Sharpie.

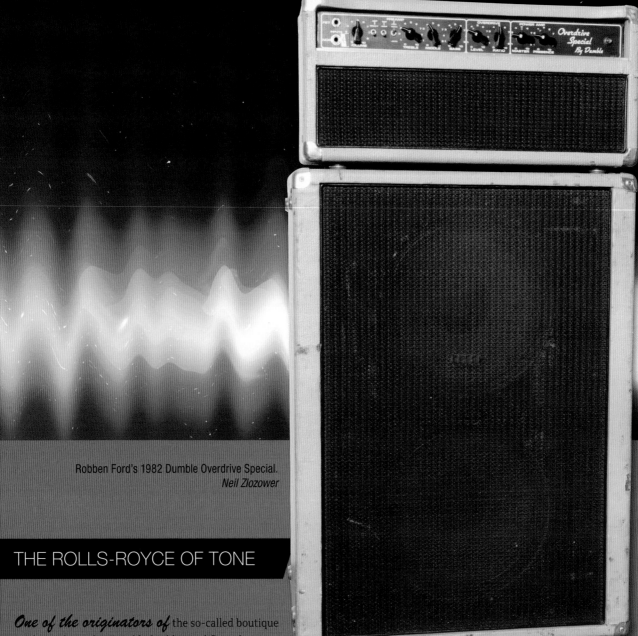

Robben Ford's 1982 Dumble Overdrive Special.
Neil Zlozower

THE ROLLS-ROYCE OF TONE

One of the originators of the so-called boutique market, Alexander Dumble builds amplifiers that now reach far, far above even that gilded label. Easily one of the two most desirable names out there, alongside Ken Fischer, Dumbles are also somewhat like Fischer's Trainwrecks in that specific long-running Dumble "models" do exist, although no two amps are quite the same. Each is crafted one at a time, by hand, by the man himself and is tweaked toward his idea of tonal perfection along the way—with the desires of the paying client supposedly given consideration too. If there has been any semiconsistent template of Dumble tone, however, it has to be the Overdrive Special, and one could do a lot worse than to probe the example that we have on hand: Robben Ford's very own amplifier.

Known as one of the premier tone machines in the history of guitar, thanks in no small part to Robben Ford's own fingers, this blond Overdrive Special simply drips with the good stuff. This amp is thick, creamy, and warm leaning, but with plenty of definition and harmonically saturated edge and cutting power. In short, it is archetypal Dumble. Alexander Dumble built the first Overdrive Special in 1972 and has continued to manufacture them in his southern California shop more or less steadily ever since, by custom order only, alongside other models such as the Dumbleland, Overdrive Reverb, and Steel String Singer, the latter frequently used by Stevie Ray Vaughan later in his career.

Backed by his Dumble, Robben Ford performs at the Montreux Jazz Festival in Montreux, Switzerland, on July 16, 2007. *Lionel Flusin/Gamma-Rapho via Getty Images*

Dumble Overdrive Special. *Amp and photos courtesy Bruce Sandler/Guitar Exchange*

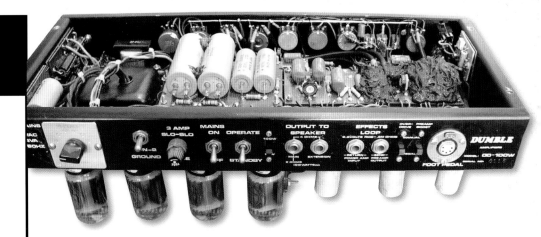

1982 DUMBLE OVERDRIVE SPECIAL

- Preamp tubes: Three 7025s (12AX7 types)
- Output tubes: Four 6L6GCs, fixed-bias
- Rectifier: Solid state
- Controls: Volume, Treble, Middle, Bass, Overdrive Level and Ratio, Master, Presence
- Output: Approximately 100 watts RMS

Are Dumbles really the holy grail of tone or just slightly overblown custom amps inflated out of proportion by the difficulty of acquiring one and the eye-popping list of major artists who swear by them? In 2008 Ford himself told a video team from Harmony Central, with this very amp glowing in the background, "Dumbles are just incomparable amplifiers. You just can't touch them. People have gotten close here and there, but overall Dumble's the king."

More workaday players who have experienced a Dumble in person report a broad range of reactions, though the majority do fall into the "blown away" category. Certainly endorsement by the likes of Larry Carlton, Eric Johnson, Carlos Santana, Sonny Landreth, our pals Ford and Vaughan, and others attests to something. For one, this list points us toward the smooth, singing, thousand-pound-violin-tone camp, perhaps not the preferred voice for players seeking raw, gut-bucket rock 'n' roll tones. Refinement of tone might be one way of putting it.

Regardless, if the stork left a surprise Dumble on your doorstep, you would take it in and feed it, given that recent new builds purportedly go for upward of $20,000 and that used examples can sell in the $30,000 to $40,000 range and have gone for as much as $50,000 thanks to the fact that fewer than three hundred of these amps exist out there. Not too bad a return on an initial investment of some $2,000 thirty years ago, which no doubt seemed like a lot at the time.

An existing 1990 price sheet tells us that Dumble offered the same amp at three different prices according to how long you were willing to wait. An Overdrive Special, for example, cost $2,135 for a "standard" wait (twenty-four to thirty-six months), $3,650 for "express-180" (days, that is), and $5,150 for "express-60," with a guaranteed two-month completion on the latter. The only problem, however, was that this price sheet has "CLOSED" hand scrawled over the prices in the "standard" column, so your short-of-pocket but willing-to-wait player was out of luck. Interestingly, the same price sheet offered Dumble's telephone consultation services at $200 for chats of ten minutes or less.

The Overdrive Special is essentially a high-gain American-style amplifier based on a quartet of 6L6 output tubes, although a handful have been made with EL34s for a more British flavor. As the name implies, its raison d'être is the generation of "smokin' lead tones," the kind of tube-generated overdrive that induces a creamy, tactile playing feel and a fat and harmonically rich soundstage. It apparently has its roots in highly modified Fender amps, but the model, as evolved, is so far away from Leo's template as to be an entirely original design, and then some. That said, Dumble has always retained the basic eyelet board construction technique.

Circuit topology aside, some keys to the Overdrive Special's sonic virtuosity are Dumble's use of individually hand-measured and -matched components, custom spec transformers, immaculate wire dress, careful signal path routing, and other fine points of the amp builder's art.

Using two 12AX7s in the preamp and another in the long-tailed pair phase inverter, the amp includes foot-switchable clean and overdrive channels. The former takes the signal through a gain stage, then a passive three-knob tone stack and volume control, and then a gain makeup stage before sending it on to the output stage. In lead mode, another two gain stages are brought in after those of the clean mode, governed by additional gain and level controls, with a final master volume to set the output level of both channels. There's also a Fenderish presence control to tweak high-end content and three mini-toggle switches labeled Bright, Mid Boost (or Deep), and Rock/Jazz to voice the preamp. In addition to the Normal input, the amp includes an FET input originally intended for piezo pickups, which routes the signal through an FET preamp stage prior to the first tube gain stage. In all, the Overdrive Special offers a lot of sizzling goodness for the guitarist who wants to drive home that chewy, saturated tone.

You want one? Suffice to say, the chances are slim—very slim—unless you want to go with the copyists. Despite Dumble's longtime practice of covering much of his circuit in masking epoxy, plenty of "cloners" have undertaken the effort of reproducing some degree of the Dumble mojo. Makers such as Two Rock, Bludotone, Brown Note, and others offer their homage to the Overdrive Special, while Malaysian maker Ceriatone sells a popular Overtone Special as a kit or prebuilt amplifier. Do they come close? We could ask Robben Ford, but he is probably too busy groovin' on the real thing.

AN AMP NAMED NANCY

The world's most desirable amplifier? Aside from any "standard" vintage amps that have been elevated through their associations with major artists, the few original-design, made-by-hand amps out there that wear the Dumble and Trainwreck brands have long been the most desirable lines on the planet.

Given that tone guru Ken Fischer is no longer with us, Trainwrecks are arguably fixed to an even higher standard by the laws of supply and demand. Please welcome, then, this rare appearance of "Nancy," an early Trainwreck Express model built by Fischer in 1986 in his New Jersey shop. One of what is believed by its maker's own estimation to be "probably one hundred Trainwrecks in the world," Nancy (Fischer used women's names on his amps rather than serial numbers) is nevertheless no under-glass collector's piece but a living, (fire) breathing tone machine that has continued to pay her way in the hands of hardworking musicians since rolling out of the shop more than twenty-five years ago, and that's more than you can say for a lot of the $35,000 vintage gear out there.

Owned for the past five years by guitarist and producer Matte Henderson, who has worked with everyone from Henry Kaiser and Robert Fripp to Jewel and Natalie Merchant, Nancy was previously played for many years by a hard-gigging guitarist from Texas, whose taped-on notes "5" and "6" still adorn the input and speaker outs, reminders of which cable goes where.

Although Fischer maintained two relatively steady models in the Liverpool and the Express, and added the Rocket to the lineup a few years later, each amp really was an individual creation, and no two were exactly alike. Each was tweaked to suit his evolving notions of perfect tone and to meet the desires of the player for whom he was building it. Components also varied throughout the decade and a half that he was manufacturing amps. Recalling his first encounter with Trainwreck, Henderson tells us, "Henry Kaiser invited me to California to record with him in 1990, and he had eight Dumbles at the time, so I was really looking forward to trying those. When I got there, he said, 'I just got this amp here' and plugged me into a Trainwreck Liverpool. I just went, 'Oh my God, I've got to get one of these!' So I bought a Liverpool from Kenny and an Express after that." In addition to becoming a customer, Henderson also acted as a handy phone demo guy for Fischer: potential customers would discuss the amps with the maker, then call Henderson for a quick over-the-phone playing demonstration to hear what they sounded like.

Trainwreck fan Mark Knopfler performs onstage in 1996. *Simon Ritter/Redferns/Getty Images*

Brad Paisley often plays through a Trainwreck Liverpool model. Here, he performs on June 13, 2002 at the 31st Annual Fan Fair in Nashville, Tennessee. *Rusty Russell/Getty Images*

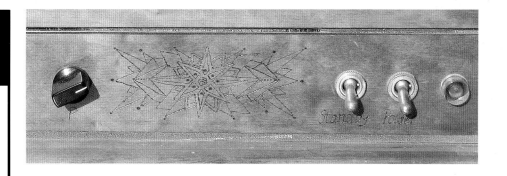

1986 TRAINWRECK EXPRESS "NANCY"

- Preamp tubes: One ECC83, one 7025, one 12AX7 (all NOS 12AX7 types)
- Output tubes: Two Mullard EL34s, fixed-bias
- Rectifier: Solid-state
- Controls: Volume, Treble, Middle, Bass, Presence, Bright switch
- Output: Approximately 40 watts RMS

The Liverpool and Express are differentiated, most obviously, by their use of four EL84s and two EL34s, respectively. As a result, the former is usually referred to as being "Voxy" to the latter's "Marshally," though every one of each model is also quite different from either of those vintage British brands. Nancy further differentiates itself from later Expresses by being one of the earlier versions made with the Stancor transformers from the Chicago Standard Transformer Company, which Fischer used from 1985 to 1989. As Fischer himself related, "In 1989 . . . Stancor stopped making those transformers, so I bought up all they had left of those to get me through the year with a few spares." Post-1990, he used "about twelve different transformer companies."

Aside from merely being historically interesting, the use of Stancors in the earlier Expresses such as this one also signaled a different sonic signature. Where later "black tranny" Expresses leaned more heavily toward high-gain tones, the Stancor Trainwrecks, though still plenty gainy when you wanted them to be, had a slightly browner, more vintagey blues rock vibe. "It's more of a small-box '68 Marshall," Henderson confirms. "Tube tuning is what these amps are all about; they run fairly low plate voltages (around 380 volts DC on the EL34s)." What really makes Trainwrecks tick, of course, is the circuit going on underneath the hood and, more than that, the way Fischer laid out the components, connected the wires, and selected individual resistor and capacitor types and values by hand to fine-tune the overall tone and feel of the amplifiers. The intense skill the man applied to his craft is further attested to by the fact that, while other makers have lifted the lids on existing Trainwrecks and copied their circuits, any experienced Tranwreck player will tell you that none of these so-called clones ever quite attains the sensitivity and complexity of Fischer's own creations.

In addition to—arguably in contrast to—their unparalleled electrical workings, Trainwrecks sported decidedly DIY-looking cabinets and cosmetics. As a case in point, check out Nancy's polished hardwood shell and front panels, the wood-

burner-etched control legends and starburst motif, and the stick-on DYMO labels that tell you what's what 'round the rear. Guitarists who were not in the know years back could be forgiven for passing one of these over as some tubehead's basement Marshall-like project, but any player who had a shot at one for reasonable money in the late 1980s or early 1990s and didn't bite is certainly kicking himself now.

The first Trainwreck Liverpool rolled out the door in 1983 at a price of $650. A year later that was raised to $1,000 for either model. Then, through the course of the 1990s, inflation took it to $1,200, then $1,600, then finally $1,800 as the cost of parts increased. Long unable to build any new amps due to a raft of illnesses, Fischer saw the price of used Trainwrecks rise to $22,000 or more during his lifetime, and in the years since his death on December 23, 2006, good Trainwrecks have pushed past the $30,000 mark. While he was still making amps, he not only offered customers a two-week trial with a full money-back guarantee but declared that he would refund the cost of shipping both ways if a buyer wanted to return his amp. None ever did.

Shortly before his death, Fischer revised the offer. "Several years back I instituted a policy: any Trainwreck amp out there has a 'triple-your-money-back' original-purchase-price guarantee. So if you've got a Trainwreck and you don't want it anymore, send it back to me, and I'll look up the original purchase price and refund it triple." As it happens, the new policy had no takers either. ●

PURE MODERN TONE

A leader of what we might call the second wave of high-end, high-gain tube amps, Soldano has been making a big noise since 1987. That year, Michael J. Soldano released his first production model, the Super Lead Overdrive (SLO-100), and this remains the amp most associated with the Soldano line. The SLO's ability to churn out searing lead tones with a certain sonic depth, clarity, and dynamics that another high-gain monster might have lacked at the time made it a quick favorite with several big-name players. The likes of Eric Clapton, Mark Knopfler, George Lynch, Gary Moore, Vivian Campbell, Lou Reed, and Joe Satriani—to name but a few—have all flown the Soldano banner at one time or another.

Our star here is from the very early days of the company, a 1990 SLO 100-watter head with no FX loop. It's a really primo example for an amp with twenty-one years of rock mayhem under its belt.

For sonic references, you might call the SLO a kind of Boogie crossed with Marshall crossed with hot-rodded Fender crossed with—well, by the time you

stir that pot and season liberally, the stew is gonna taste like something original enough to not require any specific references in the first place, so we can pretty much leave it at that. Simple tonal descriptions are more apt, and players tend to be drawn to the big, thick, creamy drive, which can also be plenty nasty and aggressive as desired while retaining musical highs and firm, chunky lows. In short, you could call the SLO a high-concept modern design rather than a modified vintage circuit, and Soldano certainly burned some midnight oil to get this one sounding its best.

Like many amps by Mesa/Boogie, Rivera, Egnator, Bogner, Budda, and a handful of other top-shelf high-gainsters, Soldanos are built on printed circuit boards (PCBs) but are assembled by hand. These aren't your grandfather's PCBs (or your cheesy Uncle Lou's); Soldano uses thick, high-quality PCBs (though not the double-sided boards here, which would appear in later years and would no doubt tell you that it opts for this topology for the sake of consistency and reliability rather than reasons of economy. While we are used to seeing plenty of high-gain 100-watters with EL34 output tubes, and might be expecting them here, this SLO—and its standard brethren—is based around

Amp courtesy Keith Welchel/photos Robin Lane

THE SLO 100.

The legendary Soldano 100w Super Lead Overdrive is the finest hand built all tube guitar amp available. Whatever your musical style, the infinite tonal variations, ease of use, versatility and rugged road-tested construction make it the ultimate guitar amp. It's a classic, definitely an investment that will last a lifetime. The SLO 100 incorporates two totally independant preamps, Normal and Overdrive. It features individual gain controls and separate master volume controls with absolutely noise free channel switching.

The Normal channel can be set up for Clean or Crunch, Bright or Normal. It is incredibly responsive and alive, producing sounds ranging from clean, full, undistorted warmth to a tough, metal-edged crunch.

The Overdrive channel supplies a grinding crunch. The low notes really growl and the high notes scream with infinite sustain and definition. This is an amp you can feel, with the versatility to produce an overdriven sound to fit any style of guitar playing.

The available options for the SLO 100 are a tube buffered effects loop, a variable level "slave" output, rack mountable chassis and custom tolex colors. Standard tolex choices are purple, black, grey and boa.

Soldano's unique design philosophy and demanding attention to detail contribute to the outstanding performance of the SLO 100. Only the highest quality components are used and each amp is thoroughly tested before it leaves the shop.

The heavy duty 2x12 and 4x12 speaker cabinets are ruggedly constructed of 3/4" birch plywood. They are available either loaded, with Soldano "PowerSpeakers" or optional Celestion "Vintage 30" speakers, or unloaded in tolex colors to match the amp heads. A slant front option is offered on the 4x12 cabinet. The cabinet dimensions are: 2x12/18"h x 28"w x 14"d. and 4x12/28"h x 28"w x 14"d.

Demand the best.

THE SM 100. (not shown)

Available on a custom order basis through your dealer, the Soldano 100w Super Manobloc is the **ultimate** guitar power amplifier. This amp is the power section of the world class SLO 100 housed in a super rugged road-tested four space rack mount chassis. It features volume and presence controls and can drive 4, 8, or 16 ohm speaker loads. Meticulously hand built in the true Soldano tradition, the SM100 is the perfect compliment to any of the Soldano family of fine preamps or as a slave amp for the SLO 100 or HR 50.

Soldano fan Joe Satriani performs at Heineken Music Hall in Amsterdam, the Netherlands, on October 29, 2010. *Mark Venema/WireImage/ Getty Images*

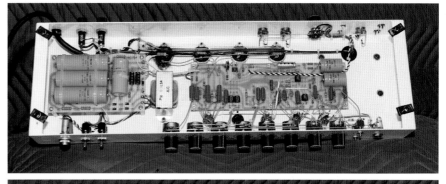

1990 SOLDANO SUPER LEAD OVERDRIVE SLO-100

- Preamp tubes: Four 12AX7s
- Output tubes: Four 6L6GC (or 5881s), fixed-bias
- Rectifier: Solid-state
- Controls: Normal (volume), Overdrive (volume), Bass, Middle, Treble, Normal (master), Overdrive (master), Presence
- Output: Approximately 100 watts RMS

four 6L6GCs (although some are modded to use EL34s). One goal achieved by this choice is the firm, tight low end that the amp is known for, along with its generally more American high-gain tone, which can generate some Brit rock crunch, certainly, but has an overall flavor that is more Yank than Limey.

The SLO's Normal channel, which is selectable between "Clean" and the slightly grittier "Crunch" mode on a mini-toggle switch, runs through two 12AX7 gain stages. Select the foot-switchable Overdrive channel and the signal is rerouted after the first shared triode to another two stages for plenty of thick, controllable preamp tube distortion. The two share a cathode-follower tone stack with the full three-knob complement of Bass, Middle, and Treble, as well as a Presence control, and each channel has its own independent Master volume control placed just prior to the long-tailed pair phase inverter.

When there's an effects loop on the SLO, it is driven by another tube, but as the blanked-out holes on the back of this one indicate, there is no loop on board, a configuration that plenty of purists swear yields a truer tone thanks to the less cluttered signal path. To the same end, this one also lacks the optional line-out.

As befits an amp with intentions for sizzling front-end overdrive and firm, hefty output tube girth, the SLO wields enormous iron, with an output transformer that is virtually indistinguishable in size from the power transformer at the other end of the chassis. Further supporting its bovine back end are design elements such as solid-state rectification, massive amounts of filtering (including three 200uF electrolytic caps and an in-the-chassis choke), and fairly high DC voltages on the 6L6GC output tubes, around 497V on the plates. A look under the hood would reveal several signs of Soldano's quality workmanship: neat and linear wire runs, a board

loaded with Mallory electrolytics, "orange drop" signal caps, metal film resistors to keep the noise down (a priority in any high-gain circuit), and tube sockets mounted directly to the chassis rather than to the main circuit board or even a supplemental board, as is often done in more mass-manufacture-grade PCB-based tube amps.

Patch this SLO through a 4x12 with Celestions, or indeed a 2x12 with EVs, and prepare to move some air and to feel a mighty thump in the gut when you hit those low-string runs and power chords. Step on the switch to kick it up a gear and expect searing, creamy overdrive, with just a little jaggedness to its edge for bite and endless sustain when desired. The SLO was never intended to be a "metal amp." It was really designed more for the contemporary rock soloist, but dial down the mid-range, crank bass, and tweak treble to taste, and you can pound out a mighty wallop, no problem, and the amp's firm bedding and fast response have no trouble nimbly translating all the shred you want to throw at it. In short, it's a modern classic of a high-octane rocker and a still a rival for any screaming new pretender. 🎱

soldano
AMPLIFIERS BUILT TO ROCK

1992 PRICE LIST

	RETAIL
SLO 100 BASIC HEAD (includes nylon slip cover)	2,800.00
OPTIONS:	
Rack Mount Chassis	230.00
Effects Loop	230.00
Slave Out	60.00
Custom Color Tolex*	120.00
HR 50 AMPLIFIER	1,050.00
Custom Color Tolex*	120.00
PREAMPLIFERS	
X99 (Soldano/Caswell)	2,600.00
X88R (3 channel, handbuilt)	2,600.00
SP 77 (2 channel)	800.00
Optional Channel Switching Foot Controller For X88R only	173.00
CUSTOM CABINETS	
we use only Celestion Vintage 30 speakers	
2x12 loaded	499.00
2x12 empty	299.00
4x12 loaded	799.00
4x12 empty	399.00
4x12 slant	(additional) 30.00
Custom Color Tolex*	120.00
* Standard colors available at no extra charge are black, purple, grey, or boa skin	
CUSTOM ANVIL CASES	
Amp Head Case	349.00
2x12 Cabinet Case (w/casters)	599.00
4x12 Cabinet Case (w/casters)	649.00
AMP SLIP COVERS	
Delux Vinyl	70.00
Standard Nylon	25.00
SOLDANO T-SHIRTS (black, white or purple)	15.00
SOLDANO SWEAT SHIRTS (purple only)	25.00

With a varied back line including at least one Soldano head, Warren Haynes and Derek Trucks of the Allman Brothers Band perform at New York City's Beacon Theater on March 19, 2009. *Gary Gershoff/WireImage for New York Post/Getty Images*

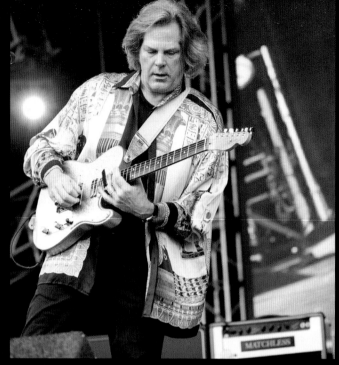

John Jorgenson performs at Fairport's Cropedy Convention on August 14, 2009 in Banbury, England. *Steve Thorne/Redferns/Getty Images*

THE AC30 THAT WOULDN'T BREAK

While one-man operations like Dumble and Trainwreck might have kicked off the boutique amp phenomenon, Matchless was arguably the first well-established "production boutique" company to succeed at selling significant numbers of point-to-point amps in the post–printed circuit board (PCB) era.

Matchless was founded in 1989 by Mark Sampson and Rick Perrotta, and the company's flagship model was designed soon after, following Perrotta's desire to "build an AC30 that wouldn't break," according to Sampson. As it turns out, the resultant DC30 is far more than a Vox copy, though it does stem from the Matchless founders' love of shimmering, saturated British class A tone. And it shares many AC30 touch points such as a four-EL84 output section in cathode bias with no negative feedback, GZ34 tube rectification, and other details we'll examine. Internally, however, it looks nothing at all like a vintage AC30—and that's probably one of its top selling points.

As great as vintage Vox AC30s in good condition can sound, they are difficult amps to service, thanks to a complex internal layout. And they can be prone to breakdown on the road. Sampson and Perrotta sought to build an amp that was both roadworthy and sounded outstanding. As the chief designer, Sampson found himself naturally led toward a genuine hand-wired, point-to-point design, and Matchless amps are the epitome of this topology. Many players and marketing departments alike often refer to any hand-wired tube amp as being "point-to-point," but strictly speaking the term doesn't apply to amps built with circuit cards or turret boards, such as vintage Fenders, Marshalls, Voxes, and others, even though every solder joint and wiring connection is completed by hand. Genuine point-to-point circuitry involves connecting each point in the signal chain and power stage with the components themselves—which is to say that capacitors and resistors are usually soldered directly between tube socket contacts, pots and input jacks, and so forth. That's exactly how Sampson did it with Matchless and how the current company still does it.

Accordingly, preamp tubes are mounted close to the inputs and volume and tone potentiometers in the front panel, and the internal components within the chassis flow logically toward the output, almost as if the circuit was rendered literally from a schematic diagram. This style of building is very labor intensive and doesn't suit every amp maker. But it certainly eliminates excess wire runs within the chassis, generally provides a very robust circuit, and sometimes makes component failure easier to diagnose and correct.

CIRCA 1990 MATCHLESS DC30

- Preamp Tubes: One EF86, three 12AX7s (one for PI)
- Output Tubes: Four EL84s in class A, cathode-bias
- Rectifier: GZ34
- Controls: Channel 1: Volume, Bass, Treble; channel 2: Volume, Tone; shared: Cut, Master
- Speakers: One Celestion G12M greenback, one Celestion G12H-30 (modified)
- Output: 30 watts RMS

The DC30 and its brethren TC-30 (2x10-inch combo), SC30 (1x12 inch), and HC-30 head are two-channel amps of the old school, which is to say the channels are not foot switchable but independent (though many players switch between them or use them in parallel with an A/B/Y pedal). The first channel effectively gives a Vox Top Boost–style sound, with one 12AX7 for the first gain stage (with its two triodes wired in parallel for a higher signal-to-noise ratio) and another 12AX7 for the cathode-follower tone stack feeding a Bass and Treble control. The second channel is a modified AC15/early AC30 preamp using a high-gain EF86 (6267) pentode preamp, with a six-position "varitone" Tone switch that routes the signal through different coupling caps to revoice the channel as desired. The channels share a cut control and Master Volume; the former reduces highs at the output stage, while the latter provides a much more tone-friendly volume reduction than many such controls used in the 1970s and 1980s—reducing the level after the phase inverter rather than just after the preamps—and can be rendered invisible when fully clockwise.

As used in the DC30—and the Vox AC15 (and briefly the early AC30) that inspired it—an EF86 pentode preamp tube helps create a sound in the amp's second channel that is quite different from the Top Boost chime and shimmer that most consider the classic Vox sound. This tube yields a thick, rich tone with a full and relatively even reproduction of the frequency spectrum (as relates to the electric guitar) without the mid-range grit or occasionally harsh highs heard in a 12AX7 used in a high-gain preamp stage. The word probably used most to describe it is *fat*, but it is also very firm and well defined, and while it has a lot more gain than a 12AX7, it also carries a lot of body along with it. In the DC30, the EF86 is used in an extremely simple preamp circuit, with a signal path that runs straight from the tube's output to the volume control via a single coupling capacitor, whichever of six is selected via the rotary tone switch. The first channel provides tones that are far more familiar but equally useful, best summed up as "sparkle with bite" at lower volume settings and "harmonically saturated grind" when cranked up. Between them, they offer an extremely versatile package.

Other aspects of Matchless' design and construction are equally impressive. They gave the combo a rugged, punchy cab with a mixed pair of Celestion 12-inch speakers—a G12M greenback and a modified G12H-30—for a broad, complex sound stage; a speaker-phase-reverse switch to ease pairing the DC30 with another amp; a useful half-power switch; and top-notch touches like shock-mounted tube sockets and star grounding for low noise.

These points and other little touches, such as 1-watt carbon-comp resistors throughout the circuit rather than the .5-watt resistors found in most boutique amps, show to what extent Matchless set out to build the best amp it possibly could. The DC30 is a modern classic on so many levels, and its continued use by a multitude of pros is further testament to the achievements of Sampson and Perrotta.

In 1999 Matchless closed its doors for a time after being hit hard by the crash of the yen and a confluence of other circumstances, at which point Perrotta and Sampson moved on to work for Bad Cat. About a year later, Matchless fired up again with Phil Jamison—the company's production manager since 1991—at the helm. He continues to run the company today. The cornerstone models are still made by Matchless in Los Angeles, with the same specs and rigorous quality control they had when their designer was still with the company. Sampson has since designed amps for Sonic Machine Factory and currently offers his own Star Amplifiers line. ◉

A TONAL JEWEL

How many knobs does stellar tone require? We humbly suggest that two—volume and tone—will do it for most occasions, at least when an amp packs all the juicy good stuff of the little Matchless Spitfire. Sure, there are actually three knobs on this control panel, so let's say three for bijou clubs and home studio use when you need to bring that master into play, but as often as not you can ignore that one and craft your requirements from its neighbors to the left. No disrespect for amps, players, or makers who need or provide more, and certainly there are occasions that demand a broader feature set, but there is something glorious about such simplicity: set your gain level, decide how much high end to bleed off, and you know exactly what is going on behind the hood. Forget the tweaking and fine-tuning and just get on down to playing your damn guitar.

With outstanding little boutique amp companies busting out all over the shop these days, it's easy to forget there was a lot less happening in this field in the mid 1990s, when Matchless was one of just a handful of major names (if still a relatively small operation), both in reputation and achievement. The company built its name on constructing bulletproof and über-roadworthy point-to-point creations inspired by vintage British templates, and it continues to ply that trade today, applying the same uncompromising quality to several designs that helped make its name, as well as plenty of clever new models introduced in recent years.

This "small box" 1x12-inch combo from 1994 hails from not long after the introduction of the model. It is even simpler than its sibling the Lightning, which had four knobs total, including Bass and Treble, for its Top Boost–style tone stack, but includes all the cornerstone Matchless build points and the same robust hand-wired topography under the hood. You will sometimes see pre-1999 Matchless amps billed as "Sampson-era," a nod to the days when company cofounder Mark Sampson was still at the helm. Sampson did design many of these models, but construction was overseen by Phil Jamison, then production manager and the head of Matchless today. Trust us when we tell you that they build them just as well now as they ever did. In fact, the only notable difference on many amps is that Matchless has done away with the nifty-looking little Lucite handle that appears on this one, mainly for its lack of reliability over the long haul. Otherwise, the innards of any bona fide Spitfire to roll out of the factory today will look virtually identical to those of this one manufactured more than sixteen years ago.

1994 MATCHLESS SPITFIRE

- Preamp tubes: Two 12AX7s
- Output tubes: Two EL84s, cathode-biased, no negative feedback
- Rectifier: GZ34
- Controls: Volume, Tone, Master
- Speaker: One custom-order Celestion 12-inch
- Output: Approximately 15 watts RMS

Metallica's Kirk Hammett often uses a Matchless Spitfire to record. Here, he performs live on July 11, 2003. *Mick Hutson/Redferns/Getty Images*

Also extremely cool is that the innards of this one look very much like a smaller rendition of Matchless' bigger and more celebrated amps, such as the DC30 (often billed as a more reliable Vox AC30 for the touring musician). Pull the chassis and you are looking at that same delightfully logical circuit flow, with tubes and components positioned as close as possible to the circuit stages in which they are used. The socket for the first preamp tube, for example, lurks just behind the front panel between the inputs and volume control, right where the circuit wants it to be. Pots, tube sockets, and other fixed parts are connected directly by the quality capacitors and big 1-watt carbon-comp resistors that provide the voicing and current-carrying functions for each stage, with just a few tag strips in between to give support and solidity and no circuit board in sight. Transformers are oversize and weighty (you can find trannies this size on many 50-watt 6L6-based amps), and an extensive effort is made to achieve a "star grounding" topology, with all ground points going to the same central point in the chassis and all metal components lifted from ground, with barriers between component body and chassis, such as the insulating fiber washers that surround the barrels of the input jacks.

Other nifty Matchless hallmarks are here, such as the light-up control panel (this combo is too small for a light-up logo), Teflon insulation on all cap and resistor leads, and grommet-mounted tube sockets. One of the niftiest things a glance inside the Spitfire chassis reveals, though, is how *little* is in there. If you want to avoid extraneous tone sucking from input to output, this kind of workmanship is likely to give it to you. Design-wise, the premise is also simplicity incarnate: one 12AX7 in the preamp (a single gain stage, but with both triodes wired in parallel for increased headroom and lower noise), a passive treble-bleed tone

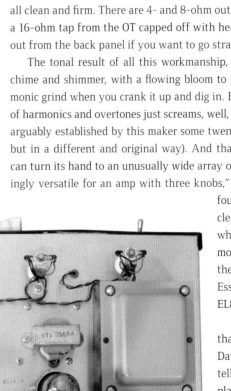

control, another 12AX7 in the long-tailed pair phase inverter, two EL84s in the output stage, and a GZ34 rectifier tube. A choke, plus some fairly heavy filtering, helps keep it all clean and firm. There are 4- and 8-ohm outs to match a range of speaker cabs (plus a 16-ohm tap from the OT capped off with heat shrink inside the chassis) and a line-out from the back panel if you want to go straight to the board or into a larger amp.

The tonal result of all this workmanship, arguably, is that archetypal Matchless chime and shimmer, with a flowing bloom to notes and chords and a rich, thick harmonic grind when you crank it up and dig in. Even in this little 15-watter, the balance of harmonics and overtones just screams, well, Matchless, and defines a genre that was arguably established by this maker some twenty years ago (on the heels of Vox, sure, but in a different and original way). And thanks to this sonic splendor, the Spitfire can turn its hand to an unusually wide array of playing styles. "The spitfire is surprisingly versatile for an amp with three knobs," says Phil Jamison. "It has an excellent foundation to start with, very simple and clean. It became very popular to the point where people began to ask for them with more power and headroom, so I designed the 30/15 to be based off the Spitfire. Essentially it's a 30-watt Spitfire [with four EL84s and a half-power switch]."

So feel free to pile on the features if that's what floats your boat, but if Henry David Thoreau were here, we know he'd tell you to cast aside the clutter and just get playing through this simple little Spitfire.

THE RISE OF THE BOUTIQUE CLUB RIG

My Morning Jacket's Carl Broemel wails through his TopHat amp on March 6, 2007. *Chris McKay/WireImage/Getty Images*

Guitarists experienced a revolution of the "club amp" beginning in the 1990s. Smaller tube amps were always with us and were always the club rig of choice for players who knew how to match the gear to the gig, but the insiders' secret bloomed into a greater awareness with the guitar community et al over the past couple of decades, and the past few years in particular.

A handful of manufacturers—certain boutique makers in particular—helped this movement proliferate, and TopHat has been among the leaders of the charge. Its Club Series, namely the Club Deluxe and Club Royale models, has turned out some of the most popular handmade club amps of the modern era. These designs from company founder Brian Gerhard neatly encapsulate the "crankable amp in a small package" ethos and are eminently worthy of examination.

When we say "smaller" amp, we really mean amps you could categorize as the larger of the small-amp breed or the smaller of the midsize. We're talking 15 to 20 watts, with 1x12- or 2x10-inch speaker configurations. For vintage reference points, from this side of the pond think Fender Princeton Reverb/Deluxe Reverb or Gibson GA-40 Les Paul. From the other side of the pond think Vox AC10/AC15 or Watkins/WEM Dominator. The Club Deluxe falls right into this category, and though TopHat has sold a few more of its Club Royales over the years, we'll look at the Club Deluxe here, partly to consider its update of the classic American club combo and partly because it no longer exists in the TopHat catalog and is therefore riper for the probing of posterity (and there's little difference between the two other than output tubes—6V6s in the Deluxe, EL84s in the Royale—and the requisite minor revoicing of EQ, bias, and output transformers).

- Preamp tubes: Three 12AX7s
- Output tubes: Two 6V6GTs, cathode-bias, no negative feedback (EL84s in the similar Club Royale)
- Rectifier: Solid-state this example, with switchable Normal/Soft response
- Controls: Volume, Treble, Mid, Bass, Cut, Master, and Bright/Fat Boost switch
- Output: 20 watts

TopHat's creations have generally fallen into the Brit-inspired camp, and in many ways so does the Club Deluxe, but this model can also be viewed as a direct evolution of two of the most popular tweed-era American amps of all time; marry Fender's 5E3 Deluxe of the late 1950s with the 5F6-A Bassman of the same era, and this is what might arrive in the delivery room nine months later. It's equipped with the cathode-biased, dual-6V6 output stage with no negative feedback loop that just screams "tweed Deluxe" every time you see it. In front of this, though, comes a cathode-follower tone stack with Treble, Mid, and Bass controls that is a direct descendent of the tweed Bassman, and the phase inverter is the noble long-tailed pair configuration, also first used by Fender in the Bassman and high-powered Twin. Between them, these stages help deliver more fidelity to the 6V6s than you're ever going to hear in a Fender 5E3 Deluxe, and a much broader range of tone sculpting. The results make themselves felt in greater headroom and increased clarity, yet the Club Deluxe still roars when you get it up toward noon on the Volume.

The Cut control is a hanger-on from vintage Vox designs and reduces high frequencies in the output stage. It's more essential in the EL84-based amps from which it is derived because many of them can be too glassy and spiky without it, but it's still a useful tweaker in a 6V6 amp. Another groovy bonus—and a very useful one at that—is the three-way Boost switch. A simple on/off/on switch that toggles between two cathode bypass caps (or none), it yields (left to right) Bright boost, off, Fat boost.

Rather than performing this trick with the cathode bypass cap of the first gain stage, however—the way it's done in so many other amps that carry such a switch—Gerhard tied his boost to the cathode of the first triode of the 12AX7 in the cathode-follower tone stack (the EQ circuit "follows" the cathode in the second triode). The results are a little smoother and more nuanced than the boost switch in many preamps, and it serves as a great thickener for guitars with thin-sounding pickups or a great brightener of dark humbuckers.

The overall result of this design is an amp centered in 6V6-based American tones but one that can easily cop Vox- and Marshall-style British voices, depending on where you set the gain and tone controls. Conversely, the EL84-based Club Royale sits right in Vox territory, but it mimics blackface and tweed Fender tones with ease, according to how you balance the highly interactive Treble, Mid, and Bass controls, while also doing great mini-Marshall impersonations as bidden. On top of these general voicings, both models exhibit great depth and dimension, with excellent swirly chime in the clean tones and juicy dynamics in the overdrive when you crank up and dig in.

Models in the Club Series have evolved through several iterations, and our example (built in 2000) is from the middle of that road from then to now. Until the most recent changes in TopHat's Mark II Series, notable for its new art deco styling, much of the tweaking centered noticeably around the rectifier, with other component and circuit changes inside. They were launched with tube rectifiers but moved to solid-state rectification with a Normal/Soft switch to give a choice of playing feels, and that's how this Club Deluxe is equipped. They went back to tubes in 2004, all models carrying a GZ34 (5AR4), but more recently the EL84-based Club Royale has adopted an EZ81, while the 6L6-based (but 6V6-capable) Super Deluxe uses a GZ34. Gerhard feels the tube rectification gives the amps a little more breadth and dimension, but they are also plenty dynamic with the solid-state configuration.

Although they're also available as 2x12-inch combos, the 1x12-inch Club amps have always been delightfully compact at 19 inches wide x 19 inches high x 9 inches deep. Shortly after this one was manufactured, TopHat increased the cab depth to 11 inches to increase low-end response. Gerhard's speaker of choice, the Celestion G12H-30, also helps with the solidity and punching power. All around, they're great-sounding little combos and surprisingly reasonable—new or used—considering the made-in-the-U.S.A. craftsmanship, as well as the immaculate circuitry and wiring inside. It's an unassuming modern classic. ◉

GOOD MEDICINE

Before the dawn of what might be called the boutique amp movement, Michael Zaite, a Cleveland-based engineer working in medical electronics for General Electric, himself a drummer rather than a guitarist (a story similar to that of Jim Marshall), decided to start his own company to build tube amps. In doing so, he established a handful of core principles for his work: avoid copying the oft-emulated classics, keep the circuits and features simple, and keep prices realistic for workaday guitarists. To this day, his Dr. Z company has retained its tri-pillared stand along those lines and has a reputation for consistently superlative tone right alongside them.

No design embodies all four of these credos more than Dr. Z's Carmen Ghia model, a petite yet powerful EL84-based design that blends a simplicity Henry David Thoreau would have admired with a surprising wealth of sonic versatility, all for a refreshing $499 (in head form) when it first hit the market in the mid 1990s.

"This design is twenty-one years old now," Zaite reflects from his workshop in Cleveland. "And it was pretty meaningful to me because it was one of the base products for Dr. Z, and it's still a mainstay in many, many studios."

Outwardly looking much like a no-count practice amp from days gone by, the little Carmen Ghia has gathered a whole shopping list of name-artist users and rave reviews in its time on this planet. And as unassuming as this little two-knob amp is, its circuit contains a number of twists and turns that remain unique in the tube-amp world to this day, and it continues to echo the origins of its far-from-secret history. During his transition from GE engineer to renegade amp designer, Zaite scrounged and repurposed tubes, parts, and transformers where he could find them. In so doing, he came upon the roots of the Carmen Ghia via one particularly fortuitous personal association.

"I've been very fortunate in that, for some reason or other, fate or a power above me or whatever has constantly directed me toward individuals who have helped me with Dr. Z amplifiers," he says. "One of them was Ken Fischer. But prior to Kenny there was a guy named Charlie Jobe, and Charlie was a Hammond Organ guru. He was the first guy to chop a B-3—they called it his coffin mod—and if you look at some of Jimmy Smith's albums, you'll see credits to Charlie Jobe.

"Anyway, I was buying stuff from him because he had a lot of parts, and one day I went to his house and saw these five little chassis on this steel shelf. I go, 'Charlie, what are those?' He said, 'Hammond reverb amps. It was an option we used to put into A100s to give reverb to the organ. I never liked it. A Hammond don't need no damn reverb!'

DR. Z CARMEN GHIA

- Preamp tubes: 12AX7, 5751
- Output tubes: Two EL84s, cathode-bias, no negative feedback
- Rectifier: 5Y3
- Controls: Volume, Tone
- Output: 18 watts

"I was looking at those thinking, 'Those would look really cool. They would make great little guitar amps.' I bought them and took them home—they were the old Hammond Model 35 reverb amp—and I'm looking at the schematic at these really unique circuits. There was a global negative feedback circuit that was really unusual and a conjunctive filter on the output circuit. . . . This was all from the minds of these Hammond guys. So I played with it and played with it and designed this really neat tone circuit to go with it, which shapes the EQ more like the way a wah pedal works than a guitar amp tone control—and to this day it is exclusive and unique."

Having sold a couple hundred of his tricked-out Hammond chassis as guitar amps for $350 a pop, Zaite realized he could go through these rebuilds faster than he could acquire them. He set about reengineering the components and building the 18-watt amp from scratch. Circa 1995, he placed his first ad in *Vintage Guitar* magazine for a model that was then officially called the Carmen Ghia: "18 Watts of Tone to Kill For: introductory price of $499."

The "Hammond reverb amp as Ghia" legend has proliferated such that this enormously successful Dr. Z model's origins are etched in the footnotes of gear lore and discussed daily in tubehead chat rooms. The good doctor has never tried to say that this amp was anything other than a design with its feet in prior origins, but an exploration of what makes it tick as a guitar amp reveals that Zaite certainly put a lot of his own skill into making it what it is today.

He retained the high-quality M6 laminates of the original Hammond output transformers in his reengineered OT, along with certain essential basics of the circuit. His tweak of the phase inverter to use a less gainy 5751, however, and the aforementioned EQ network are all proprietary twists, and they sit alongside a handful of other modifications and upgrades intended to better suit the Carmen Ghia to its purpose when compared to a stock Model 35 Hammond reverb amp.

"I really liked a 5751 in the phase inverter," Zaite relates. "In other amps, you can get to the point where it sounds like you're just pushing the EL84s too hard [with a 12AX7], and you get that splattery kind of distortion; so I decided to use a 5751 for a couple of reasons. One, that it wouldn't push the EL84s so hard. But another is that it has this scooped tone, this hollowness in the mids that gives it a big-amp sound that was very, very natural to me."

Ultimately, the Carmen Ghia speaks for itself. Breathy, rich, and dynamic at all volumes, it is beloved for its ability to run textured, high-fidelity clean tones at studio levels to juicy, thick EL84 overdrive tones at club volumes, at a price (Zaite still makes it) that's still a bargain in the boutique amp world. All that, and its two-control simplicity lets you concentrate on playing rather than knob twiddling. Sounds like the definition of a modern classic. ●

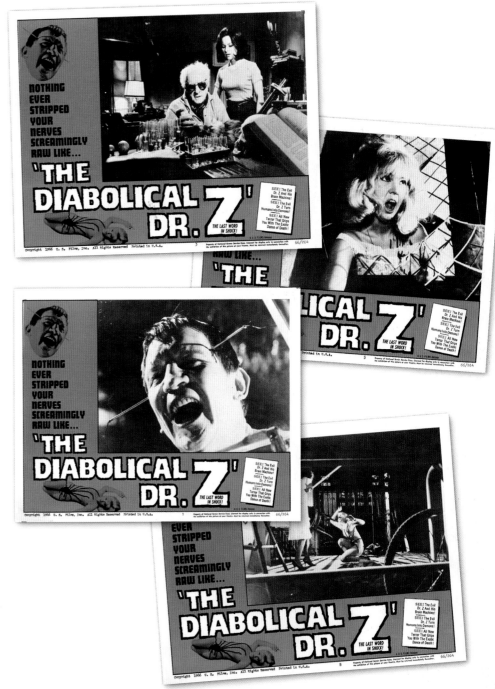

First published in 2012 by Voyageur Press, an imprint of MBI Publishing Company, 400 First Avenue North, Suite 400, Minneapolis, MN 55401 USA

With a big, loud thanks to Ward Meeker and everyone else at *Vintage Guitar* magazine where many of these essays first appeared in a different form.

Voyageur Press titles are also available at discounts in bulk quantity for industrial or sales-promotional use. For details write to Special Sales Manager at MBI Publishing Company, 400 First Avenue North, Suite 400, Minneapolis, MN 55401 USA.

To find out more about our books, visit us online at www.voyageurpress.com.

ISBN-13: 978-0-7603-3972-5

Editor: Michael Dregni
Design Manager: Cindy Samargia Laun
Cover and text designed by: John Barnett/4 Eyes Design

Printed in China

10 9 8 7 6 5 4 3 2

ON THE FRONTISPIECE: *Photos Deke Dickerson, Fender Musical Instruments Corporation, Michael Dregni, Christopher Kontoes/fStop/Alamy*

ON THE TITLE PAGE: Fender's Twin Reverb reissue. *Fender Musical Instruments Corporation*

ON THE FINAL PAGE: Marc Bolan of T Rex casts a shadow over his stack of Vamp amps while performing at Wembley Empire Pool in London on March 1, 1972. *Estate of Keith Morris/Redferns/Getty Images*